Memorializing Violence

Genocide, Political Violence, Human Rights Series

*Edited by Alexander Laban Hinton, Nela Navarro,
and Natasha Zaretsky*

For a complete list of titles in the series, please see the last page of the book.

Memorializing Violence

Transnational Feminist Reflections

EDITED BY ALISON CROSBY AND HEATHER EVANS

Rutgers University Press
New Brunswick, Camden, and Newark, New Jersey
London and Oxford

Rutgers University Press is a department of Rutgers, The State University of New Jersey, one of the leading public research universities in the nation. By publishing worldwide, it furthers the University's mission of dedication to excellence in teaching, scholarship, research, and clinical care.

Library of Congress Cataloging-in-Publication Data

Names: Crosby, Alison, editor. | Evans, Heather, editor.
Title: Memorializing violence : transnational feminist reflections / edited by Alison Crosby and Heather Evans.
Description: New Brunswick, New Jersey : Rutgers University Press, [2025] | Series: Genocide, political violence, human rights | Includes bibliographical references and index.
Identifiers: LCCN 2024016378 | ISBN 9781978843257 (paperback ; acid-free paper) | ISBN 9781978843264 (hardcover ; acid-free paper) | ISBN 9781978843271 (epub) | ISBN 9781978843288 (pdf)
Subjects: LCSH: Memorialization. | History—Philosophy. | Mourning customs. | Atrocities. | Suffering.
Classification: LCC D16.9 .M3175 2025 | DDC 901/.9—dc23/eng/20241017
LC record available at https://lccn.loc.gov/2024016378

A British Cataloging-in-Publication record for this book is available from the British Library.

This collection copyright © 2025 by Rutgers, The State University of New Jersey
Individual chapters copyright © 2025 in the names of their authors
All rights reserved

No part of this book may be reproduced or utilized in any form or by any means, electronic or mechanical, or by any information storage and retrieval system, without written permission from the publisher. Please contact Rutgers University Press, 106 Somerset Street, New Brunswick, NJ 08901. The only exception to this prohibition is "fair use" as defined by U.S. copyright law.

References to internet websites (URLs) were accurate at the time of writing. Neither the author nor Rutgers University Press is responsible for URLs that may have expired or changed since the manuscript was prepared.

♾ The paper used in this publication meets the requirements of the American National Standard for Information Sciences—Permanence of Paper for Printed Library Materials, ANSI Z39.48-1992.

rutgersuniversitypress.org

In loving memory of Malathi de Alwis

Contents

	Preface	xi
	Introduction: A Transnational Feminist Approach to Memorialization ALISON CROSBY AND HEATHER EVANS	1
1	Tracing Absent Presence MALATHI DE ALWIS	17

Part I   The Colonial, Imperial Logics of Memorializing

2	Law's Racial Memory CARMELA MURDOCCA	29
3	Toward a Queer Diasporic Remembrance of Air India Flight 182: Memorializing Transnational Flows of Loss and Desire AMBER DEAN	43

Part II   Inhabiting Loss, Exceeding the Frame

4	"I Am Here for Justice and I Am Here for Change": Reflections on Anticolonial Remembering within the National Inquiry into Missing and Murdered Indigenous Women and Girls in Canada KARINE DUHAMEL	59

viii • Contents

5 Transnational Contestations: Remembering Sexual
Violence in Postgenocide Guatemala   72
ALISON CROSBY, IRMA ALICIA VELÁSQUEZ NIMATUJ,
AND MARÍA DE LOS ÁNGELES AGUILAR

6 Poetics and Politics of Sound Memory and Social
Repair in the Afterlives of Mass Violence:
The *Cantadoras* of the Atrato River of Colombia   87
PILAR RIAÑO-ALCALÁ

Part III   Invoking Revolutionary Present Pasts

7 Figures of Dissent: Women's Memoirs of Defiance   105
SHAHRZAD MOJAB

8 Filming Disappearance: An Account of a Visual Battle   119
CHOWRA MAKAREMI

9 Dialita Choir: Women Survivors Reclaiming
History in Indonesia   130
AYU RATIH

Part IV   Care in/as Collective Mourning

10 Ceremonies of Mourning, Remembrance, and Care
in the Context of Violence: A Conversation about
Performing *Song for the Beloved*   147
HONOR FORD-SMITH AND JUANITA STEPHEN

11 Maternal Activism and the Politics of Memorialization
in the Mothers of the Movement: A Black
Feminist Reading   160
ERICA S. LAWSON AND OLA OSMAN

12 The Embroidering for Peace Initiative: Crafting
Feminist Politics and Memorializing Resistance to
the "War on Drugs" in Mexico   173
CORDELIA RIZZO

13 Epigraph 24584: In Which She Talks to the Dead
and Sometimes the Dead Talk Back   187
CHARLOTTE HENAY

Contents • ix

Part V On Worlding

14 Dreams to Remember: A Conversation on
Unsilencing the Archive: An Afronautic Approach   209
CAMILLE TURNER, MILA MENDEZ, AND HEATHER EVANS

Acknowledgments   219
References   221
Notes on Contributors   243
Index   249

Preface

> Some are made articulate by grief
> others struck dumb
> As I struggle within my cage of silence
> that unravels infinitely
> in a Munchian scream
> I promise one thing
> to you who promised so much more
> The ideas you engaged
> the intellectual spaces you enabled
> the reconciliation you envisioned
> with such courage and commitment
> will be pursued now
> with renewed passion and purpose
> Your legacy will live on
> once even we are long gone
> from this scarred and embittered land
> —Malathi de Alwis, *For Neelan*

In putting together this edited volume, we have grappled with a heart-wrenching yet vital task: remembering and memorializing someone whose own work on memory, grief, and loss has been so profoundly generative to this project. Dr. Malathi de Alwis ("Mala"), the renowned Sri Lankan cultural anthropologist, feminist, and environmental activist, passed away in January 2021. She and I first met in 1995 when we were graduate students and members of the Women in Conflict Zones Network (WICZNET), a transnational group of feminist scholars and activists concerned with the gendered dimensions of militarization and war (Giles, de Alwis & Klein, 2000; Giles & Hyndman, 2004). We became firm friends. Mala had a marked—and indeed remarkable—proclivity for working with her friends; or, those who worked with her quickly became her friends. Her scholarship, activism, and friendships were deeply intertwined. As the many tributes to her have testified, she took such great care to nourish and sustain these transnational relationships and collaborations. And so, in 2008, during a WICZNET meeting in Dubrovnik, Croatia, drawing on our respective work in Sri Lanka and Guatemala, we began a conversation about whether it is possible to create, in her words, a "political community of the sorrowing" (de Alwis, this volume) in the aftermath of mass atrocity. This led to our creating *The Inhabitance of Loss: A Transnational Feminist Project on Memorialization*, which examined when and how survivor-led initiatives to memorialize loss in Guatemala and Sri Lanka can create new articulations of agency, voice, and community within and across national borders.

In the course of our collaborative research and through our encounters with other feminist scholars, activists, and artists working on memorialization practices in myriad spaces and places—particularly through our ongoing conversations with Heather Evans, Honor Ford-Smith, Shahrzad Mojab, and Carmela Murdocca—we realized that it was necessary to expand the scope and scale of our project. Hence, *Memorializing Violence: Transnational Feminist Reflections* came into being.

The chapter that Mala was intending to write for this volume was titled *Memory Walks*. She had chosen to analyze the commemorative practice of walking in two sites of past violence, Rio Negro (Guatemala) and Jaffna (Sri Lanka), to think through the complicated relationship between memory and place. In her initial chapter abstract, critiquing Maurice Halbwachs' (2011) rather static understanding of place as preserving memory, she drew on Karen Till (2005), who has argued that places are not only "continuously interpreted" but are also "haunted by past structures of meaning and material presences from other times and lives" (p. 9). Guided memory walks, Mala posited, render place "ephemeral and contingent." They are often led by "someone who bears the scars of violence or is burdened with its legacy," who "becomes the interpreter of material ruins, remains and residue while simultaneously stimulating our imagination with visual artefacts and verbal imagery, recalling Claude Lanzmann's apt phrase: 'One must know and see, and one must see in order to know' (as cited in Chevrie & Le Roux, p. 38)." And although Rio Negro and Jaffna are "very distant and disparate spaces," Mala highlighted how they are "entangled through colonial and post-colonial imbrications of violence and are crucial punctuation points in the transnational feminist conversation initiated by Alison Crosby and myself."

Sadly, Mala was unable to complete her chapter or fulfill her anticipated editorial role in this volume. We did, however, receive permission to reprint *Tracing Absent Presence* (2009). It is fitting that this chapter begins the book, given how influential it has been in terms of our collective thinking about remembrance and memorialization practices and the meaning of transnational feminist praxis.

A companion to this edited volume will be our digital archive (see https://www.memorializingviolence.com/digital-archive), which will curate research, resources, and original digital materials relevant to the remembrance and memorialization of colonial, imperial, militarized, and state violence through a transnational feminist lens. The first collection we will curate, in collaboration with Mala's colleague Hasini Haputhanthri, will be dedicated to her memory work. As we gather materials and create a timeline, it is extraordinary to see the "palimpsest of traces" (de Alwis, this volume) of her work and indeed her very being that emerge. Mala was continuously preoccupied with how survivors of violence can, in the words of Veena Das (2000), "reinhabit the world" (p. 23) in the aftermath of devastating loss and unending grief. In *Tracing Absent Presence*, reflecting on the agony of family members of the disappeared who live with ongoing absent-presence, often encapsulated in the photographs of their loved ones, she wondered about the potentiality of objects. She asked, "Does tracing absent presence in the life of objects, albeit abject objects, provide a more meaningful framework for that re-inhabiting? A space for politics?" She took up these questions in her ongoing community praxis. Most recently, just before she died, Mala and Hasini completed the Archive of Memory project (see http://www.archiveofmemory.lk/), in which they brought everyday objects to life to tell the stories of ordinary Sri Lankans over the past seventy years since independence. A pair of spectacles, a teacup, or a piece of coconut shell became the means through which Sri Lankans could narrate often untold experiences and, in some cases, even reach some degree of closure. In an interview with them for the podcast *Witnesses to History* (visit https://historicaldialogue.lk/podcast/ep-1/), which was the final interview Mala gave, the journalist Smitri Daniel described Mala and Hasini as "caretakers of living memory," with Mala adding that the people they interviewed for the project themselves became the archive, a living archive.

Mala wrote the poem in the above epigraph in memory of her friend and mentor Dr. Neelan Tiruchelvan, cofounder of the International Centre for Ethnic Studies where Mala worked for many years. He was assassinated on his way to his office in Colombo on July 29, 1999. It could also have been written to her by her legions of friends, colleagues, students, and mentees "made articulate by grief," a community-in-becoming bound by our "renewed passion and purpose" in the struggle against injustice that Mala was so deeply committed to with every fiber of her being. For those of us fortunate to have known her, we will strive to honor and emulate her extraordinary ways of being in and seeing the world. *Her legacy will live on, once even we are long gone.*

Alison Crosby
August 2021

Memorializing Violence

Introduction

A Transnational Feminist Approach to Memorialization

ALISON CROSBY AND
HEATHER EVANS

> If that is so—if it is that you have
> something terrible and right alongside
> it you also have something beautiful,
> generous, and loving and based on
> intensely enriching, enduring bonds—
> then how can we mobilize what is
> enriching to do the work of making
> justice happen in the living present?
> (Ford-Smith & Stephen, this volume)

It has been humbling to bring this volume into being during a period demarcated in part by its potential for racial and memorial reckoning. As we began work on the book in the spring of 2020, the emergent global COVID-19 pandemic had already abruptly altered the contours of our individual and collective daily lives. In its relative suspensions of time and mobility, as well as the predictably disproportionate attentiveness to some lives over others by local, national, and international governance systems, the pandemic brought into stark relief what Brand (2020) has termed the "calculus of the living and dying" (para. 4) of the anti-Black "endoskeleton of our world" (para. 1). In so doing, it simultaneously delivered the conditions that rendered tens of millions of people available and willing to join immediate calls to action by the Black Lives Matter movement in response to the 2020 police murders of Breonna Taylor on March 13 and of George Floyd on May 25. The mass demonstrations against anti-Black violence, police brutality, and racialized and gendered imperialism, although ignited in the United States, were almost instantaneously taken up around the globe in connected yet distinctly context-specific ways.

These transnational uprisings have been most prominently characterized by street demonstrations and by renewed attention to monuments and memorials as key material markers that uphold and spatialize heteropatriarchal colonial and imperial cultural memory. Demonstrators located in various cities and countries rushed en masse to sites of statues, plaques, headstones, sculptures, and other forms of memorialization that commemorate figures associated with the transatlantic slave trade, Indigenous genocide, European colonialism, and racial injustice to deface, topple, protest, and demand their removal, using the hashtag #TakeItDown to document and disseminate their contestations in real time. This confrontation with the neocolonial memorial landscape was—and still is—met with stiff defense, whether immediately in the form of overtly aggressive police responses or later in the form of the levying of resources, legal expertise, and political clout to ensure that "national heritage" remains intact. Here in Toronto, where we as editors are located, the police arrested three artists on July 18, 2020, for applying pink paint to the statues of Sir John A. Macdonald and Egerton Ryerson, architects and propagators of Canada's genocidal residential school system, as part of a Black Lives Matter Toronto action. Word of their arrest spread rapidly through local networks and social media, and hundreds of protestors rallied at the Toronto Police 52 Division where they were being detained on charges of public mischief and denied access to their legal counsel. Demonstrators, including several contributors to this volume, demanded the artists' release, holding vigil overnight. Meanwhile, mounted police officers encircled the protestors in an egregious display of power and a testament to the threat that the painting of the statues, which we read as a radical act of memorialization itself in the form of what Gossett and MacManemin (2020) called a "counter-aesthetic" (para. 29), posed to the white order.

At the time of this project's inception many years ago, we could not have foreseen this transnational groundswell of direct contestations to monuments that would loudly punctuate our global social consciousness in 2020, nor could we have predicted the scope of renewed attention to memorialization that would resultingly infuse our sociocultural, political, and scholarly spheres. That is not to say that this wave of encounters emerged precipitously; in fact, a welcome outcome of this period has been the renewed visibility of what Badilla and Aguilera (2021) termed "repertoires of decolonial de-monumentalization" (p. 1227) in the United States and beyond. Although the toppling and defacement of statesponsored statues are as old as the invention of such nationalist relics themselves, the current moment builds directly on "memory movements" (Ghoshal, 2013, p. 331) of the past two decades that have challenged confederate and white supremacist monuments in the United States, particularly in the South (Beetham, 2016; Leathem, 2020; Toppled Monuments Archive, 2022), with counterdemonstration clashes in Charlottesville in 2017 notably igniting a first wave of nationwide memorial protests (Beetham, 2016). Corresponding initiatives by organizations such as the Philadelphia-based Monument Lab (https://monumentlab.com/), which envisions and enacts more liberatory public memorial landscapes through creative, community-based interventions, have significantly enhanced the impact and reach of these North American-based mobilizations, notably engaging younger generations in a dimension of public life often written off as archaically static and mundane. But, as Badilla and Aguilera (2021) and Frank and Ristic (2020) have argued, it would be myopic to underestimate the formative connections to these U.S.-based actions in other contexts as well, including, respectively, the 2019–2020 anti-neoliberal, decolonial monument protests in Chile and the 2015 #RhodesMustFall, or "fallists," decolonial student movement that originated in Cape Town with the defacement of a statue of Cecil Rhodes—and which quickly evolved into a global phenomenon. #TakeItDown would never have existed without the inspiration of and transnational sociopolitical groundwork laid out by #RhodesMustFall; contextualized in this way, we can understand the monumental contestations of the 2020 racial uprisings as building from and continuing a transnational momentum of decolonial mobilizations. We can also appreciate that the number and density of actions at memorial sites across several continents over a span of just weeks in June and July 2020 and into 2021 offered a poignant reminder of the persistent centrality of these material and symbolic markers to the logics and maintenance of oppressive orders and, thus, to liberatory efforts. A colonial reckoning without a memorial reckoning—or vice versa—would, at this juncture, be difficult to imagine.

The layered contours of these intertwined reckonings sit at the heart of this volume, which brings together feminist reflections on the transnational lives of memorializations to colonial, imperial, militarized, and state violence. We attend here not to remembrance in all its variegated senses but rather pointedly to the communally generated and oriented memorializing practices and rituals through which collective memories and grief are "made material, to be spoken, to be witnessed" (Ford-Smith & Stephen, this volume) by those most touched by disparate yet always already entangled experiences of such violence. Statues, performance, novels, ceremony, memoirs, sonic rituals, documentary film, paintings, comic books, embroidery, poetry, archival initiatives, national inquiries, and legal sentencing hearings are the nontraditional sites and forms of memorial praxis from contexts and experiences across and crossing the globe and spanning decades that the contributors to this volume engage and put into reflexive transnational dialogue. In so doing, they animate their dynamic imbrication and foreground shared curiosities about the role of memorialization in grappling with loss, mourning, and desires to collectively remember and commemorate, as well as urges to forget, amidst and against ongoing conditions of harm and injustice produced by and sustaining a white supremacist global capitalist empire. How, for example, do community-based memorializing initiatives in seemingly unconnected remembrance landscapes speak to, with, and through each other in a world order inflected by racist-sexist colonial, imperial, and neoliberal logics, structures, and strictures? How do they formulate within and move through complex transnational flows and circuits, and what transpires along the way? What ways of being, knowing, and languaging are drawn on to navigate subjectivity, agency, and relationality in these transnational memorial landscapes, and how do they constitute the form the remembrance practices take? When the "right to remember" (UNGA Resolution 60/147, 2005) is the purview of the neocolonial and carceral nation-state and international regimes that beget the violence in the first place, what is at stake in inhabiting grief, mourning, resistance, refusal, and desires for otherwise worlds through caring practices of memorializing? What lives on and becomes newly alive through such inhabitance?

The assumption undergirding these and other curiosities, namely that the contemporary order is predicated on the revision, burial, erasure, and fabrication of national and supranational cultural memory enacted in no small part through hegemonic memorialization practices, is, of course, far from a novel insight. Reflections on the relationship between cultural memory and power are ubiquitous in critical scholarship, certainly including feminist studies, although the subject of memorializing is perhaps most centrally attended to in the interdisciplinary field of memory studies that took shape in Europe and, to a certain degree, North America in the 1980s. Although its philosophical origins lie in Maurice Halbwach's (1925) theory of "collective memory," which first proposed memory as socially mediated and imbricated with a subjective temporality, Huyssen (2003), Olick et. al. (2011), and Winter (2006) have traced the field's more contemporary formulation to the poststructuralist turn of the late 1960s and cultural studies insights of subsequent decades. This included a shift from an early twentieth-century teleology of memory characterized by European modernity's preoccupation with the nation-state, national identity, the building of sovereign futures, and monumentalism's essential role in it all to a postmodern critical consciousness and skepticism over nation-state sovereignty, monumentalism, and claims to historical truth, objectivity, and justice. This shift from "present futures to present pasts" (Huyssen, 2003, p. 11) emerged at a moment characterized by increasing transnational ties and encounters and the movement, migration, and circulation of people and information—and cultural memory—through material and digital spaces at unprecedented rates and speeds. Experiences of and social responses to harm and injustice caused by the deepening global asymmetries produced through neoliberal globalization and by contemporary political violence such as military dictatorships in Latin America, apartheid in South Africa, and the Vietnam War among others could be shared more easily and in relative real time across borders and continents. This was always unevenly skewed, of course, toward Western geopolitical investments in some forms and instances of violence over others, as evidenced in the priorities of the concurrent institutionalization of international human rights and transitional justice paradigms that encoded the "right to remember."

The field drew heavily from insights in nascent cultural studies about the centrality of representational practices to acts of remembrance and the dynamic, techno-sociocultural processes by and through which individual and collective memory and identity are produced, mediated, and inflected locally and transnationally (Erll, 2008; Pethes, 2019). Memorialization, particularly nontraditional, artistic, and embodied forms, as a key "act of transfer" (Connerton, 1989, p. 39) of these contestations has always figured prominently in the discussions, the theorizing of which has been significantly influenced by Young's (1992) notion of "counter-monument." He used counter-monument (now interchangeable with counter-memorial) to describe the self-effacing, ironic, antiheroic, interactive, and impermanent monuments erected in Germany post-WWII that challenged the totalitarian nature of monumentality and foregrounded both a distrust in national narratives of justice and an ambivalence to acts of memorializing painful pasts writ large. Young's intervention put into the spotlight the memorializing practices through which contestations over traumatic pasts manifest, a focus in the field that has evolved significantly since and has recently been preoccupied with decolonial memorial contestations, as previously referenced, and with digital forms of counterhegemonic memorial efforts (see Ernst & Parikka, 2012; Hoskins, 2017; Locke, 2020; and Reading, 2016 for discussions in digital memory studies).

Thus, concerns within memorialization studies about who and what gets remembered or forgotten, whose losses are mourned and grieved, and how and what kinds of memories are assigned cultural value and others made absent have from the outset been inextricable from an evolving consciousness around transnationality, albeit from a distinctly Western vantage point. That is not to say that transnationality has always been theorized as a unit of analysis in this literature; in fact, it is only in the last decade and a half that a subfield that some are calling transnational memory studies—arising in what is commonly referenced as the "third wave" of memory studies—has given the term more rigorous attention. This scholarship emphasizes memory's unboundedness to any nation-state, community, or social movement and animates the inherent dynamic mobility of remembrance, with conceptualizations such as "travelling memory" (Erll, 2011) and "multidirectional memory" (Rothberg, 2009) adding complexity to considerations of locatedness and the processes through which memory is transnationalized and illuminating the unexpected interconnections between differently situated memory movements. Wüstenberg and Sierp's 2020 volume, *Agency in Transnational Memory Politics*, brings together nuanced theorizing about the role of agency in these transnational dynamics, demonstrating how transnational memory is made not through global connectedness but through the deliberate "practices of transnational agents" and the relational commitments therein (p. 4). We find a productive feminist grounding of these deliberations in Altınay et al.'s (2019) edited volume *Women Mobilizing Memory*, which privileges performance and the arts in looking at women's cross-border conversations in relation to mobilizations of memory for justice and the collective building of alternative futures in Chile, Turkey, and the United States. Although not exclusively focused on memorialization practices, their volume's centering of diverse gendered perspectives on and experiences of remembrance in the aftermath of political violence, as well as their efforts to show how remembrance is foundationally shaped by racialized and gendered histories, ideologies, subjectivities, and imaginaries, is a refreshing critical feminist contribution to a memory studies field that has only marginally attended to feminist analyses of gender, sexuality, and race, and rarely intersectionally so (see Hirsch & Smith, 2002, for an overview of early international feminist memory scholarship). In our own review of the memorialization literature of this field, when feminist work does appear, it has historically tended to revolve around the remembrance of sexual violence in conflict, following sensationalizing trends circulated through international human rights regimes that have been a focal point of critique in transnational feminist scholarship (see Crosby et al., this volume; Crosby, 2023; Crosby & Lykes, 2019; Jaleel, 2021).

This collection offers something different, and we believe needed, to academic inquiries into our transnational memorial landscape. The roots of its unique contributions can be traced over a decade ago to a research project housed at the Centre for Feminist Research at York University in Toronto, Canada, titled The Inhabitance of Loss: A Transnational Feminist Project on Memorialization (2014–2019), which centered around dialogues between transnational feminist scholars Alison Crosby and the late Malathi de Alwis about their respective work on survivor-led memorialization initiatives in Guatemala and Sri Lanka (see preface, this volume). Their curiosities around the potential for a "political community of the sorrowing" (de Alwis, this volume) organically evolved to engage other feminist scholars doing research on memorial practices, including Heather Evans, Honor Ford-Smith, Shahrzad Mojab, and Carmela Murdocca. The opportunity to converse about otherwise relatively siloed research interests within our various fields—anthropology, sociology, law, women, gender and sexuality studies, adult education, and performance studies among others—was a source of much-needed vitality and reflection. A memory reading group formed and opened to a broader network of thinkers based in Toronto, and several of its members participated in a conference organized by Mojab in October 2019 titled Reclaiming Justice: Memory and Memorialization of Violence. This edited volume, along with our forthcoming companion interactive digital archive, materialized out of these earlier conversations and initiatives and has dynamically stretched the original project's scope, breadth, and theoretical concerns through the involvement of an even wider array of artists, performers, and scholars who responded to a public call for contributions. In June 2021, we gathered volume contributors for a three-day virtual workshop to reflect on our framings of the transnational as we read each other's initial drafts. The workshop also served as the catalyst for the dialogues taken up in the chapters by Ford-Smith and Stephen and by Turner, Mendez, and Evans.

Throughout its various iterations, this project has remained anchored in a transnational feminist methodology that brings into conversation this plurality of feminist lenses and research on memorialization practices to theorize from within the frame of the transnational. By this we do not mean "transnational" in the comparative international or global sense that is commonly deployed in liberal women's movements and scholarship, as well as other scholarly, sociopolitical, and public discourses. Rather, we reference critical understandings of transnationality developed by the scholarly lineage of transnational feminist thought and praxis that came into articulation in the early 1990s through the work of self-identified women-of-color—postcolonial, diasporic, and Black feminist intellectuals, including Chandra Talpade Mohanty, Inderpal Grewal, Caren Kaplan, and Jacqui Alexander, among others. Situated within academic institutions in the Global North but organizing and thinking with feminist scholars and activists through and beyond the Western axis, they were contending with the global impacts of a reordering of heteropatriarchal racial capitalism primarily via the U.S. empire and its concurrent manifestation in an internationalizing white feminist political and epistemological hegemony. They generated analyses of the racist-sexist inequities and violence produced through neoliberal globalization and embedded heteropatriarchal nationalisms, demonstrating how they overdetermined the conditions of and opportunities for enacting agency in emergent transnational relations, spaces, and processes lauded as inherently progressive and liberatory by mainstream perspectives. In other words, transnational feminist scholars have from the outset understood studies of the transnational as not primarily about movement, transit, expanding connections, solidarities (i.e., "global sisterhood"), and so forth. Rather, they have emphasized the ways that transnational linkages, encounters, processes, and spaces and the formations of non-states around which they are anchored are foundationally constitutive of and reproduce a white supremacist heteropatriarchal and capitalist global empire, and how and what kind of coalitional work is required and being done in this transnationalizing milieu. Crucially, we must remember that their approach did not emerge in isolation. It built on intersectional feminist analyses that had been developing for decades within nonwhite/non-Anglo feminist activist and intellectual spaces and networks around the globe (see Blackwell & Naber, 2002; Moghadam, 2005 for overviews of international organizing and thought in this moment). And notably, as Falcón and Nash (2015), Nash (2021), and Aikau et al. (2015) have reanimated, transnational feminist praxis emerged alongside Black and Indigenous feminist thought, and, particularly, the Black feminist concept of intersectionality (Crenshaw, 1991), which present different genealogies, accountabilities, and analytical foci but also share more historical and theoretical overlap than is commonly acknowledged (James, 2017).

One such overlap is a vested interest in the "*how* of decolonization" (Aikau et. al., 2015, p. 87), particularly the imperative to decenter (feminist) Western epistemologies. As such, a transnational feminist approach must consider the scale of global empire and the "scattered hegemonies" (Grewal & Kaplan, 1994) that are insidiously reproduced through benevolent imperialisms and militarisms, liberalism and liberal feminisms, and development and interventionist paradigms, including human rights and transitional justice mechanisms, to name a few (see also Bueno-Hansen, 2015; Crosby & Lykes, 2019). It also must attend to the complex ways that people's lives are configured within dynamic, multidirectional flows and circulations of people, goods, discourses, information, and so forth if it is to levy transnational analyses that will materially impact people's lives (Alexander, 2005; Trotz, 2006). There is, therefore, a need to prioritize self-reflexive cross-cultural, cross-border work that fervently avoids pulls to universalize or find unity and instead values deeply the particularities and specificities of heterogeneous, differently situated knowledge and experiences as the grounds from which to explore connections, similarities, and coalitional possibilities (Mohanty, 2003; Swarr & Nagar, 2010). This also requires constant scrutiny over our attachments to and investments in stable notions of nation upon which the very existence of transnationality rests (Grewal & Kaplan, 2000). In this way, transnational feminist theorizing has perpetually inhabited and enacted the paradox of mobilizing around and through, yet always working to unsettle its own analytic grounds. As Swarr and Nagar (2010) have articulated, "transnational feminist studies [is] a necessarily unstable field that must contest its very definition in order to be useful" (p. 12).

This volume is that quintessentially postmodern paradox made manifest. Many of the chapters directly mobilize understandings and analyses of the transnational attributed to this lineage, and others trouble, challenge, and even refuse such terms. In her contribution, Dean points out the limits of transnational feminist theorizing of remembrance that assume heterosexuality as the default and argues, drawing on the work of Gopinath (2005), for the usefulness of a queer diasporic framework that looks beyond hetero and homonormative frames of subject, nation, and location. Diaspora is also centered in the chapter by Lawson and Osman, which explores the politics of grief among diasporic Black mothers, and by Henay who, invoking Clark (2009), offers it as a modality to denote the liminal space inhabited and navigated by Black and Indigenous womxn and womxn of color as one of poesies and as one from which flow rich traditions of what she terms "memorying." In another vein, thinking with Afrodiasporic and Indigenous movements in Colombia, Riaño-Alcalá takes up the lens of translocality, which, drawing on Alvarez et. al. (2014), she argues works differently from the transnational feminist frame to "decenter the nation-state as the interlocutor for recognition and move towards an anti-colonial agenda that links issues of gender and race with the defense of their territories and the restoration of harmonious and balanced relations with the environment and sentient beings" (this volume). Resonant concerns, even if more implicit, of whether the vantage point of the transnational can adequately attend to marginalized or non-Western ontologies of locatedness and relations are found in other chapters as well, enriching ongoing conversations about the possibility of doing decolonial and anti-imperial feminist work while carrying vestiges of transnationality's geopolitical origins. This, one might say, is transnational feminist methodology's enduring appeal: that its imperatives and commitments can facilitate such tensions coming to the surface and nuancing our feminist theoretical investments, a process of epistemic decentering that can radically transform our worldviews.

Such matters of epistemology harken back to a talk by curator, writer, and researcher Candace Hopkins.[1] In a presentation at the John H. Daniels Faculty of Architecture, Landscape, and Design at the University of Toronto on February 10, 2016, Hopkins drew on her research in Albuquerque, New Mexico, to talk about the spirits and histories that are exorcised and released when monuments are defaced (UofTDaniels, 2016). Starting with the severing of the bronze foot of the notoriously brutal conquistador Don Juan de Oñate's statue on the 400th anniversary of his arrival, she unpacked the colonial violence and Pueblo resistance that the statue had covered up and that were reanimated with its defacement. She elaborated on several new settler monuments to Oñate that were subsequently erected over the next decade in response and eventual attempts by Albuquerque city officials to quell the controversy by inviting a Native artist to participate in a different memorial interpretation of Oñate's arrival. They approached Santa Clara Pueblo artist Nora Naranjo Morse, who after research and reflection, decided against taking part in their memorial initiative and instead created her own response at Tiguex Park near the Albuquerque Museum, the site of the city's new sculptures. Hopkins described a spiral earthen path with a metal plaque at the entrance that, translated, reads, "Our Center Place" and that tells the story of the Pueblo worldview through its emphasis on earth, water, and plant life. She explains how the embodied act of journeying along the path leads visitors to the center of the spiral where a simple, unassuming rock sits in stark contrast to the grandiose bronze monuments, shifting "the perspective of what's worth honoring: not this violent, murderous man, but the land itself" (UofTDaniels, 2016, 38:32).

In what could easily be missed by those unfamiliar with the memory studies literature, Hopkins referenced Young's (1992) notion of counter-monument, which, as already mentioned, has come to mark the postmodern turn toward critical memorialization studies. Yet in her talk, Hopkins remarked that Naranjo Morse's intervention should be seen as "not a counter-monument, but *something else* [emphasis added]" (UofTDaniels, 2016). A curiosity—perhaps an anxiety—is thus provoked: if it is not a counter-monument, *what is it, then?* With just a few passing words, Hopkins called into question not just the analytical framework but the very worldview through which many have come to understand memorializing practices, gesturing to ways of being, knowing, and remembering that remain elusive within the existing terms of reference.

What it is and isn't, then, can be understood as a broader onto-epistemological provocation around which many of the interventions in this volume find generative convergence as the authors seek articulation of ontologies of remembrance that are not wholly legible within dominant epistemes but are very much alive in our memoryscapes and scholarship. Our use of onto-epistemology draws from Barad's (2007) notion of "ethico-onto-epistem-ology" (p. 90), which explicates the inherent entanglements and inseparability of ontology, epistemology, and our ethical responsibilities in and to the world, positing that "intelligibility is an ontological performance of the world in its ongoing articulation" (p. 379). Barad's formulation gestures to extensive theorizing that has challenged the master coding of Western regimes of being and knowing Human. One example of this is Wynter's (2003) elucidation of the white Western conception of "Man as the political subject of the state" (p. 264) and its "ontologically absolute self-description" (p. 283) in relation to the racialized Other, an ontology of Human that has empirically and epistemologically institutionalized itself as the center and gauge of civilized, rational intellectuality. Wynter's formative assertion that "one cannot 'unsettle' the 'coloniality of power' without a redescription of the human outside the terms of our present descriptive statement of the human, Man, and its overrepresentation" (p. 268) makes clear an ontological imperative that has always been distinctly pertinent to transnational feminist commitments to Western epistemic decentering, and, specifically for our purposes, to theorizing remembrance and memorialization. Engaging questions of what it is and isn't demands that, rather than heeding Radstone and Hodgkin's (2003) caution to privilege the study of memory's epistemological concerns—the "regimes of memory"—over its ontological ones to avoid essentializing, universalizing, objectifying, or romanticizing memory, we instead join a chorus of emergent decolonial memory scholarship in recognizing how the project of coloniality, that of Western science, depends on and normalizes this bifurcation and positivist interpretation of ontology, erasing heterogeneous worldviews and the rich, situated onto-epistemological frameworks that they generate.

This volume has thus neither been organized around nor aimed to arrive at a cohered theorization of or approach to mourning, remembrance, or transnationality, or violence, for that matter, but has endeavored to facilitate a space capacious and reflexively rigorous enough to center a plurality of onto-epistemologies and articulations of "something else" in regard to memorializing practices as its core commitment; for, as Henay warns in this volume, "How we language grief and memory has the power to enclose our imaginations, and futurities." Unsurprisingly, in the same way that counter-monument or counter-memorial failed to describe Nora Naranjo Morse's memorial response to Oñate, so, too, have such conceptualizations and the philosophical traditions from which they originated been insufficient entry points to the remembrance practices discussed in many of these chapters. Some contributors engage concepts and arguments from the memory studies literature, and generatively so; however, the theorizing of remembrance most consistently referenced across the chapters emerges from elsewhere, even if they are increasingly invoked in memory scholarship. This is the case with de Alwis's notion of "tracing absent presence," put forth in her reprinted essay that opens this volume and that has shaped thinking herein around the contours of living with loss that arises from enforced disappearance and with maternal grief (in this volume, also see contributions by Lawson and Osman; Mojab; Murdocca; and Rizzo). In contemplating the afterlife of violence as an absent-presence, theorizations of "haunting" are also widely mobilized, with Gordon's (2008) landmark *Ghostly Matters: Haunting and the Sociological Imagination* serving as a methodological anchor point for some in considering how to "confront the ghostly aspects" of our complex contemporary social lives, of which "haunting is a constituent element" (p. 7; in this volume, see Crosby et al.; Turner et al.). For volume contributors thinking along lines of Blackness, Saleh-Hanna's (2015) theory of Black feminist hauntology and thinking on remembrance in relation to Sharpe's (2016) theory and praxis of "wake work" are more resonant, as their formulations of haunting and ghostliness animate differently the ways that the enmeshments of colonization and slavery permeate all aspects of our social existences. Their works highlight the complexities that arise in thinking through "ghosts" when the perspectives of those who "never achieve, in the eyes of the other, the status of the living" are centrally considered (Holland, 2000, p. 15; in this volume, see Lawson & Osman; Turner et al.). Reasons why these articulations, contextualized within the "hauntological turn" in the humanities and social sciences in the last several decades following Derrida's (1994) *Specters of Marx*, have served as more apt entry points to questions of memorialization than, for example, Megill's (2011) conceptualization of memory as the "other that continually haunts history" (p. 193), merit further elaboration that is beyond the scope of this chapter.

These are only a few of the variegated theoretical lineages and articulations of remembrance brought to bear on questions of memorialization through this project, which together with the divergent approaches to transnationality herein, rendered decisions around how to organize the chapters a formidable challenge. Interestingly, what arose as the most thematically coherent in the way the contributions dialogue is how they speak to the question of what it is and isn't with regard to the forms of remembrance they bring forward. We begin with what it isn't. Part 1, The Colonial, Imperial Logics of Memorializing, renders visible the insidious ways that memorialization practices anywhere—even, and perhaps especially, countermemorializing practices—are embedded in and shaped by racialized gendered colonial and imperial logics that travel and (re)assert themselves through transnational liberal regimes and related policies and practices. The menacing enmeshment of liberalism and memorialization is elucidated in Murdocca's chapter, which reads Canadian reparative sentencing hearings as commemorative national practices of racial capture enshrined in colonial liberal law. Murdocca builds on Lowe's (2015) attenuation to liberal archives to underscore how remembrance of injustice is appropriated by and mobilized in "transnational economies of liberalism" (p. 48) that shore up the white order. This has been ubiquitous in the wake of 9/11, Dean's analysis of remembrance of the 1985 Air India Flight 182 bombings reminds us, as state-sponsored memorializations to racialized "terror" have become a core component of how the U.S. and British empires justify and deflect opposition to increased police, military, and border control securitization.

If Part 1 pays cautionary heed to the slippery entrapments of liberal memorializing projects, Part 2, Inhabiting Loss, Exceeding the Frame, turns to considerations of *what is it* by invoking Indigenous and Black decolonial practices of inhabiting such institutionalized spaces in ways that exceed their very terms, demonstrating onto-epistemic refusal and nuanced negotiations of agency. In this volume, Duhamel foregrounds the anticolonial remembrance practices of Indigenous communities in settler colonial Canada as they engaged the state's National Inquiry into Missing and Murdered Indigenous Women and Girls. These included community-led artistic, creative, and ceremonial expressions of memorialization that nourished affected communities, reclaimed power and place, and recentered "good relations." Crosby, Velásquez Nimatuj, and de los Ángeles Aguilar's chapter in this volume animates the memory work of Maya Q'eqchi women struggling for redress for military sexual harm suffered during Guatemala's genocidal armed conflict. They read an educational youth comic and the testimonies on which it is based through the lens of *testimonio*, a practice of collective remembrance wherein "the individual is a refraction of the community" and through which there emerges a public memory of racialized and gendered violence grounded in a Maya Q'eqchi' worldview that seeks to suture land and body, attending to the systemic dimensions of colonial harm. Riaño-Alcalá turns our attention to the affective and poetic practices of sound memory of the Afro-Colombian *cantadoras* of the Atrato River as they performed by invitation at the signing of the internationally mediated peace accord after decades of armed conflict. Upending expectations of a performance to commemorate the end of violence, the cantadoras used the sonic medium of *alabaos*, which are regional Black traditional funerary chants sung during burial and mourning rituals, to hold local and international officials accountable and to reinscribe into public memory ongoing violence against Black and Indigenous peoples, a practice of "re-membering the world" (this volume) that brings to vibrant life the offerings of this section.

Part 3, Invoking Revolutionary Present Pasts, casts light on those who use creative memorial practices to carry forward memories of women's revolutionary pasts. Mojab weaves her own memories of being an activist with the women's movement and the Kurdish autonomous movement in postrevolution Iran from 1979–83 with political memoirs—which she reads as counter-memorials—of other women from this period in Iran, Oman, and Turkey, a layered exploration of what it means to mourn defeated revolutions and the collective, transnational dreams that nourished them. Postrevolutionary Iran is also the focus of Makaremi's contribution to this volume, in which she reflects on the process of making *Hitch: An Iranian History*, a speculative diasporic documentary film that memorializes her mother and aunt, political prisoners who were disappeared and executed and whose stories are only available through "traces left behind." Subverting and distorting the "fact-finding episteme" that dominates in the afterlife of violence and animating the intergenerational hauntings that breathe life into so much of our memory work, Makaremi offers her film as a means to gather and interpret these traces in the context of a state-sanctioned collective memory "infused with a violence that is busy erasing its own contours" (this volume). The intergenerational dimensions of memorializing are also taken up in Ratih's analysis of the Indonesian Dialita choir, made up of female ex-political prisoners of anticommunist violence from 1965–66 and their daughters. Ratih unpacks how the choir's performances memorialize the ex-political prisoners who did not survive through a sonic practice of collective mourning that celebrates repressed histories of revolution and transnational solidarities in the Global South. Read together, these essays posit that the "transnational archive of women's defiance" (Mojab, this volume), excluded from hegemonic archives of resistance, finds refuge and life in the creative ways we memorialize and care for their legacies and dreams.

Part 4, Care in/as Collective Mourning, moves this theme of care to the fore. As Ford-Smith asserts in her conversation with Stephen, "memory is a labor of care" and one that "affirms the reciprocity and the reliance on others that is required to dismantle violence in its myriad forms" (this volume). The focus of their dialogue is Ford-Smith's immersive performance-installation *Song for the Beloved*, which remembers racial urban violence in Kingston, Jamaica, as a locally inflected manifestation of the violence produced through neoliberal globalization and which has been performed transnationally, and Stephen's *Son*, a multimedia installation in Toronto, Canada, that responds to the threat of racial violence from the perspective of a Black mother parenting a Black son. They reflect on what it means to curate embodied, caring spaces for people to grieve and mourn racialized violence while remembering the love, joy, and relations that emerge alongside as a project of radical social transformation. Lawson and Osman explore the ways that Black women in the U.S.-based Mothers of the Movement continue to care for their children murdered by gun violence at the hands of police or private citizens through the strategic occupation of public political and media spaces to memorialize, seek justice, and reclaim their children's humanity. They locate their memory work in a transnational Black feminist tradition of maternal bereavement in the afterlife of slavery. Rizzo's discussion of the transnational Embroidering for Peace Initiative that protests the logics of the "war on drugs" in Mexico considers how the practice of collective embroidering as an act of memorialization and its anchoring in touch has facilitated space for unique exchanges of care through which enduring relations across difference have been formed. Henay's creative contribution to this volume blends poetics, critical autoethnography, metaphor, images, and archival documents in a practice of ethnographic refusal that renders accessible a "perceived ongoing exchange between living and deceased" through which she grieves *with* her matrilineal Bahamian ancestors as a Black diasporic process of dreaming Afro-Indigenous futurities and of caring for the dead, a practice she terms "sitting with the bones."

Here we return to Hopkins's gesture to "something else" and its deeper implications. We read in Henay's contextualization of "sitting with the bones" as a tradition of "memorying," a casting that "exceeds the temporal" (this volume) and that is done in active dialogue with the dead, an attempt to signal to an understanding of being in relation to grief, remembrance, and memorialization that exists beyond dominant Western frames of reference. A similar effort to language otherwise is found in Duhamel's articulation of "anticolonial remembering," which she explains as a process of "leaning into those things we know and have always known and using this knowledge to reclaim our identities in concrete and radical ways" (this volume). Less straightforward but no less potent interventions in the form of questions percolate through the chapters. What understandings of the human as a relational being are embedded in the centering of "good relations" (Duhamel, this volume) in memorializing missing and murdered Indigenous women and girls? What are the contours of memory in Maya Q'eqchi' worldviews that "seek to suture land and body" and that hold a nonlinear and collective conceptualization of the experience of violence such as the Q'eqchi' *muxuk* (Crosby et al., this volume)? How are grief, memory, and memorialization understood from the perspectives of those who, in the afterlife of slavery, have not been endowed with the privilege of being considered human (Lawson and Osman, this volume)? These and other formative inquiries permeate the chapters of the first four sections, reminding us that it is in how we collectively mourn and memorialize that our onto-epistemologies of memory come to light.

It is also in how we dream. In Part 5, On Worlding, Turner, Mendez, and Evans explicitly foreground such questions through a reflective discussion of the Afronautics lab that Turner facilitated for volume contributors in June 2021. They zoom out from the specificities of memorialization to contemplate what the methodology of Afronautics, which Turner, as a descendant of ancestors who were enslaved, developed as an approach to finding Blackness in colonial archives, reveals about an Afrofuturist understanding of memory and the possibilities for building worlds that it engenders. In Turner's understanding of reality and in her art, remembrance is a practice of critical dreaming, a project of "worlding," of "evoking a speculative world, and of bringing into the mind, body, and existence the possibility," that starts from, rather than leads to, "the dream" (this volume); in other words, remembering is anchored in the collective, heterogenous space of dreaming that conjures futures liberated from the human order of Man and its social and political structures and systems. "The dream" is something that even if one inhabits it for, per Mendez, just "two seconds," then "in that embodied moment, the two-second dream or the two-second vision, you *are* inhabiting it. It is not future, but it is *a* future accessed in the present dream" (this volume). Those of us who participated in Turner's lab were fortunate enough to experience, if briefly, the permission, spaciousness, and invigoration that this onto-epistemology of remembrance offers, an experience that illuminated instantaneously that what threads together our work is not loss, grief, violence, transnationality, or even memory, but rather *a* dream through which each of us, from a distinct location, perspective, worldview, and desire, seeks connection, refuge, and inspiration.

When we reflect on this experience of *a* dream now, we find ourselves recalling the imagery and sounds of Atlantic Ocean water off the coast of Newfoundland that Turner played for us in the workshop, a preview of her multimedia installation *Nave* (2022). Long a symbol of both transnational connection and the Middle Passage, Turner also invokes water often in her work as a living witness to what has been, is, and is yet to come. Can water, then, offer a vantage point from which to conjure *a* dream that, like water, can neither be fully contained nor defined but that is the life-giving and living substance that nourishes, seeps through, carries, and makes possible our collective transnational remembrance? What would the weight of our memories be if not buoyed by such dreaming?

They say, however, that dreams are inevitably bound by the fallibilities of their dreamers, and in that spirit, we would be remiss in a failure to acknowledge some of this collection's shortcomings. Foremost is the absence of trans memorialization practices or some focus on remembrance through the lens of transness. This reflects the ways that transphobia has manifested in and continues to shape many transnational feminist communities, organizing, and scholarship, often despite stated politics otherwise, and unquestionably extends to the grounds and terms of the theorizing itself. Although the analytical frameworks that transnational feminisms mobilize are not inherently incompatible with trans insights into the logics of white cis-heteropatriarchal orders, nor with concomitant visions of coalition, liberation, and what it means to inhabit desire, joy, grief, and care in this moment, such theorizing is not often formatively taken up within them. This erases an abundance of examples of trans remembrance through art, memorials, commemorative events and actions, performance, literature, film, and digital media, and the vibrant contributions to memorialization studies that have much to say about the flows of our transnational remembrance landscapes and their trappings and possibilities (for examples, see Bhanji, 2018; Gossett, 2013; Hatfield, 2019; Lamble, 2008). This gap is a silence that haunts this volume.

Another regret is that the volume does not reflect the salience of the digital in the ways we mourn, remember, and memorialize painful pasts. One chapter contribution attends to digital media as a contemporarily central space and means of mobilizing, engaging, documenting, and sharing in grief and memory (see

Lawson & Osman, this volume), but there is much to be excavated about the layered implications of what Hoskins (2011) termed the "connective turn" in cultural memory studies, referencing the impacts of the "sudden abundance, pervasiveness, and immediacy of digital media, communication networks and archives" on "what memory is and what memory does" (p. 1). We diverge from Hoskins's (2017; 2021) assessments that memory broadly is in a state of crisis due to the digitalization of our world, although imperial and colonial mnemonic epistemes most certainly are, albeit for other, if related, reasons. However, the fact that the digital era has reconfigured the contours of our remembrance landscapes is undeniable, and its implications are both profound and provocative, as reflected in the growing interest in digital memory studies. The digital-transnational nexus birthed through the historically contingent processes of digitalization and neoliberal globalization adds layered complexity to questions of locatedness, difference, discursive flows and travels, agency, and formations of racialized gendered subjectivities and world orders. The relevance of these questions to our memorialization work will be taken up more centrally in our interactive, public digital archiving project (see http://www.memorializingviolence.com/digital-archive).[2]

This volume puts forward generative and provocative reflections at a critical juncture for studies of memorialization. Brand (2020) poignantly noted, "The statues are falling" (para. 7), and this potential for reckonings that continues to reverberate in our remembrance landscapes in the wake of the 2020 uprisings and of those that came before asks that we take seriously the role of our memorializing practices, rituals, and creative expressions in shaping, caring for, and enacting worlds and relations. As the contributions herein attest, doing so must take into account our transnational remembrance entanglements—culturally, politically, and onto-epistemologically—and their racist-sexist colonial and imperial grounds. In this moment of renewed attention to the role of memorials in our interconnected, interdependent struggles for liberation, *how* we engage these contexts, worldviews, and histories-crossing dialogues and what analytical, political, and ethical commitments we mobilize in the process have profound implications. To this end, we believe that the diverse feminist approaches to the transnational dimensions of memorialization included in this volume, individually and in dialogue, generate refreshing insights into and gesture toward otherwise possibilities for engaging pedagogies and practices of memorialization in our transnational remembrance landscapes.

Notes

1   Our deepest gratitude to Suzanne Morrissette for introducing Hopkins's lecture to the memory reading group, a resource that has offered such generative reflection for the project.
2   See also the Transformative Memory Digital Archive project led by Riaño-Alcalá, https://omeka.irshdc.ubc.ca/s/Transformative-Memory/page/welcome.

1

Tracing Absent Presence

• •

MALATHI DE ALWIS

> Upon mountain ranges, across scorching
> plains
> Amidst twining lianas, in gurgling
> streams
> Along highways and byways
> In all my comings and goings
> I trace your beloved face
> Always
> —Adapted by author from a mother's
> lament, May 1992

Forced disappearance is one of the most insidious forms of violence as it seeks to obliterate the body and forestalls closure. The lack of an identifiable body of evidence, as it were, not only confounds the investigations of those who seek the disappeared and thwarts the assigning of accountability but also makes "chronic mourners" (Schirmer, 1989, p. 25) of those left behind.

In this brief essay, I want to think about how such chronic mourners "rein-habit the world" (Das, 2000, p. 223) in the face of continuously deferring loss and what might be its political outcome(s). This re-inhabiting, I wish to suggest, is a constant tracing of traces given the ambiguous nature of the disappeared's status of absence, and thus presence. Although I am much indebted to Derrida's theorization of the trace—with its multiple implications of mark, wake, track, spoor, footprint, and imprint—as an undecidable that is neither fully present nor fully absent, I nevertheless remain steeped in a nostalgia for lost presence (i.e., bodies that matter), which is decidedly un-Derridian (Spivak, 1974, p. xvi).[1]

It seems unavoidable to not valorize presence in contexts of forced disappearance, of fraught absence: Is s/he dead or alive? What proof is deemed adequate to confirm death when no body is available as evidence? Does one mourn permanent absence of presence or a temporary one, which nevertheless carries with it its own anxieties and fears for any moment that absent presence could be made permanent. The terror that one's own feverish search for the disappeared, one's own aggressive inquiries regarding perpetrators and witnesses, could lead to the termination of his or her existence. A simultaneous horror that one's investigations may be too tardy, that the one missed opportunity to pursue the abductors' jeep, to enlist the beneficence of an influential minister, to track down that elusive witness, or to follow up yet another dubious lead could mean the difference between life and death.

How long does one wait expecting return? One, five, ten, fifteen years? Does it ever end, the waiting?

Sri Lankans have become very adept at waiting. One could visit most any district on the island today and hear tales of a father, a sister, a teacher, a friend, the postman, or the fishmonger who went to the store, got on a train, headed to school, and was last seen walking on the beach, never to return home: *athurudahan vuna* (Sinhala), *kanamal podathu* (Tamil), *disappeared*; it has happened during an anti-Tamil riot, a militant attack, a youth uprising, an army cordon and search operation, and most recently, the tsunami. There are still several thousands of people, many of them children, who remain unaccounted after the tsunami. Another estimated twenty-five thousand, predominantly young Tamil men, have been forcibly disappeared from the north and east of the island, which has witnessed almost twenty-five years of civil war between the Sri Lankan armed forces and militant Tamil groups, now primarily the LTTE (Liberation Tigers of Tamil Eelam).

But the dubious honor of recording the highest number of forced disappearances within the briefest span of years goes to the southern regions of the island where between 1987 and 1990, around thirty-five thousand predominantly Sinhala youth and men went missing.[2] Although the militant Sinhala youth group seeking to wrest power from the state, the Janatha Vimukthi Peramuna (JVP), were responsible for some of these disappearances, the state mobilized this form of terror and violence on a much more coordinated and extensive scale. "Bodies rotting on beaches, smouldering in grotesque heaps by the roadsides and floating down rivers were a daily sight during the height of state repression from 1988–1990" (de Alwis, 1998a, p. 185).[3] Many of us had stopped eating fish.

How do people continue to have a "life after atrocity" (Langer, 1997, p. 63)? How do they cope with waking up day after day to ambiguous absence and lacerating loss, to face another day rife with memories, of forgetting, of waiting? There exists today an extensive literature on many variations on this theme of abject life,[4] including survivor guilt and psychic numbing (Lifton, 1967), *testimonio* (Douglass, 2003; Menchú, 1984; see also Crosby et al., this volume), witnessing (Agamben, 1999), a "descent into the everyday" (Das, 2000), melancholia (Jeganathan, 2004), but these have primarily focused on how survivors live with death—a permanent loss, an irrevocable absence. Dominick La Capra (1999), who has made an important distinction between loss (involving particular events and thus specific and historical) and absence (transhistorical, abstract, evacuated, and disembodied), has noted that in posttraumatic situations where such distinctions are conflated and loss is converted into absence, one "faces the impasse of endless melancholy, impossible mourning, and interminable aporia in which any process of working through the past and its historical losses is foreclosed or prematurely aborted" (p. 698). This very conflation, he further noted, "attests to the way one remains possessed or haunted by the past, whose ghosts and shrouds resist distinctions" (p. 699). Though La Capra quite rightly seeks to forestall our all too easy descent into such a maelstrom, I, on the contrary, wish to pause awhile at this moment of conjuncture between loss and absence; to explore its texture and tone, and to understand the affectual burdens of such a haunting. Indeed, I would argue that one cannot adequately comprehend political outcomes of such "life after atrocity" without first addressing and interrogating these moments and spaces of conflation. Could the uncertainty and anxiety, often even a glimmer of hope, that is produced by disappearance and its concomitant evocation of the temporariness of loss and revocability of absence structure the reinhabiting of worlds differently? Does it keep the spirit of resistance alive—that is, "the absence of bodies creates a presence of protest" (Schirmer, 1989, p. 5; de Alwis, 1998, p. 187)? How do such tracings unfold? Does tracing absent presence in the life of objects, albeit abject objects, provide a more meaningful framework for that re-inhabiting? Does it provide a space for a politics?

In the course of extrapolating on the idea of articulation, Derrida (1974) remarked that the trace "does not lend itself be summed up in the simplicity of a present" (p. 66). What he sought to argue is that in the same way that an absence defines a presence and a signified is always a signifier in another system (thus meaning is always deferred, dispersed, and delayed), the present can be known as the present only through the evidence of a past that once was a present: "Since past has always signified present-past, the absolute past that is retained in the trace no longer rigorously merits the name 'past'" (p. 66). The temporalities of lived experience, in the wake of forced disappearance, are similarly complex and exemplified in the comment of a staff member of the Asian

20 • Malathi de Alwis

Human Rights Commission, which documented stories of the families of the disappeared, in 2003:

> The families' emotional retelling of the disappearance of a spouse or child gave the impression that their loved one had disappeared 15 days earlier rather than 15 years earlier. Their pain had not subsided and will probably never do so. This impression of a tragedy that has freshly taken place is reinforced by the families' recollections of dates, times, places, suspected perpetrators and other details of their loved one's disappearance. The future of that entire family was affected too at that fateful moment. Thus those responsible for the disappearances painfully touched the past, present and future of these families. (van Voorhis, 2004, p. 128)

Indeed, the mother's lament too (see above), while evoking her endless tracings and retracings through both natural and manmade scapes in her quest for her disappeared, simultaneously articulates a subtle layering of temporalities through the trace of the disappeared—his face—which appears to her wherever she goes and in whatever she looks. It is as if this very absent presence/present absence of the disappeared is what holds death in check; he is everywhere, always.

This play of past-present, presence-absence in the traces of the disappeareds is also discernible in their families' recountings of nightly hauntings—the disappeared's familiar footfalls pacing through the house, the feel of his fingers "running ants" through an ailing mother's hair (Menike, personal communication, May 1993), an instantly recognizable voice calling out to his mother to make his favorite curry, "almost as if he were in the next room" (Asilin, personal communication, June 1992), or the creak of the well's pulley during the disappeared's favorite bathing time. I have written previously of more complicated, "umbilical" traces that are reiterated through mothers such as Yasawathi, who insisted, "I gave birth to that boy. Surely, won't *I* sense it if he dies?" (de Alwis, 1998a, p. 187) and Seela interpreting her frequent blackouts as moments in which she was communing with her disappeared son, wherever he was incarcerated (de Alwis, 2001, p. 203). However, when the trail of the disappeared grew cold, and weeks and months of absence extended to years, it was in tracing traces in specific objects and mementos, that families of the disappeared seemed to acquire greater solace (see Argenti-Pillen, 2003; de Alwis 1998a, 1998b; Galappatti, 2004; Perera, 2001; Samarasinghe, 1999).

Of all mementos, the photograph still remains the quintessential abject object for it takes its shape and poignancy from death and loss and absence (Mavor, 1995, p. 5).[5] Its unique ability to simultaneously encompass both presence and absence—by signifying absence but simultaneously keeping absence at bay by producing a simulacrum of presence—was particularly palpable when I would visit the homes of members of the (southern) Mothers' Front,[6] a large grassroots women's movement that was protesting the disappearances of their kin during the JVP youth uprising in the early 1990s. No conversation would be complete without the invocation of the absent presence of the disappeared, an almost imperceptible tilting of the head or a casting up of the eyes toward a photograph of the disappeared, which would be given pride of place upon the hallway wall or upon the single glass cabinet, the repository of prized crockery and knickknacks. The photograph(s),[7] often garlanded with fresh or plastic flowers and "brought alive"[8] in the flickering glow of an oil lamp, lit every evening, and joss sticks wafting smoke and ash were accorded reverence equivalent to a religious icon that would be similarly propitiated within the domestic space. Similarly, the clothes (and importantly, used towels) left behind by the disappeared and to a lesser extent other mementoes of their lives such as schoolbooks, sports trophies, certificates, and letters were preserved and treasured items, lovingly brought out, caressed, and commented upon at great length during such visits. Frequently, the very name of the young man or boy either written in his own hand or in that of another would bring tears to his parents' and siblings' eyes as their fingers gently retraced the curvilinear, Sinhala script that proclaimed an entity, an identity, now untraceable.

For many families, however, seeing an object that belonged to the disappeared, outside the context of his home—that is, out of place—was the most shattering and painful. One mother recalled how she fainted when one young man who had escaped from an army camp brought her the amulet her son always wore around his neck. Newspapers carried similar stories of mothers and wives swooning over segments of sarongs and false teeth they insisted belonged to their sons and husbands, which were unearthed from a mass grave in Suriyakande between 1993 and 1994. The parents of Hemantha Chandrasiri, who went to a commemoration of murdered law students to meet someone they thought could intercede on behalf of their disappeared son, collapsed when they saw their son's photograph included among those being commemorated (Puvimanasinghe, 2004). Most poignant, however, is the daily torment of 19-year-old Lichchowi Nishanthe Weerasinghe's 72-year-old mother who frequently encounters a man wearing the shoes she had gifted her son and which he was wearing the day he was abducted. She has opted not to report this man, fearful that other members of her family will be harmed (Puvimanasinghe, 2004).

Although such mementoes, and, in particular, photographs of the disappeared, play almost a sacral role in the everyday life of those who mourn their absence, their function outside the space of the domestic was equally crucial during a particular moment in Sri Lankan history.[9] Following the example of the Madres of Plaza del Mayo in Argentina, the members of the Mothers' Front also riveted a nation by marching with photographs and other mementos of their disappeared along the streets of the capital city, Colombo, as well as in other regions of the island between the years 1990 and 1993.

In a context where the state was denying that its armed forces and paramilitaries were abducting young men and where local police stations were refusing to record entries regarding abductions, in a context where the site of incarceration was unknown and bodies missing or so mutilated that they were unidentifiable, the often sole photograph of the disappeared that was possessed by his family was the primary document that authenticated existence—in most visually visceral terms. This person was flesh and blood; he lived and breathed. There he stands sweating in his Sunday best at the local studio; here he is accepting a gold medal for athletics, receiving his degree, getting married, and holding his first child. He was there! It is this "evidential force" of the photograph, simultaneously evoking "the past and the real," observed Barthes, that bears testimony "not on the object but on time" (Barthes, 1981, pp. 88, 82).[10] Indeed, from a phenomenological viewpoint, Barthes further noted, a photograph's "power of authentication exceeds the power of representation"; it is a veritable "certificate of presence" (Barthes, 1981, pp. 89, 87).

Likewise, an unforgettable moment at one of the public meetings of the Mothers' Front in 1992 came when a mother seated in the audience suddenly disrupted the speech of a politician by holding up a pair of blue shorts (commonly worn by junior schoolboys in Sri Lanka) and wailing and lamenting loudly: "They are my most precious possession because they still bear the scent of my child. I won't wash them until he returns and wants to wear them to school again. . . . I have been waiting for two years." The size of this piece of clothing stirred the hearts of all those present for it was very clear that this was a very young boy who had been disappeared.[11]

Particularly poignant was how this mother continued to articulate her relationship to this piece of clothing through her materialized labor of caretaking through doing laundry. Such a labor also invoked her caretaking of her son—of washing him and of washing his clothes—and neither task could be performed because of his (physical) absence as well as his absent presence (his scent). Physical absence, which in this instance is not perceived as finite, makes the identificatory logic of maternity (imbricated in caretaking) particularly traumatic because the mother cannot "take care" of her son's clothing—that is, wash it— because it still carries the trace of his absent presence.[12]

Such chronicles of loss and absence reassert the presence of the disappeared and "*publicly* [emphasis added] break the state's monopoly over memory" (Schirmer, 1994, p. 202; cf. Taussig, 1992). The very bodiliness of massed women in public spaces which "highlight viscerally the very lack of bodies" (Schirmer, 1994, p. 189) in the discourses of the state are thus doubly bodied through the traces and markers of other bodies with which they clothe their own bodies.[13] The disappeared who are denied names or identities by the state, who are assumed to "occupy no space," now "have a place" (Franco, 1985 p. 420) upon the bodies that birthed them and "mothered" them.[14]

This poignant formulation recalls Walter Benjamin's (1972) insistence on the centrality of the photographic caption that "literarises the relationships of life" (p. 25). It is these women's bodies that caption the photographs they carry of their kin as disappeared. This implication of doubled authenticity, as it were, not only gives credibility to the "realness" of the disappeared but also asserts the "realness" of the women's relationship to their disappeared; it echoes a previous placeness of the disappeared *within* the bodies of these women—a crucial link in the structuring of sentiment and the engendering of a critique of a repressive state (see de Alwis, 2000).

It is such echoes that also produce a *punctum*, that wounding or piercing that Roland Barthes (1981) described so eloquently as being effected by certain photographs (pp. 26–27).[15] An additional gift, "the grace of the *punctum*," Barthes further noted, is also that "additional vision," the "power of expansion" (p. 45) that enables us to see beyond the photograph through "*what is nonetheless already there* [emphasis original]" (pp. 55–59) in the photograph.[16]

This "subtle *beyond* [emphasis original]" of the punctum (Barthes, 1981, p. 59) is exemplified in the lament of this 70-year-old mother: "*Aney*, it is not I who should be carrying this picture [of her son]. It is my son who should be carrying pictures. . . . *Aiyo*, he should be carrying *my* picture, at *my* funeral."[17] A similar poignancy and untimeliness of loss were evoked by the wedding photographs that several women carried around their necks; frequently, the only photographic record they possessed of their recently betrothed disappeared.

Barthes (1981) has also written movingly of the "umbilical" connection between a photograph, its referent, and its viewer: "From a real body, which was there, proceed radiations which ultimately touch me . . . light, though impalpable, is here a carnal medium, a skin I share with anyone who has been photographed" (pp. 80–81, also p. 5; see also Sontag, 1973). Barthes's evocation of a shared skin also recalls another kind of skin—the child's clothing—that I referred to above. Thus, the trace of the disappeared—that is, his image, his scent, and his touch—takes hold of the be(holder); it becomes a tie that binds.[18]

For Judith Butler (2004), grief, too, is a tie that binds. It is "the thrall in which our relations with others hold us, in ways that we cannot always recount or explain, in ways that often interrupt the self-conscious account of ourselves we might try to provide, in ways that challenge the very notion of ourselves as autonomous and in control. . . . I am gripped and undone by these very relations" (p. 23). Unlike La Capra (1999),[19] who is concerned that allowing ourselves to be interminably caught up in the thrall of our grief is intellectually unproductive and psychically debilitating, Butler revels in this relational undoing and insists that to grieve is not to be resigned to inaction. For it is in this undoing, this submitting to a transformation due to loss, that a space for politics unfolds.

This undoing, for Butler (2004), is both psychical (see above quote) and physical: "One is undone, in the face of the other, by the touch, by the scent, by the feel, by the prospect of the touch, by the memory of the feel" (p. 24). Thus, at the same time that we struggle for autonomy over our bodies, we are also confronted by the fact that we carry the "enigmatic traces of others" (p. 46) and that we are interdependent and physically vulnerable to each other. This unboundedness of flesh and fluids, this corporeal vulnerability, argued Butler (2004), must surely engender an imagining of another kind of political community that implicates us in "lives that are not our own" (p. 28) and develops "a point of identification with suffering itself" (p. 30).

It is clear that Butler's envisioned audience resides primarily in the United States or other Western nations who, having been made vulnerable through violence (including 9/11), have resorted to war, to defining who is human, and to deciding whose deaths are grievable and whose are not. Butler (2004) posits an alternative way of dealing with injury and grief and the "dislocation of First World privilege, however temporary": "To be injured means that one has the chance to reflect upon injury, to find out the mechanisms of its distribution, to find out who else suffers from permeable borders, unexpected violence, dispossession, and fear, and in what ways. . . . It offers a chance to start to imagine a world in which that violence might be minimised, in which an inevitable interdependency becomes acknowledged as the basis for global political community" (p. xiii).

Although Butler (2004) acknowledged that she did not yet know how to theorize this interdependency, I find her resolve to rethink international political coalitions, in light of this and previous feminist critiques and stress on requiring "new modes of cultural translation," particularly productive (p. 47). Butler remained unclear about what such translations would exactly entail but was nevertheless certain that they would differ from "appreciating this or that position or asking for recognition in ways that assume that we are all fixed and frozen in our various locations and 'subject positions'" (p. 47). Such a formulation pushed me to rethink my previous arguments regarding political communities in Sri Lanka in the wake of atrocity (de Alwis, 1998a, 1998b, 2000). While criticizing the ethnically majoritarian Sinhala community for translating their perception of vulnerability to that of further discriminating and waging war against the Tamil minority, I had suggested that it might have been more productive for Sinhala and Tamil women to have politically allied under the aegis of "motherhood," using such a subject position contingently, of course. But maybe what we should really aim for is the formation of alliances under the mark of grief, a political community of the sorrowing.

Notes

Ironically, this essay, too, is a palimpsest of traces having poorly weathered several computer crashes, and I am grateful to Dilki de Silva and Pradeep Jeganathan for so generously lending me their computers at crucial moments of this writing process. My thanks also to Piya and Parama for coaxing this essay out of me and thus enabling me to finally confront some of my own hauntings. This essay is dedicated to Diga, who cannot "with simple grief assuage dismemberment" (from Fernando, n.d.).

1 It is also important to keep in mind that Derrida evokes the trace in a very different context—that of writing (see especially Derrida, 1974, part I, ch. 2).

2 This is an estimate on which most local and international human rights organizations have settled. Journalistic accounts of that period such as Chandraprema (1991, p. 312) list the number as forty thousand. The more accepted figure, however, especially among families of the disappeared, is sixty thousand. This is the figure I have also used in my previous work (see, for example, de Alwis, 1998a, 1998b, 2000).

3 Of the 7,761 cases that were heard by the Commission of Inquiry into Involuntary Removal or Disappearance of Persons in the Western, Southern and Sabaragamuwa Provinces, the bodies of the victims were found only in 1,513 (19.4 percent) of the cases. Others had disappeared "without a trace," and the commission was quick to point out that in such a context, the word "disappearance" was only a euphemism for death caused by extrajudicial killings (see *Final report of the Commission of Inquiry*, 1997, p. 27; see also de Alwis, 1998b, p. 11, fn1).

4 I am using abjection here *pace* Butler to designate "a degraded or cast out status within the terms of sociality" (Butler, 1993, p. 3, fn2).

5 In this regard, Christian Metz's (1990) comment that a "snapshot . . . is an instantaneous *abduction* of the object out of the world into another world, into another kind of time [emphasis added]" is chillingly ironic (p. 158).

6 I am appending a locational qualifier here to differentiate this group from a similarly named group that was formed in the north and east of the island, ten years prior, to protest the disappearance of Tamil youth by the Sri Lankan armed forces.

7 There were many tragic instances where a family had lost more than one member to violence: a father disappeared while seeking his abducted son, daughters were raped and sons taken in lieu of the father, who was later murdered as well, three sons were abducted on the same day from different locations, one son was killed while fighting the LTTE in the north and the other disappeared, and one father died of a "broken heart" a week after his son was abducted.

8 One of the interns who documented the stories of the families of the disappeared for the Asian Human Rights Commission recalls how once when she asked to see a photograph of the disappeared, "One mother who had lost her son went to the kitchen and brought a towel, with which she carefully cleaned, then polished her son's photo on the table before us. To me, she looked as if she was going to dress her son in his best clothes, tie his shoelaces and comb his hair. She treated the photograph as if it were her son alive" (Jeong-ho, 2004, p. 124). Many mothers, as well as children, sought to perpetuate this notion that their disappeared was still alive, and his return was imminent by keeping his share of each meal they partook, imagining he was incarcerated in a "dark, unknown place," living in another town or city, or gone abroad. See discussion in previous section.

9 Photographs also play a central role at the Wall of Tears, part of the Monument for the Disappeared, in Seeduwa, which commemorates disappearances from that region and was built by activists from the Seeduwa area with financial support from the May 18 Memorial Foundation in Gwangju, South Korea, and the Asian Human Rights Commission in Hong Kong. Ironically, in 1994, a much larger national monument to the disappeared, designed by installation artist Jagath Weerasinghe and located enroute to the new Parliament in Kotte, was erected by the Peoples' Alliance government, which suppo4rted the (southern) Mothers' Front and routed the regime that perpetrated these disappearances; that monument, however, has

26 • Malathi de Alwis

fallen into ruin while this smaller monument in Seeduwa is well maintained, much visited, and linked with annual commemorative ceremonies on October 27—declared as Disappearance Day to memorialize when two key activists from the Seeduwa area were abducted—and World Human Rights Day on December 10. Two important reasons for this, I argue, are that the monument at Seeduwa is a much more organic memorial, built with the active participation of people in that region, and it incorporates photographs of the disappeared, which provides a tangible link for the visitors to the memorial, unlike the national monument at Kotte, which is much more abstract in its symbolism.

10 Sontag (1973), in her assertion that photographs "furnish evidence," calls our attention to the fact that a photograph "seems to have a more innocent, and therefore more accurate, relation to visible reality than do other mimetic objects" (p. 5).

11 The majority of those who were disappeared were aged between 20 and 45. However, there were about thirty schoolboys who were disappeared from the Embilipitiya region (in southwestern Sri Lanka), supposedly to avenge a personal vendetta of the principal of their school.

12 Christian Boltanski, who has noted the shared heritage of clothing and photographs as "simultaneously presence and absence . . . both an object and a souvenir of a subject, exactly as a cadaver is both an object and souvenir of a subject," nevertheless fails to capture the complexity of "presence" that is embedded in such "souvenirs," such as a person's scent or sweat stains (quoted in Mavor, 1997, p. 111).

13 One father of a disappeared who participated in a march also attended by the Mothers' Front chose to make this statement in a slightly different fashion by wearing a blood-spattered T-shirt, which, he announced, bore evidence of the great fight he had put up in an attempt to stop those who had abducted his teenaged son two and a half years previously. The photograph and caption documenting this were published in *The Island* on March 3, 1992, p. 3, and on the same day on the front page of its sister paper, *Divaina*).

14 Jennifer Schirmer (1994) goes so far as to suggest that the photographs hanging from the necks of the madres in Argentina echo the dog tags worn by soldiers and "demonstrate the nonhumanity of war (appearing as replaceable parts, as luggage)"; these women thus use the "public grammar of war" only to counter it through "intense bodily metaphors" that they wear on their bodies (p. 189).

15 Interestingly, Derrida (1978), in a play on the German/English word *Spur*—trace, wake, indication, mark—noted that it is a word "which perforates even as it parries" (p. 41).

16 Benjamin (1972) referred to a similar potency in photographs when he noted, "The spectator feels an irresistible compulsion to look for the tiny spark of chance, of the here and now, with which reality has, as it were, seared the character in the picture; to find that imperceptible point at which, in the immediacy of that long-past moment, the future so persuasively inserts itself that, looking back, we may rediscover it" (p. 7).

17 *Aney* and *aiyo* are common exclamations of despair somewhat akin to "Alas!"

18 Mavor (1997) captured well this "evidence" of bodiliness in clothing and (to a lesser extent in photographs) when she noted: "For me, wearing the clothes of a loved one or a friend, in which their smells come forth, in which their body has worn the cloth smooth or through, is akin to carrying a photographic image with me . . . I sense them skin to skin" (p. 121).

19 La Capra's (1999) arguments stem from different political stakes, which are equally laudatory but which I cannot go into in this essay.

Part 1

The Colonial, Imperial Logics of Memorializing

● ●

2

Law's Racial Memory

• • • • • • • • • • • • • • • • • • • •

CARMELA MURDOCCA

In 2018, commenting on the need to weigh individual and historical experiences of anti-Black systemic racism in the imposition of a prison sentence, Justice Shaun Nakatsuru of the Superior Court of Ontario stated: "Social structures and societal attitudes that were born of colonialism, slavery, and racism have a very long reach. We must not forget this. Our memory of past injustices must be long enough to do justice in an individual case" (*R. v. Morris*, 2018, p. 37). The sentencing decision concerned Kevin Morris, a young Black man living in Toronto, who was subjected to a police chase, detention, and injury by Toronto officers, P. C. Keefer and D. C. Moorcroft. In 2014, instead of pursuing an investigation of a nearby home invasion, the police surveilled and detained Morris and three other young Black men. None of the four men were involved in the home invasion. Morris was ultimately charged and found guilty of possession of an unauthorized firearm and sentenced to fifteen months in jail (*R. v. Morris*, 2018, p. 8). In the decision, Justice Nakatsuru relied on biographical and documentary evidence concerning the history of anti-Black racism in Canada, as well as the social history and experiences of Kevin Morris, to determine a prison sanction. Significantly, all parties to the case—the defense and the Crown—agreed that systemic and background factors should be considered when sentencing Black Canadians. They did not agree, however, on how such evidence should be weighed, nor on the appropriateness of the fifteen-month sentence imposed by the judge. The Crown appealed the ruling on the basis that the sentence was too lenient given the seriousness of the offense and maintained that a causal link must be established between Morris's experience of anti-Black racism and the commission of the offence in order for the realities of anti-Black racism to be factored into a sentencing calculus (Sharma, 2021).

Raising the profile of the case, ten community legal advocacy organizations were granted standing in the appeal. These organizations included the Black Legal Action Centre, Canadian Association of Black Lawyers, Aboriginal Legal Services, South Asian Legal Clinic of Ontario, Chinese and Southeast Asian Legal Clinic, Colour of Poverty/Colour of Change Network, Canadian Muslim Lawyers Association, and the Urban Alliance on Race Relations, among others. The Court of Appeal found that judges can take judicial notice of anti-Black racism at sentencing but cautioned that social context evidence cannot be used to mitigate the seriousness of the offence (*R. v. Morris*, 2021). This precedent-setting case raises important sociolegal questions about how judges may consider individual and group-based experiences of historical and systemic anti-Black racism when considering confinement and imprisonment. The invocation of past and ongoing experiences of systemic racism throughout the case animates carceral law as a collective site of racial memory-making.

R v. Morris (2018, 2021) followed an established trend in Canadian criminal law that incorporates restorative justice measures when a person is confronting the racial violence of the carceral state through confinement and imprisonment. Since the 1990s, reparative and restorative justice measures have been increasingly prioritized in criminal justice reforms; however, this emergent sociolegal field raises practical and fundamental questions about how reparative justice practices shore up and legitimize racial carceral violence. This trend is driven in part by a unique sentencing provision in Canada's criminal code that instructs sentencing judges to consider historical and social context in the lives of Indigenous people in the "criminal punishment system" (Kaba, 2021, p. 2). Known as the Gladue principle, named after the first supreme court case that interpreted and applied this provision, the statute requires a consideration of the social and contextual factors that bring an Indigenous person before a criminal court (*R. v. Gladue*, 1999). Sentencing decisions have attempted to extend a Gladue approach to consider the application of this legal provision to the sentencing of Black Canadians, who also experience gendered systemic racism and the legacies of slavery, segregation, and anti-Black racism in Canadian society. In these cases, judges have considered how systemic racism and structural disadvantage have affected the lives of Black Canadians facing criminal charges (Murdocca, 2013). Although this sentencing trend is not a panacea for the overincarceration of Black and Indigenous people in Canada, the aim involves a new methodology for alternative sentencing and the use of incarceration as a last resort.

As rituals of law's violence, sentencing hearings offer a rich site to consider how the conjuring of the past and the use of broader social and historical context work to legitimize the racial violence of the prison. As Balfour (2013) maintained: "It is important to consider the legal narratives of sentencing decisions as they provide a glimpse of the practice of law as distinct from the text of the law . . . sentencing decisions can be read as social practices that are expressions of dominant cultural meanings and relations of power that operate within particular cultural and institutional contexts (p. 88)." Sentencing decisions provide a window into the individual and collective relational dynamic at play when a project of liberal reparative justice is incorporated into national racial governance. Individual sentencing decisions can thus be read, in part, as a collective repository of legal responses to histories of anti-Black and anti-Indigenous racism in the criminal punishment system. The drama of the sentencing hearing is to perform and legitimize this system of racial capture. Reparative practices in sentencing should thus be viewed as a project of racial governance that work to sustain the criminal punishment system (Murdocca, 2013).

To show the case of *R. v. Morris* as part of a trajectory of restorative or reparative practices in sentencing, it is necessary to unpack the reasoning advanced in the trial decision, reasoning that proceeded by considering the weight given to histories of anti-Black racism and the utility of analogizing anti-Black and anti-Indigenous racism and that then concluded with the imposition of a prison sanction. I propose a framework that considers the sentencing hearing a site where a violent system of racial capture functions as commemorative national practice. For this reason, this chapter prioritizes an analysis of the trial level decision in this case.

Despite effort to consider anti-Black racism, Kevin Morris and his friends were nevertheless subject to the violence and surveillance of policing, detention, physical and psychological injury, and imprisonment. Given these experiences, for whom is this practice reparative? In the first section, I situate an analysis of sentencing hearings (and law more broadly) as sites of commemorative national practice within the transnational economies of liberalism in which this reparative practice is embedded. The reparative juridic evidence how this sentencing practice functions as a repository of the collective memory of colonial, racial, and anti-Black violence in service of liberal forms of racial rule. In particular, I chart a route through a consideration of law as archive to show how law carries the symbolic, material, and representational archival traces of histories of gendered anti-Black and racial colonial violence.

Attending to the transnational economies of liberalism in which this reparative provision is embedded shows how a national judicial ritual of sentencing participates in and mobilizes global dimensions of differently situated histories of slavery and settler colonialism constitutive of genealogies of liberalism. In using the phrase "transnational economies of liberalism," I follow Lowe's (2015) transnational feminist methodological imperative to delve into the liberal archive—in this case, the liberal archive of law—for how global and transnational genealogies of slavery, colonialism, and empire find expression in the institutionalization of racial governance. This approach brings into view how circulating modern ideas of reason, progress, and reparation in liberal law are deeply commensurate with ongoing processes of racial violence, anti-Black violence, colonialism, and empire (Lowe, 2015). I argue that it is imperative to consider law as a site of racial memory-making in service of liberal projects of racial rule. Law's racial memory, I suggest, is a useful register to consider how legal discourse seizes and contains histories of anti-Black and racial colonial gendered violence to consolidate what Lowe describes as the global and transnational "economy of affirmation and forgetting that structures and formalizes the archives of liberalism, and liberal ways of understanding" (p. 3). The "economy of affirmation and forgetting" central to liberalism is constitutive of "race" because, as Eng and Han (2019) have explained, "Race may be considered the historical trace of what remains between the affirmation of a universal (European) liberal human subject and the forgetting of a long history of African slavery, Asian indentureship, and indigenous dispossession on which that universalism was constructed" (p. 13).

In the second section, I consider how legal attention to histories of slavery and colonialism in the laws of sentencing displays an interpretive practice where a reparative moral ideal delivers a punitive blow. I follow the logic of the "economy of affirmation and forgetting" in the sentencing decision, attending to the plotting of a continuum from the particular facts of the case to the historical contingencies of gendered anti-Black racism, the legacies of slavery and segregation, and processes of settler colonialism. I use the invocation of the past in *R. v. Morris* to consider how particular versions of Blackness inform a consideration of law's racial memory. In focusing on one sentencing decision, I do not intend to overdetermine the role of one judge or one decision in a broader system of racial carceral violence. Indeed, as will be examined, this decision is constitutive of relational genealogies of gendered colonial racism alive in the racial carceral process. I draw particular attention to how a transnational feminist framework compels an analysis of relationality as a methodological imperative for considering law's racial memory. Relationality signals the ways that broader structures and logics of gender, race, and white supremacy travel within and across racial formations and colonial frontiers (Alexander & Mohanty, 2010; Grewal, 2017). A relational approach to understanding processes of racialization and redress is of critical importance because such an approach prioritizes the role of individual and group-based experiences in pursuing an analysis of history, race, gender, and power in sociolegal culture.

Law as Racial Memory

Scholarly discussion on the connections between law, history, and memory generally proceeds through two lines of inquiry. The first focuses on how historical change shapes law. In this formulation, law is an object that is refined or produced by historical forces. The second line of inquiry prioritizes a perspective internal to law and examines "law for the way it uses and writes history as well as for the ways in which it also becomes a site of memory and commemoration" (Sarat & Kearns, 1999, p. 2). I follow this latter thread and position law as an active site of memory-making and commemorative national practice that is embedded in transnational economies of liberalism in which reparative juridics play a central role. Law as an active site of commemorative memory-making attends to how "law writes the past, not just its own past, but the past for those whom law seeks to exercise dominion.... Law constructs a history that it wants to present as authoritative ... and law uses history to tell us who we are" (Sarat & Kearns, 1999, p. 3).

This approach is consistent with Pierre Nora's view that memory is "above all archival. It relies on the materiality of the trace, the immediacy of the recording, the visibility of the image" (Nora, 1984, as cited in Sarat & Kearns, 1999, p. 12) and evokes Derrida's use of the idea of trace. Borrowing from Levinas, Derrida described memory as trace to signal the absent presence of meaning in the constitutive and repetitive production of memory. As de Alwis describes in this volume, attending to trace as a mode of signification in textual, visual, or legal practice requires the recognition that "the present can be known as the present only through the evidence of a past that once was a present." Borrowing from Raymond Williams, Lowe (2015) explained that the modifying word "residual" refers "to elements of the past that continue, but are less legible within, contemporary social formations" (p. 19). In this vein, attention must be given to how the traces of historical regimes of colonial, racial, and gendered violence continue to manifest in symbolic, institutional, and legal practices.

Adjacent to the line of inquiry that situates law as a residual site of remembrance for colonial, racial, and anti-Black violence is a consideration of law's archive, of the role of law in creating an archive of collective memory and national commemoration. Collective memory refers to shared meanings and representations of memory and the past constructed through social institutions and structures (Halbwachs & Coser, 1992). Sociolegal scholars describe how law's archive is formed through the daily procedural activities of law. Sarat and Kearns (1999) asserted that cases create "a record, courts can become archives in which that record serves as the materialization of memory" (p. 13) and that connected lines of precedent through evidence, transcripts, documents, visual representation, and written decisions, for example, ultimately form law's memory. Sarat and Kearns further stated that the temporal dimensions of disputes in law require attention to the "slippery terrain of memory, as different versions of the past events are presented for authoritative judgement" (p. 3). These normative processes of law are embedded in historical and transnational economies formed through slavery and colonialism. As Mawani (2012) suggested, viewing "law as archive" acknowledges this "dynamic formation in which law and history morph, mutate, and bleed into one another without ever fully collapsing" (p. 351). A sentencing hearing in Canada can thus be understood as performing and codifying a system of racial capture producing a collective repository of legal and ethical responses to histories of anti-Black and colonial racism.

Law not only carries but also invents memory through a socially constructed archival practice that works to cohere and bind groups and nations, serving a collective pedagogical function (Halbwachs & Coser, 1992; Razack, 1999). Feminist transnational scholars of colonial archives suggest that in national and local contexts formed through empire, the methodological imperative is to view the use of the archive not as an "extractive exercise;" rather, the production of the archive is an ethnographic exercise that requires attention to the political, cultural, and affective designations and registers (Stoler, 2009, p. 47). Archival memory produced through law "perpetually creates itself as a legitimate form of command while always harboring the possibility that its authority and legality may be called into question by exactly those documents it produces and seeks to protect" (Mawani, 2012, p. 351). In societies structured by white settler racial capitalism, law contains the archival residue and instrumentality of power and subjectification in service of racial violence. As Lowe (2015) asserted, "Refusing the simple recovery of the past" demands attention to how liberal political rationalities instantiate race and racial and human difference as the onto-epistemological form of liberal rule (p. 136). Signaling an active process of memory-making, the archive is thus a "force field that animates political energies and expertise, that pulls on some 'social facts' and converts them into qualified knowledge that attends to some ways of knowing while repelling and refusing others" (Stoler, 2009, p. 22). Recognizing law as archive, and indeed law's archive, consolidates the view that law is a repository of racial memory-making. As Stoler (2009) suggested, "In no small part (the archive) inscribes the authority of the colonial state and the analytic energies mobilized to make its assertions. But it also registers other reverberations, crosscurrent frictions, attractions, and aversions that worked within and against those assertions of imperial rights to property, persons, and profits that colonial regimes claimed as their own" (p. 21).

Law thus carries the symbolic, material, and representational archival trace of histories of anti-Black and racial colonial violence. Memory as trace is a useful description to consider the routine activities of law because in every legal act there is "an invitation to remember" in the "testimony of witnesses at a trial, in the instruction a judge gives to a jury, in particular interpretive theories, and in the monumental buildings that honor our courts as well as our prisons" (Sarat & Kearns, 1999, p. 13). Law, and the residue of trace, forms part of the daily practices of memory-making, an archive in action, a repository, and a normative tool to build new national and public narratives. I am suggesting, then, that law's racial memory, a collective memory archive, is thus constituted by the routine, temporal, and affective dimensions of law that ultimately serve a normative function in racial governance and violence. Law's racial memory expresses the contestations and entanglements of law in the production and administration of liberal societies structured by ongoing racial violence.

In using the phrase "law's racial memory," I am mindful of Mawani's important conceptual work on law's archive. Mawani (2012) claimed that "law is the archive" and builds an argument that "refers to 'law as archive' or 'law's archive'" (p. 340, fn6). Mawani aligned this phrasing with work in sociolegal historical studies that makes a conceptual distinction between "law and ..." and "law is ...". As Tomlins and Comaroff (2011) have explained, the tradition of historiographical scholarship invoking "law and ..." relations signals conceptual and analytical distance between law and other forms of social and political relations. "'Law and' relies on empirical context to situate law as a domain of activity. It explains law through its relations to cognate but distinct domains of action (society, polity, economy, culture) by parsing the interactions among them" (p. 1040). Motha (2015) added that the "law and society movement," for example, "might be summed up, albeit reductively, as the tendency to lodge the problem of law elsewhere ("law and ...")" (p. 327). The conceptual turn to "law is ..." signaled in *law is racial memory* or *law's racial memory* "dwells instead on the conditions of possibility for critical knowledge of the here and now" (Tomlins & Comaroff, 2011, p. 1044). The conceptual form of "law is ..." is indebted to genealogical analysis where law is a constitutive practice in which the past operates as points of emergence and contingency, modulating the present with meaning and resonance.

Reparative Juridics

The racial violence of the prison is shored up and performed through sentencing decisions. As Rodríguez (2006) explained: "The prison's fundamental logic of power becomes apparent and comprehensible through the drama of racist state violence that creatively renders (that is, materially practices and discursively represents) the physical subjection of the racially overdetermined captive body" (p. 10). The drama of the sentencing hearing is to perform and legitimize this system of racial capture. In Canada, the use of social and historical context when a person's liberty is at stake is a practice deployed to determine what the law describes as the mitigating and aggravating factors to be weighed when a person is confronting imprisonment and confinement. As I argue, this is a pernicious practice because its racial structure binds reparative juridics with state retribution (Murdocca, 2013). The existing jurisprudence in this domain contains lively and impassioned attempts to insert the progressive teachings of movements for racial and gender justice into the machinations of a sentencing hearing.

Justice Nakatsuru has built a reputation as an exceptional jurist, one who writes "poetic" and "inspiring" decisions concerning how histories of colonialism and racism in Canada should factor into a prison sanction (Friscolanti, 2017). His accessible decisions are consistently described as "beautiful judgements" (Leung, 2015). *R. v Morris*, in particular, is referred to as "transformative" and a "game-changer" concerning how histories and experiences of anti-Black racism should be considered in law (Burns, 2021; Leung, 2015; Ibrahim, 2018). Hailed as a compassionate and humanitarian moral crusader, Justice Nakatsuru is not without critics who most often charge him with imposing lenient, race-based discounts in sentencing and "dumbing down" the legal process through the use of plain-language written decisions (Leung, 2015, para. 5). In this section, I follow the plot constructed in *R. v. Morris* from the particular facts in the case to the historical contingencies of anti-Black racism. Of particular interest is Justice Nakatsuru's reasoning concerning how the Gladue principle may be appropriately applied to Black Canadians in conflict with the law. *R. v. Morris* provides a rich portrait of how histories and genealogies of anti-Black systemic racism are understood to circulate globally and yet indexed through deeply local conditions of racialized and gendered subjugation and exclusion.

After outlining the facts of the case, the decision in *R. v. Morris* (2018) begins with a review of two significant documents submitted as evidence: an expert social science report about anti-Black racism in Canada and a presentence report prepared by a social worker described as summarizing the "social history of Kevin Morris," which included "how anti-Black racism, education, socio-economic factors, mental health, social influences, and criminal justice involvement have affected [him]" (p. 46). Together, these reports proved influential in assessing how histories of anti-Black racism were relevant to this particular case. As noted, the use of such documentary evidence is paradigmatic of a trend in criminal law in Canada where a consideration of biographical, systemic, and social experiences and circumstance form part of the calculus to arrive at what the law deems as a "fit and proportionate" sentence. The sentencing calculus is meant to mitigate the moral blameworthiness of a defendant through a consideration of how historical systemic and racial injustice has structured their experiences and interactions with the criminal punishment system. Although this sentencing principle is almost exclusively applied to Indigenous people in conflict with the law, *R. v. Morris* is among a few decisions where judges have attempted to apply this trend to a consideration of historical and ongoing injustice and racism in cases concerning Black defendants (for other examples, see Murdocca, 2013).

Couched in the language of restorative and reparative justice, the social histories of colonial, racial, and anti-Black violence and systemic exclusion is made use of by lawyers, judges, advocates, and academics in crafting biographical and socially contextual portraits of people positioned in conflict with the law to mitigate, lessen, and illuminate what the law describes as proportionality and deterrence in the weighing of an "appropriate" form of punishment. Justice Nakatsuru waded into this legal morass and asked the following questions concerning how histories of racial injustice should be weighed in the laws of sentencing: "Thus, I pose the question, is it right that we harshly deter and denounce the conduct of people who have been subject to such injustices by giving them stiffer sentences? Is it right to denounce their conduct when that conduct was constrained in choice; a constraint that was inequitably imposed upon them?" (*R. v. Morris*, 2018, p. 58). Justice Nakatsuru ultimately reasoned that historical, systemic, and case-specific factors concerning anti-Black racism are relevant in the case and mitigate, but will not render unnecessary, the imposition of a prison sanction for Morris. He explained that histories of "colonialism, slavery, policies and practices of segregation, intergenerational trauma, and both overt and systemic racism continue to affect Black Canadians today" and that these histories of racial and anti-Black violence carry case-specific resonance (*R. v. Morris*, 2018, p. 9). Summarizing the social science evidence, Justice Nakatsuru wrote directly to Morris:

> Anti-Black racism has shaped your life in a way that has brought you into the criminal court. It shaped your mother's life as well. It has negatively impacted your opportunities in life to date. You lived in a poor neighborhood, with a number of socio-economic challenges. This was an environment that was affected by anti-Black racism. You yourself have wondered why Blacks seem to live a lot in certain neighborhoods. Yours was affected by danger in the streets, both real and perceived. You did not find a way out through the public education system. I have no doubt that anti-Black racism affected how you were treated in school. . . . That failure in the education system makes a child vulnerable to becoming involved in the criminal justice system. Because your mother was working so much and the death of your father impacted you so hard, you became vulnerable to the bad influences of others. You are a follower and not a leader. Your feelings of frustration and powerlessness as you grew up in this environment made the possibility of possessing a gun real to you; something that given your life experiences, you decided that you wanted to do. (*R. v. Morris*, 2018, p. 74)

Examining Justice Nakatsuru's analysis of how the content of the social science and social history evidence informed his decision reveals how Black defendants are narrativized and constructed in sentencing decisions. How does Nakatsuru's reasoning construct Morris as a particular kind of Black subject? Indeed, it is not the role of a sentencing decision to indict the state for histories and ongoing injustices; however, this decision provides an opportunity to consider discursive frameworks advancing a particular racial ontology in service of restorative or reparative justice. Historical and ongoing anti-Black violence and racism are transformed into the identification of a range of "vulnerabilities" that Black Canadians experience because of anti-Black racism. Through the recognition of some of the effects of anti-Black racism in Morris's life, Justice Nakatsuru showed how histories of anti-Black systemic racism provide content to individual and collective subject positions in law. These subject positions restore and reinvent a politics of anti-Black subjectivity and subjection through the very reparative juridics that claim to work toward the undoing of such politics. Indeed, the perceived progressiveness of this decision—the plain language through which it narrates a partial account of Morris' life—is constitutive of how reparative justice shores up particular versions of Black and racial subjectivity.

38 • Carmela Murdocca

Recognizing histories of anti-Black racism in this way is an expression of liberal forms of racial governance through the production of a particular ontology of Black subjectivity in service of carceral law. The instrumental deployment of history, or history being used as the affirmation of legal memory, leads to an unsettling premise that binds seemingly progressive jurisprudence with an ontology of systemic racial and carceral disenfranchisement. Justice Nakatsuru provided a narrative link between anti-Black police racism and constructions of Black masculinity. Speaking directly to Morris, Nakatsuru J wrote,

> First are the systemic issues that have led to distrust between the police and Black men. These are set out in the reports. This has caused many Black men to fear their interactions with the police. In this case, there is specific information about your own past experience with the police and how you view them. You did not feel you would be fairly treated by them. I have little doubt that this all contributed to your impulsive reaction to take flight. It was not a considered action, but a reflexive one given the situation existing at the time. This fear was aggravated by the fact you collided with a police car as you ran. It also likely contributed to your ditching of the gun. I note that the gun was not thrown away into a place that was easily accessible to a passersby or innocents. It was left in an unused stairwell, concealed in a jacket, amidst a pile of debris and water. (*R. v. Morris*, 2018, p. 65)

Through constructing an ontology of gendered Black experience in antagonistic relation to police violence, anti-Blackness is relegated to residual experience for young Black men. A focus on personal experiences with law enforcement denies a more historically situated analysis of how anti-Blackness is constitutive of carceral policing practices. Anti-Blackness is affirmed through occluding how histories of slavery and segregation have resulted in a project of racial capture that relegates Black subjects to processes of surveillance and carceral violence. Following how histories of slavery, segregation, and other forms of anti-Black racism show up in the facts of a case leads to an unsettling premise that binds reparative jurisprudence and racial ontology with a narrow view of individual Black experience with the police. Law's racial memory thus contains an ontology of Blackness at the intersections of liberalism (or liberal forms of racial governance), criminalization, and reparation that is narrowly focused on individualizing Black experience with carceral systems.

As noted at the outset, in framing the issues concerning how anti-Black racism mitigates the imposition of a prison sanction, the judge situates this sentencing framework as an expression of collective memory. Justice Nakatsuru wrote, "Social structures and societal attitudes that were born of colonialism, slavery, and racism have a very long reach. We must not forget this. Our memory of past injustices must be long enough to do justice in an individual case" (*R. v. Morris*, 2018, p. 76). Collective memory is narrated in this carceral practice as integral to a temporal demand that urges a progressive teleology for national identity. The collective and national *we* invoked positions a system of racial capture as commemorative national practice. Asserting that "social structures and societal attitudes that were born of colonialism, slavery, and racism have a very long reach" demands attention to the temporal and referential dimensions of carceral practices. The linking of historical and contemporary anti-Black racism shows the laws of racial capture to be "facing backward, engaged with the past, constructing majestic narratives of continuity with occasional flaws in the tapestry" (Sarat & Kearns, 1999, p. 6). In this case, law's racial memory is revealed to be a practice that uses the ascendency of history (histories of slavery, colonialism, and racism) to authorize its legitimacy. These discourses demonstrate law's racial memory to be facing backward, engaged in historical reconstruction to explain present realities. The genealogical continuities at play show anti-Black racism, slavery, and colonialism as a temporal process where locally articulated historical phenomena are anchored through contemporary processes of criminalization and punishment.

The decision in *R. v. Morris* presented a unique opportunity to clarify the legal quagmire of whether a legal provision applicable to Indigenous people can be followed when weighing histories of slavery, segregation, and anti-Black racism. Through the application of this legal provision, the parsing of distinct, though related, histories of colonial and racial systemic violence is played out in the drama of a sentencing hearing. Justice Nakatsuru sought to establish a precedent by articulating a triangulation between Black Canadians, Indigenous people, and colonial and racial histories and experiences of violence and exclusion. He issued the following dictum concerning the legal requirement to address social and historical context for Indigenous people in sentencing:

> The criminal law has recognized that there are cases where, in order to determine a fit and proportionate sentence, consideration must be given to an individual's systemic and social circumstances. These circumstances may extend beyond a person who is being sentenced to include factors such as systemic discrimination and historical injustice. This has been recognized by the criminal courts, particularly in the case of Indigenous offenders. While the distinct history of colonial violence endured by Indigenous peoples cannot simply be analogized to Black Canadians, I found that the ability to consider social context in a sentencing decision is extended to all under section 718.2(e) of the *Criminal Code*. (*R. v. Morris*, 2018, p. 9)

In response, the Court of Appeal stated clearly: "We do not agree that this court should equate Indigenous offenders and Black offenders for the purposes of s. 718.2(e)" (*R. v. Morris*, 2021, para. 118). However, the trial level decision provides an invitation to consider the productive function of analogy when an individual is confronting the violent apotheosis of the racial carceral state at sentencing.

Justice Nakatsuru's reasoning exposes the racial fault line of reparative justice as national commemorative practice. In this formulation, the reparative process obliges judges to consider how histories of slavery, segregation, and anti-Black racism are manifest in particularized social experience. Despite marshaling a narrative that appears attentive to the historical particularities of anti-Indigenous and anti-Black racism, analogy is a serviceable tool in the racial process of criminalization and confinement. It is worth noting that Wilderson (2010) has called attention to what he describes as the "ruse of analogy," which is the impossibility of analogizing the violence that subjugates racialized people and the violence that subjugates Black people (p. 37). A relational analytic thus compels an approach that recognizes how particular subjects are differently positioned in relation to settler colonialism and racial capitalism through this legal mechanism. The practice can be said to advance an ontological and temporal framework that ultimately codifies particular discourses about Black and Indigenous people in the criminal justice process. This legal reasoning brings into stark relief the version of liberalism at play when the racial carceral violence of the prison is secured by a moral reparative ethos. As Grewal (2017) articulated, "the interrelation between the sovereign right to kill and the right to 'rescue' has constituted liberal modes of state power for centuries" (p. 9).

A framework that considers law's racial memory may be usefully employed to consider the transnational economies of liberalism in which this uniquely Canadian reparative sentencing provision is embedded for two reasons. First, these trends in the laws of sentencing show a response to historical change through codifying historical narratives of racial injustice in carceral law. The legal ritual of sentencing can be viewed as a site of collective memory-making because it is one significant judicial form for asserting historical discussion in law. The legal assertion that particularized attention to histories of colonialism, slavery, and policies and experiences of segregation and intergenerational trauma must be weighed in the laws of sentencing displays an interpretive practice where a moral ideal attached to the collective memory of colonial, racial, and anti-Black violence binds reparation with retribution (Murdocca, 2013). As explored, these rhetorical moves are anchored in compelling legal and judicial practices, including the submission of social science evidence and socially and historically contextualized portraits of Black and Indigenous people positioned as in conflict with law. Legal precedent of this kind designates acceptable historical narratives and produces particular kinds of Black and Indigenous subjects that take on a moral and epistemological form in a carceral system of racial capture. This kind of reparative juridics provides a local index of transnational dimensions of continued histories of racial subjection constitutive of genealogies of liberalism.

Second, understanding the judicial ritual of sentencing as a form of collective memory allows for the recognition of processes of occlusion in the archive of liberalism. In the ritual of legal punishment, racial carceral violence continues despite efforts to consider how Black and Indigenous people have survived the effects of colonial and racial gendered violence. The criminal punishment system is an iconic liberal form of rule. Invoking Drucilla Cornell's phrase, "Legal interpretation demands that we remember the future," Sarat and Kearns (1999) explained, "There are, in fact, two audiences for every legal act, the audience of the present and the audience of the future ... (law) reenacts the past, both intentionally and unconsciously, and it is one place where the present speaks to the future through acts of commemoration" (p. 13).

Conclusion

Racial carceral violence continues despite efforts to consider how Black and Indigenous people have survived the effects of colonial and racial gendered violence. These historical and contextual experiences are in stark contrast to the individualized and punitive nature of law and legal processes. This chapter calls attention to viewing the law of punishment in racial colonial contexts as a repository of law's racial memory that ultimately functions as commemorative national practice produced through transnational economies of liberalism. This use of the past and ongoing lived experiences of racial injustice in the criminal punishment system recalls Brown's (2001) analysis of Walter Benjamin's "formulation of the bearing of history on the political present" (p. 171). Brown uses the word "suffering" to describe the limits of a liberal politics premised on the identification of social injury as the basis of political or legal action. She wrote, "Suffering that is not yet finished is not only suffering that must still be endured but also suffering that can still be redeemed; it might develop another face through contemporary practices. Making a historical event or formation contemporary, making it 'an outrage to the present' and thus exploding or reworking both the way in which it has been remembered and the way in which it is positioned in historical consciousness as 'past,' is precisely the opposite of bringing the phenomena to 'closure' through reparation or apology (our most ubiquitous forms of historical political thinking today)" (p. 171). This trend of reparative juridical intervention in sentencing requires "reworking" of the past and ongoing suffering through the creation of memory and national commemoration in service of law.

This form of legal memory-making enables a consideration of how the invocation of racialized and gendered subjectivity is made use of as a resource for extraction in liberal sociolegal remediation. The liberal redemptive gesture of affirming histories of colonialism and slavery in law epitomizes how a reparative aspiration exemplifies a national commemorative practice that proceeds through force and violence of law. As Lowe (2015) explained, "Liberalism comprises a multifaceted, flexible, and contradictory set of provisions that at once rationalizes settler appropriation and removal differently than it justifies either the subjection of human beings as enslaved property, or the extraction of labor from indentured emigrants, however much these processes share a colonial past and ongoing colonial present" (pp. 10–11). Indeed, the flexibility of liberal forms of recognition materialize through the distinctive positioning of racial bodily violence in formations of Black and Indigenous subjectivity as a normalized ground of reasoning in liberal reparative juridics. Such judicial reasoning ultimately reveals the interdependence of histories of racial violence and reformist liberal recognition politics that seek to advance the discursive avowal of histories of systemic racial injustice through processes of criminalization that construct particular gendered versions of Black and Indigenous ontology and subjectivity. The reparative juridics canvased in this chapter assist in outlining how law's racial memory materializes through this racial structure of carcerality. The naming of histories of colonialism, slavery, and segregation gives way to the necessity of considering the production of racial subjectivities relationally in order to address the shared, and particular, contexts of domination, subordination, violence, dispossession, and criminalization (Murdocca, 2013). Creating affirmative memory in service to law and nation requires a consideration of the connections between how the pursuit of reparation or restraint in law proceeds through racial carceral violence. I suggest this trend in criminal law be considered a site of confrontation that constructs memory in service to liberal legal regimes constituted by racial difference.

3

Toward a Queer Diasporic Remembrance of Air India Flight 182

• •

Memorializing Transnational Flows of Loss and Desire

AMBER DEAN

> Queer desire does not transcend or remain peripheral to these histories [of colonialism and racism] but instead it becomes central to their telling and remembering: there is no queer desire without these histories, nor can these histories be told or remembered without simultaneously revealing an erotics of power. (Gopinath, 2005, p. 2)

On June 23, 1985, a bomb detonated in Irish airspace on Air India Flight 182 en route from Montreal (via Toronto) to New Delhi, killing all 329 people on board: 268 Canadian citizens, 27 British citizens, and 24 citizens of India, including the crew members.[1] Initially, the Canadian government was very slow to recognize this act of violence and the losses arising from it as distinctly Canadian

(Chakraborty, 2012, 2015; Chakraborty et al., 2017; Failler, 2009). Only after the events of September 11, 2001, did the Canadian government develop a strategic and troubling interest in claiming the Air India bombing as a Canadian tragedy; as Failler (2012) noted, "The 1985 Air India bombings are being strategically remembered in the present in order to justify a racist mandate of state securitization as the only 'reasonable response' to terrorist threat" (p. 3). Such strategic remembrance has become ubiquitous in the wake of 9/11 and has taken the form of state-sponsored permanent memorials created in Toronto, Ottawa, and Vancouver (all after 2001), as well as of dedications and speeches offered by government officials at subsequent anniversary memorial events at these sites (see Chakraborty, 2012, 2015, 2016; Chakraborty et al., 2017; Dean, 2012, 2013; Failler, 2009, 2010, 2012). Similar mobilizations of remembrance of the losses of Flight 182 are evident in forms such as documentary film (Failler, 2012) and in the National Inquiry that was belatedly called to review the government's handling of the bombing (Razack, 2017; Chakraborty et al., 2017).

Beyond these more hegemonic, state-sponsored frames of remembrance, there is also a growing number of "artistic memorializations" (Chakraborty et al., 2017, p. xvii) of the bombing that take the form of dance, fiction, poetry, visual art, and film.[2] Turning to two such creative memorial responses, this chapter explores how remembrance of the bombing might be productively expanded through a queer diasporic framework (Gopinath, 2005). Queer, here, is determinedly *not* the subject of rights and signifier of progress deployed by many Western states today to continuously justify violence against and exclusion of racialized Others deemed incapable of equality, democracy, and freedom (Puar, 2007; see also Haritaworn et al., 2014). Instead, following Gopinath (2005), I deploy the term queer in a way that aims to "[contest] the logic that situates the terms 'queer' and 'diaspora' as dependent on the originality of 'heterosexuality' and 'nation,'" and to "[disorganize] the dominant categories within the United States [and, I would add, Canada] for sexual variance, namely 'gay and lesbian'" (p. 13). In other words, queer in my usage here is not positing or imposing an identity category but works instead to name and reflect on the significance of forms of desire and loss that exceed and challenge the purported naturalness of the nation and the heterosexual, as well as the too-oft-presumed whiteness of the categories of gay and lesbian. In this chapter, I consider how a queer diasporic frame of remembrance can productively move us outside nationalist and hetero/homonormative frames of remembrance of the bombing by focusing remembrance instead on the transnational flows of loss and desire arising in its aftermath.

Creative memorial responses to the Air India bombing might make a queer diasporic frame of remembrance possible in ways that more strategic state-initiated memorials cannot; to demonstrate this potential, I turn to two memorializations that offer quite a different approach to engaging with the aftermath of the losses aboard Flight 182: Farzana Doctor's (2015) novel, *All Inclusive*, and Eisha Marjara's (1998) docudrama, *Desperately Seeking Helen*. These works are identifiable as memorializations to Flight 182 because they are dedicated to those who were killed on the flight and because they memorialize Flight 182 by returning this event to public consciousness and by inviting their audiences to attend not just to the losses occasioned by the bombing but to the aftermath of those losses in the lives and desires of those in greatest proximity to the people killed (for other examples of writing and film as memorialization, see chapters by Mojab and Makaremi, this volume). Both creative memorializations invite contemplation on (queer) desire in relation to what it means to live (on) in the aftermath of loss, productively calling into question the gender and heteronormativity that pervade remembrance of Flight 182. Desire in Doctor's novel and Marjara's film can be traced as a practice of self-making and world-making evocative of Judith Butler's (2004) insistence that loss and desire undo us: "Let's face it. We're undone by each other," she wrote, adding, "If this seems so clearly the case with grief, it is only because it was already the case with *desire* [emphasis added]" (p. 23). Desire drives a practice of learning to commune with those loved ones who were lost on Flight 182 in these creative works, and ultimately, I argue that these memorializations invite reflection on the urgency of attending to the transnational flows of loss and desire for living (on) in the aftermath of violence.

I am compelled to trace not just loss but also desire as it arises in these works, in part because of a long-standing debate in queer theory about whether we should orient to the (queer) past through loss (Love, 2007) or through desire (Freeman, 2005). Elizabeth Freeman (2005) argued compellingly that there are risks to attaching a queer reading of the past too profoundly to loss, as she further argued for attending to the importance of desire in collective remembrance practices. Drawing on psychoanalytic understandings of desire (and of the relationship between loss and desire), Freeman urged us to "imagine the 'inappropriate' response of eros in the face of sorrow as a trace of past forms of pleasure located in specific historical moments" (p. 65). Positing a practice of "erotohistoriography," Freeman wrote, "I would like to take the risk of the inappropriate response to ask: how might queer practices of pleasure, specifically, the bodily enjoyments that travel under the sign of queer sex, be thought of as temporal practices, even as portals to historical thinking?" (p. 59). Doctor's novel and Marjara's film offer two such productive portals to historical thinking, as both imaginative responses to loss insist that loss and desire are neither opposites nor even easy to differentiate in the wake of events of historical trauma such as the bombing of Flight 182. Instead, in these imaginative works, both loss and desire seem critical to what it means to live in relation to the traumatic losses of the bombing and to keep the past in living memory without being consumed by it.

A queer diasporic remembrance of the bombing of Air India Flight 182 has the potential to deepen our collective understanding of the event in several ways. First, I argue that such a framework ensures that the bombing is remembered as a transnational event that cannot be understood without attending to the ongoing legacies of the British Empire and especially to the racist logics driving and arising from its colonial histories, putting an end to the long, misplaced debates about whether the bombing was more a "Canadian" or an "Indian" event. Second, it prompts us to think in more complex terms about the continued reliance of nation-states on heteronormativity (and homonormativity) as mechanisms for defining and managing sexuality. As transnational feminist analyses have long shown, violence frequently results from yoking gender and sexual norms to nationalist ideals (Yuval-Davis, 1997). I am interested here in the potential of a concept like Gopinath's queer diaspora to trouble static or conventional notions of diaspora as tied to a national origin, while simultaneously troubling predominantly white, Western understandings of queerness. In this way, a queer diasporic framework builds on the work of transnational feminist theorizing while still insisting that such theorizing falls short if it assumes heterosexuality as the default or naturalized condition of women's lives. Third, a queer diasporic framework for remembering Air India Flight 182 requires attending to the complex enmeshments and transnational flows of loss and desire by illuminating the potential for (queer) desire and loss to confound nationalist and hetero/homonormative frames of remembrance. Desire, in this understanding, becomes a mode of relating crucial to living (on) in the aftermath of violent loss, never redeeming loss and always disputing the reduction of loss or of the relations that matter to narrow, hetero or homonormative frameworks for kinship and/or belonging.

Air India Flight 182: A *Transnational* Tragedy?

I have spent over a decade now contemplating the *national* significance, remembrance, disavowal, and eventual nationalist reclaiming of the Air India bombing in Canada (see Dean, 2012, 2013; Chakraborty et al., 2017). In fact, my interest in studying memorializations of the bombing arose from my wider research on what public mourning and memorialization tell us about whose lives are framed as mattering to a wider public in the specific national context of Canada. I continue to see the value of focusing, at times, on the complexities of what memorials tell us about whose lives matter in a national context. But my research on remembrance of the Air India bombing has taught me that a deeper understanding of the complicated colonial histories implicated in the bombing requires a transnational lens (Soni & Varadharajan, 2012). Ashwin Rao, the protagonist of Padma Viswanathan's (2014) remarkable novel about the Air India tragedy, *The Ever After of Ashwin Rao*, perhaps best explains the necessity of approaching the bombing through a transnational lens when he insists,

> When I think on the Air India disaster, I hear the chain of history rattle. Its links are loops. Loops have holes. Was the bombing a Canadian or an Indian tragedy? Why pose this false division? Canada was colonized when India was,

and their fates were ever linked. There is no expiation. The declaration of any single truth is itself an act of violence. . . . Without India, could there be Empire? Without Empire, could there be radicalizing? Without Canada, could there have been a bomb? (p. 242)

Its links are loops, loops have holes, and one can get lost down the rabbit hole of trying to determine whose national tragedy the bombing really was or which nation was more at fault. Doing so, however, distracts from the bigger picture: empire. Rao curiously returns to a national frame with his final question, likely because for decades, Canadian politicians have tried to assert that the bombing itself had "nothing to do with Canada," as then Prime Minister Stephen Harper proclaimed in his 2007 speech at the dedication of the permanent Air India memorial in Toronto. Harper later corrected this claim, insisting in his public apology to the families of those who were murdered aboard Flight 182 in 2010 that "Canadians now understand that this atrocity was conceived in Canada, executed in Canada, by Canadian citizens, and its victims were themselves mostly citizens of Canada. We wish this realization had gained common acceptance earlier" (Harper, 2010, p. 154). The "we" in his claim is noteworthy for how it evacuates the Air India families once again from the category of "Canadians" who have apparently now universally achieved this belated awareness about the national significance of the bombing.

But again, even Harper's correction focuses attention back on the national context in a way that can distract us from empire as not just a historical but an ongoing transnational structure, one that clearly shapes the bombing and its aftermath. Perhaps we can shift Rao's final question a little to ask the following: without empire, could there have been a bomb? In asking this question, I follow Sara Ahmed (2000) when she insists, "Rather than saying that History determines the relationship between this and that, we can ask, 'how is the relationship between this and that determined?' as a historical question, a question that henceforth cannot be answered in a total or exhaustive manner" (pp. 9–10). The question, "Without empire, could there have been a bomb?" can never be answered definitively, but it is still a relevant question if we want to deepen our understanding of the bombing and its aftermath, and even more urgently, if we want to transform the conditions that made the bombing thinkable and doable in the first place.

If one begins with the Air India bombing and follows Rao's chain of history back, the logics and histories of the British Empire and their roots in the founding of Canada and India as nations are evident not just in the conditions that made the bombing possible but also in the bombing's aftermath and how it lives on today in subsequent acts of violence. The links on the chain weave together not just the more obvious events that have been widely connected with the bombing, such as Operation Blue Star in 1983 (the storming of the Golden Temple by the Indian Army, resulting in the violent deaths of many Sikhs); the subsequent murder of the Prime Minister of India at the time, Indira Gandhi, by her Sikh bodyguards in 1984; and the anti-Sikh violence that followed. But if we follow the links further back, they take us to the partition of British India in 1947, to the routing of the *Komagata Maru* (a ship carrying mostly Sikh men hoping to immigrate to Canada) from the shores of Vancouver in 1914 (see Dean, 2012), and to the unfulfilled promise of the British Empire that citizens of its colonies might move freely among them.

If empire is implicated in the bombing and its aftermath, then a transnational framework becomes essential for analyzing efforts to remember the bombing today. In Harper's (2010) apology to the families of those who died in the bombing, India (and by extension the East more broadly) is curiously cast both as a place full of "old roads to the blood-feuds of the past" and as a "great and forward-looking nation" (p. 156). India, an important contemporary trading partner to Canada, can only be "forward-looking" (a backhanded compliment, given that in being forward-*looking* there is still a presumption of being behind or backward in the moment), presumably through its commitment to neoliberal market capitalism. But in this framing, India also has dangerous roots in a purportedly backward-facing past full of "blood-feuds"—a thinly veiled evocation of primitivist racial stereotypes evoking the violent logics of empire that cast Brown, Black, Asian, and Indigenous races as inherently less developed or more primitive, violent, and feudal than white Europeans. In this characterization, India may be "forward-looking" but cannot escape its purportedly primitive past, which is framed as the source or cause of the violence that led to the bombing, taking attention from the life-shaping and delimiting—and crucially, following Ahmed (2000) again, determining but never fully determining—policies, practices, and legacies of empire itself. Although the histories of Canada and India as nations are yoked together through their shared ties to the British Empire, these histories are also differentiated through how Canada is understood as part of the West and India as part of the East.

My reflections on these logics of empire bring me to the question of how queerness might matter to remembrance of the Air India bombing. As Puar's (2007) analysis has shown, in the early twenty-first century, queerness has become one significant phenomenon by which East and West continue to be differentiated and hierarchized. She demonstrates how the greater inclusion and acceptance of some (white) queer lives in Western capitalist national contexts occur "at the expense of sexually and racially perverse death in relation to the contemporary politics of securitization, Orientalism, terrorism, torture, and the articulation of Muslim, Arab, Sikh and South Asian sexualities" (p. xiii). If remembrance of Air India is to be productively queered, then this queering must be attentive to the risks of falling prey to how "queer" as a category of rights-bearing subjecthood can be deployed to uphold some of those very same logics about race and the East that underpin the colonial histories of the British Empire in the first place. But a queer diasporic framework for remembering the bombing refuses this way of understanding queer, and such a framework can thus productively undermine nationalist frames of remembrance in ways that expose the false assumptions that foundationally shape empire's logics.

Toward a Queer Diasporic Framework for Remembering Flight 182

Diaspora and transnational are concepts that overlap and are often used interchangeably, even though they do have somewhat distinct histories (Faist, 2010). But because of their many enmeshments, Faist argued that "the two concepts cannot be separated in any meaningful way" (p. 12). For Gopinath (2005), "What is remembered through queer diasporic desire and the queer diasporic body is a past time and place riven with contradictions and the violences of multiple uprootings, displacements, and exiles" (p. 4). She insisted on resisting a tendency to idolize diasporic life and experience, arguing that there is nothing inherently transgressive about diaspora as a concept: it can reproduce nationalist logics that celebrate "capital and globalization" (p. 7), as well as heteronormativity, just as easily as it can challenge these things. This is not surprising, for as she noted, "All too often diasporas are narrativized through the bonds of relationality between men" (p. 5). But for Gopinath, "Suturing 'queer' to 'diaspora' thus recuperates those desires, practices, and subjectivities that are rendered impossible and unimaginable within conventional diasporic and nationalist imaginaries. . . . The urgent need to trouble and denaturalize the close relationship between nationalism and heterosexuality is precisely what makes the notion of a queer diaspora so compelling" (p. 11).

Gopinath is critical of some South Asian feminist theorizing that aims to challenge patriarchal nationalisms while still presuming heterosexuality as naturalized (pp. 9–10). She also argues that "'queerness' needs 'diaspora' in order to make it more supple in relation to questions of race, colonialism, migration, and globalization" (p. 11). A queer diasporic framework crucially builds on transnational feminist theorizing, which has long proven its suppleness for confronting white Western feminist theorizing with its inadequate theorizations of race, colonialism, migration, and globalization (Mohanty, 2003). Simultaneously, Gopinath argued that a queer diasporic framework challenges any lingering naturalizations of heterosexuality in feminist thought and takes white Western queer theorizing to task for its inadequacies in thinking through the imbrication of the figure of the queer with racism, colonialism, and empire.

A queer diasporic framework for remembering the bombing is therefore not invested in memorializing the bombing as a distinctly Canadian or distinctly Indian event and would resist any remembrance of the bombing that tried to impose such a nationalist frame. It is also thus inherently transnational, not only because it refuses nationalist frames of remembrance but also because its insistence on thinking about sexuality through terms that exceed identity poses a challenge to how nation-states tend to define and organize sexuality.

What emerges from a queer diasporic remembrance "are subjects, communities and practices that bear little resemblance to the universalized 'gay' identity imagined within a Eurocentric gay imaginary" (Gopinath, 2005, p. 12), subjects, communities, and practices that also challenge nationalist frameworks in productive ways. In the next section, I turn to the two creative memorial responses I have selected to draw out how they attend to the transnational flows of loss and desire in ways that also exceed nationalist frames.

Memorializing Transnational Flows of Loss and Desire

Doctor's novel and Marjara's film demonstrate the potential of such a queer diasporic framework for remembering transnational histories of violence, exceeding nationalist frames of remembrance by prompting us to consider how loss and desire are embedded in diaspora *and* sexuality in ways that cannot be neatly separated. Both texts traverse multiple national contexts—Canada and India, and, in Doctor's novel, also Mexico—but in both texts, the protagonist never feels entirely at home in any national setting, giving texture to the lived experience of queer diaspora that lacks firm referents in national boundaries. Ameera, the protagonist in *All Inclusive*, is a sexually confident Canadian tour representative working at an all-inclusive resort in Mexico. Her primary sexual desire lies in couples who visit the resort as tourists. As she attempts to keep her clandestine sexual encounters from her coworkers and employer, Ameera also begins searching for her biological father, a South Asian man originally from India who had a single, brief but ecstatic sexual encounter with her white Canadian mother in June of 1985 before he seemingly disappeared. All Ameera knows of him is his first name: Azeez. But Azeez, who died aboard Flight 182, is looking for Ameera as well. The novel moves back and forth between Ameera and Azeez's first-person narrations, and between India, Canada, and Mexico, as each character struggles first to find the other and ultimately, to learn how to create a good life or, in Azeez's case, a good death in the aftermath of loss.

In *Desperately Seeking Helen*, Eisha is on a passionate quest to find Helen, a Bollywood actress who frequently played the vamp in many of the Hindi films Marjara watched as a child and young adult, especially after her family moved from Amritsar to Quebec in the 1970s.[3] As Eisha's desire to find Helen in Bombay (now Mumbai) becomes more and more desperate, we learn that her passionate quest is driven in part by her desire to better understand and grieve her relationship with her mother, Devinder Marjara, who was killed on Flight 182. Eisha's desire to find Helen is desperately wrapped up in the loss of her mother, a loss complicated by the fact that were it not for her own hospitalization due to anorexia, Marjara would have been on Flight 182 with her mother and her younger sister, who was killed in the bombing as well. Neither Ameera nor Eisha identify in these texts as explicitly queer subjects; in fact, it would be impossible to straightforwardly read either character as either queer or lesbian, reflective of

Gopinath's sense that a queer diasporic remembrance is not invested in queer as an identity category. But in both texts, the protagonists' (queer) desire propels them to confront difficult memories and live with loss in ways that are potentially transformative, making it possible for them to find ways to live (on) in the wake of the undoing caused by the violent loss of loved ones in the bombing of Flight 182.

In Doctor's *All Inclusive*, desire and loss are so intertwined as to be inseparable to what it means to remember and live on in the wake of the bombing. Slowly, over a span of thirty years, Azeez—who remains unable to reincarnate, despite his strong desire to—learns of Ameera's birth and is confronted with the loss of a daughter he never knew he conceived. Upon finally locating Ameera at the all-inclusive resort where she works in Mexico, it becomes clear to Azeez that Ameera is also struggling with loss, but hers is a feeling of loss she can neither identify nor articulate to others because she has not yet learned of his violent death; as Azeez describes it, she is "too full of the yearning she couldn't name" (Doctor, 2015, p. 172). Slowly, Ameera learns to listen to Azeez, even though she never realizes it is him who is trying to tell her things about her past or trying to reassure her that she can and will learn to live with his loss. And communing with Ameera and others around her also slowly allows Azeez to grapple with his own violent death as a wound that will never be redressed. Through their fictional learning to live in relation to each other and to loss, Doctor's novel provokes considerations about desire, loss, and remembrance that remain largely unattainable through strategic, state-initiated memorials to the Air India bombing.

Sexual desire, for Ameera, becomes a practice of self-making and world-making evocative of Butler's (2004) insistence that desire, like loss, "undoes" us (p. 23). Through desire, Butler argued, we are "undone, in the face of the other, by the touch, by the scent, by the feel, by the prospect of the touch, by the memory of the feel" (p. 24). This undoing reveals our fundamental interdependence on others and is key to Butler's wider argument that "liberal versions of human ontology" cannot "do justice to passion and grief and rage, all of which tear us from ourselves, bind us to others, transport us, undo us, implicate us in lives that are not our own, irreversibly, if not fatally" (p. 25). Through its exploration of the transnational flows of loss and desire that exceed national boundaries, the novel also undoes nationalist frames for remembering the bombing. Ameera, for example, seems amply aware that unconventional desire is what led to her unexpected conception, even though she does not know the details; as readers, however, we learn that Azeez's encounter with her mother was his first and only sexual experience and that he was overly confident about his ability to pull out in time before climaxing. An unexpected, transracial, and trans-national moment of desire gave her life, and for Ameera, desire—also often enacted transnationally because Ameera's job occasions opportunities for explorations of desire across all kinds of boundaries, including those of nation—subsequently becomes a way to explore her relation to a father she never knew, and quite literally so; one "magic" sexual encounter with a lesbian couple allows

Ameera to finally be vulnerable enough to ask for help with finding out what happened to her father (Doctor, 2015, p. 191). One of the lesbians, Jessie, is an archivist who does genealogical research on the side (p. 190). After Azeez prods Ameera to seek out Jessie's assistance, he follows Jessie back to Toronto so he can try to assist her with the search. Eventually, his efforts to commune with Jessie lead to the discovery of Azeez's full identity and of his untimely, violent death as a young man aboard Flight 182, the day after Ameera was conceived.

In Marjara's *Desperately Seeking Helen*, Eisha's passionate quest to find Helen is bookended in the film by an opening emphasis on airplanes and passing mention of a trip to India to scatter the ashes of her mother and sister followed by the final scene's disclosure of how Marjara's mother and sister were killed. The mixed-genre docudrama angle of the film productively troubles our sense, as viewers, of what is real and what is fantasy. Loss and desire are deeply entwined in the film, and the revelation of loss—or, at least, of the details of what caused Marjara's loss of her mother and sister—happens even more slowly than in Doctor's novel. The film appears to be primarily about desire, specifically Eisha's (queer) desire for Helen: to find Helen, to be like her, to live the sort of life Helen is imagined by Eisha to live, that is, glamorous, fun, exciting, unconventional, and above all, brimming with passion.

More than anything else, Helen represents a challenge to the presumed naturalness of heteronormativity, of a life that culminates for women in a heterosexual marriage, motherhood, and a life of "homemaking" thereafter. As a girl, Eisha pressed her mother to tell her what happened to the characters of her beloved Bollywood movies after the films ended, and her mother explains that "unlike Helen, the heroine becomes a bride, after The End" (Marjara, 1998, 10:36). "The movie's end begins the real life of the heroine lady," Marjara (1998) narrates, "and it lasts forever and ever" (11:21). This "forever and ever" is made to seem like a dreadful outcome through Marjara's intonation, as well as through her childhood insistence, much to her mother's dismay, on her desire to be like Helen the vamp rather than like the dull heroines. *Desperately Seeking Helen* begins with seductive music and an image of Eisha as an adult walking down a street in Bombay/Mumbai, her deliberate, slow-motion movements also suggestive of her longing and desire as the scene cuts to an image of Helen performing the sort of highly seductive Bollywood song-and-dance scene for which she was infamous. As viewers, when we watch Helen's seductive performances throughout Marjara's film, we are encouraged to imagine Eisha also watching these performances as her desire for Helen—to be like her, to be with her, to be her—builds.

As Gopinath (2005) argued, "Song and dance sequences [in Bollywood films] are the primary arena in which the female body and female sexuality are on display, in a way that may be disallowed in the other components that make up the film text," disallowed because of a censorship code that Gopinath described as a "legacy of British colonialism" (p. 100). As a result, Gopinath reads "the song and dance sequence as a peculiarly *queer* form: because it falls outside the exigencies of narrative coherence and closure, it can function as a space from which to critique the unrelenting heteronormativity that this narrative represents" (p. 101). Perhaps nowhere is this queer potential of the song and dance number of the Bollywood classic more evident than in Marjara's use of such numbers to document Eisha's passionate search for a Helen she never finds. A queer reading of *Desperately Seeking Helen* (and of *All Inclusive*, for that matter) confirms Gopinath's suspicion that in South Asian diasporic texts, "Narratives that explicitly name female same-sex desire as 'lesbian' may be less interesting than those moments within the narrative that represent female homoeroticism in the absence of 'lesbians'" (p. 108). Eisha may be on a transnational quest to find Helen because Helen represents everything her mother was not and everything Eisha hoped her life might become, but the film also invites us to imagine the homoerotic potential of Eisha's desire to escape from the heteronormative family frame that is so clearly tied to the meaning of national belonging, in both Canada and India, in the film.

Eisha's (queer) desires to escape heteronormative family frames leave her feeling out of place in both contexts, affirming Gopinath's point about how deeply entrenched heteronormativity remains with nation. Perhaps to really feel at home in a national context requires aligning one's desires for a good life solely with a hetero (or more recently in some national contexts, also a (homo)normative family frame. The limited roles accorded to women within such a frame in both countries were never enough to satisfy Devinder Marjara, according to Marjara's narrations, and never enough for Eisha, either. "An Indian bride?!" (Marjara, 1998, 34:05), Eisha exclaims in response to a sari costume she is dressed up in at an acting school in Mumbai while looking for Helen. "And just when I thought she was dressing me up as a vamp! Thank god my getaway car is parked right outside" (34:10). Moments such as these suggest Eisha's unconventional desires exceed heteronormative frames, as does her experience of loss. Marjara must (re)turn to India in pursuit of Helen to confront both her desires and her losses, but neither are resolved there. Desire and loss instead become entangled in transnational flows as Eisha struggles to commune with her mother's past and find a way to live (on) in the aftermath of her loss.

In the end, Eisha does not find Helen, and as the film moves along, her passionate quest for Helen seems to become less important than learning to live (on) in the aftermath of the losses occasioned by the bombing of Flight 182. "What was I looking for?" Marjara (1998) narrates. "Oh yeah, Helen. It shouldn't be this difficult. I was close to giving up and then I wondered, what would I be giving up? Was I chasing a fantasy?" (1:12:45). Just before these lines, Eisha chases an actress, made to look like Helen but wearing a distinctive blonde wig, onto an airplane, only to touch the actress on the shoulder and have her turn to reveal Eisha's own face beneath the wig. "The dream scene," Angela Failler (2009) suggested in her analysis of Marjara's film, "links Eisha's nostalgic quest for Helen with her struggle to come to terms with the loss of her sister and her mother." It turns out, Failler asserted, that perhaps Eisha has been "desperately

54 • Amber Dean

seeking herself" after all (p. 171). We might read this scene as undoing the queerness of Eisha's desire for Helen, resolving it through the implication that Eisha's quest for Helen was about her identification with her rather than her desire for her. But I want to complicate this more straightforwardly feminist reading of the film to "hold open the possibility that modes of *desire* [emphasis added] are also at work here" (Gopinath, 2005, p. 110). Just before the ending of the film, we see footage of a profoundly emaciated Eisha in hospital, who speaks of the changes she would still like to see in her body and of how hard the current state of her body is on her back: "I have to admit, it's hard to stay straight" (Marjara, 1998, 1:15:57). It is my own queer desire that prompts me to read Eisha's admission out of context, to contemplate whether the difficulty of "staying straight" might have been one of the many factors exacerbating Eisha's complex relationship to living in the moment of her utterance. I wonder whether her subsequent passionate quest for Helen might be read as an enactment of Eisha's desires for more from life than a conventional narrative will allow, thus affording a way for Eisha to live on through the transnational pursuit of her complex desires in the aftermath of the self-shattering loss of her mother and sister.

Conclusion: Remembering Flight 182 through a Queer Diasporic Framework

Doctor's novel and Marjara's film invite us to reflect on the urgency of attending to the transnational flows of loss and desire when it comes to living (on) in the aftermath of violence. Desire in the novel and film offers no final consolation for loss; it is represented in all its complexity, as a way we are frequently "undone" (Butler, 2004, p. 24), as sometimes magical or a site of powerful fantasy, but also at times as mundane and sometimes as dangerous. But ultimately, Ameera and Eisha's desires become important means of working through how they will live (well) in the aftermath of the traumatic losses they have experienced, with the quite unbearable knowledge of their loved ones' violent deaths in the bombing. In this way, the novel and the film can be read as memorializations that prompt us, as readers and viewers, not only to remember and remain conscious of the bombing but also to reflect on the complex transnational flows of loss and desire that are so crucial to self-making and world-making in the aftermath of violence.

A queer diasporic framework for remembering the bombing of Flight 182 remains urgent in a moment when nationalist frames of remembrance continue to strategically call up the memory of the bombing to rationalize and reinforce systemic racism (Razack, 2017) and "war on terror" policies and practices (Failler, 2012; Chakraborty, 2016). Contemporary state-initiated efforts to remember the bombing risk reaffirming the logics of empire in ways that make it difficult to decipher how the histories of empire are actually chained to the bombing and its aftermath. Similarly, Gopinath (2005) has pointed out how urgent it is that we recognize "institutionalized heterosexuality as a primary structure of both British colonialism and incipient Indian nationalism" (p. 10). The creative memorials I take up in this chapter invite just such a recognition of the role of institutionalized hetero (and homo)normativity in propping up nationalism and colonialism in Canada and India, pointing to a very different remembrance of the bombing and its significance than what is on offer in state-initiated memorials. The experiences of loss and desire represented in these creative memorial works exceed nationalist frameworks as surely as they exceed hetero (and homo) normative frameworks. Loss and desire simply do not and will not adhere to national or sexual boundaries, inviting us instead to reckon, as Eisha and Ameera do, with how profoundly and transformatively they can undo us. Remembering Flight 182 through a queer diasporic frame has the potential to pry open the delimiting effects of state-initiated remembrance of the bombing, calling on us to attend instead to the complex transnational flows of loss and desire called forth in the wake of the bombing, and to (queer) desire as one means by which people can and do find ways to live (on) in the aftermath of violent losses.

Notes

1 The bomb is believed to have been transferred to the Air India flight from a Canadian Pacific Airlines flight that originated in Vancouver. A second bomb originating in Vancouver and believed to have been targeting an Air India flight to Bangkok the same day detonated prematurely and caused the deaths of two baggage handlers at the Narita International Airport in Japan.

2 For further analysis of a broad range of these artistic memorializations of Flight 182, see Chakraborty et al., 2017. In our introduction to that text, we also theorize the significance of "creative works as knowledge–as testimony, remembrance, and witness to Canada's racial past and present," suggesting that such works offer "creative modes of engagement [with the bombing and its aftermath] that complement but also complicate and extend traditional historiographic accounts" (p. xx).

3 Because *Desperately Seeking Helen* is classified as a docudrama, it seems important to distinguish Eisha, the film's protagonist, from Marjara, the filmmaker, although admittedly this separation is not always clear or easy to distinguish because the film does contain elements of more conventional documentary alongside its dramatic enactment of Eisha's quest to locate Helen in Mumbai. In an (admittedly imperfect) attempt to hold on to this distinction, when I use "Eisha" I refer to the character in the film, and when I use "Marjara," I refer to the filmmaker who narrates the film and slowly reveals her family's connection to the bombing of Flight 182.

Part 2

Inhabiting Loss, Exceeding the Frame

• •

4

"I Am Here for Justice and I Am Here for Change"

· ·

Reflections on Anticolonial
Remembering within the
National Inquiry into Missing
and Murdered Indigenous
Women and Girls in Canada

KARINE DUHAMEL

In June of 2019, the National Inquiry into Murdered and Missing Indigenous Women and Girls (hereafter National Inquiry) released its final report, *Reclaiming Power and Place*. The product of decades of advocacy by family members and survivors, as well as a call to action from the 2015 Truth and Reconciliation Commission of Canada, the National Inquiry was in its construction, mandate, and output an historic undertaking. This chapter examines portions of the National Inquiry's work through the lens of memorialization and commemoration. Specifically, this chapter focuses on the creation of the National Inquiry's Legacy Archive as a central component of the Truth Gathering Process, within which survivors, family members and allies created and donated artistic expressions to share their truths about the scale and scope of violence faced by Indigenous women, girls, and 2SLGBTQQIA+ people. It explores various ways that participants used the space of the Legacy Archive to memorialize and commemorate lives cut short by violence. It also animates how the National Inquiry centered Indigenous epistemological frameworks of memory in this work. The anchoring within Indigenous feminist praxis, in particular, importantly shaped how the National Inquiry's work, including the Legacy Archive, actively remembers loved ones in anticolonial ways that move beyond individuals or events and instead toward memory of our communities, our nations, and our collective strength. For me, remembering as an anticolonial act means leaning into those things we know and have always known and using this knowledge to reclaim our identities in concrete and radical ways.

I come to this issue as the director of research for the National Inquiry and one who met with family members and survivors to review, analyze, and compile the experiences shared during the compilation of the final report. As an Anishinaabe historian, what emerged most prominently from this process was the need to reflect on what individuals and community members found important to commemorate and how to center these understandings within a broader approach to memorializing violence directed toward Indigenous women, girls, and 2SLGBTQQIA+ people in settler colonial contexts.

This chapter begins by considering the issue of memorialization and commemoration through the lens of colonial erasure and by centering the ways in which Indigenous expressions of anticolonization generated through Indigenous feminisms provide an alternative pathway to memorialization grounded in the pursuit of good relations. Next, I explore the creation of the National Inquiry's Legacy Archive through three themes consistent in artists' submissions: anticolonial and translational expressions; challenges to the dehumanization of Indigenous women, girls, and 2SLGBTQQIA+ people; and relationality. Ultimately, I suggest that as a significant site for engaging the experiences of those who have survived settler colonial violence, the Legacy Archive memorializes and commemorates in distinctive ways that are worthy of further attention.

Decolonizing Memorialization: Relationality as Indigenous Feminist Approach to Remembrance

Indigenous people have long been imagined, understood, and defined through a colonial gaze that forms the basis of non-Indigenous state archives. As Hirsch and Smith (2002) have pointed out, "Official archives memorialize the experiences of the powerful, those who control hegemonic discursive spaces" (p. 12). This phenomenon has had important consequences for the way in which we as Indigenous people are described, objectified, and represented both historically and in contemporary ways (Tuhiwai-Smith, 2012). How settler Canadians "know" Indigenous people, and women and girls in particular, is an active process in which those with an interest in maintaining the marginalization of families, communities and nations create "memories" and "facts" about who Indigenous people are and how to maintain settler privilege. In particular, the sexualized and fetishized imagined identities of Indigenous women, girls, and 2SLGBTQQIA+ people have served to dehumanize and dispossess us, and, ultimately, to enact violence against us. We are "noble Indian princesses," enslaved "squaws," or so close to nature that we are barely recognized as human. These imposed subjectivities, taken to their most extreme conclusions, were used to justify what would come to pass and what continues today in the structures, institutions, policies, and encounters that sustain colonial violence.

Today, knowledge is created and mobilized to similar outcomes, though it has become more insidious. This includes hegemonic notions and practices of human rights and remembrance that are inherent to colonial frameworks. Sites of creation of colonial knowledge in contemporary times include reparative justice mechanisms such as state-established commissions or inquiries that often solicit experiences of atrocity or violence in "highly prescribed roles and subject positions" (Million, 2013, p. 3; see also the chapters by Crosby et al., Ratih, and Riaño-Alcalá, this volume). As Million (2013) noted, these roles suggest that inquiries represent an important site through which to evaluate what power means today. This includes the power to remember and to forget, as well as to create new narratives that actively suppress the memories and ways of remembering of those who participate. In this way, ongoing colonization takes the form of erasing and devaluing Indigenous knowledge systems by insisting on the individual rights bearer rather than the collective; by promoting rights without meaningful responsibilities to them; and, in particular, by pursuing the "fixing" of Indigenous people by ignoring the ongoing harms of settler colonialism that undergird so many of the challenges we face. Million further argued that the current focus on truth and reconciliation, for instance, "reaffirms the people's systemic inequality and endemic social suffering as a pathology, a wound that is solely an outcome of past colonial policies" (p. 6). In so doing, it denies a central truth: that Indigenous Peoples continue to be targeted in the present day by such policies and that the operation of colonial systems now contributes to a perpetual re-wounding—rather than healing—that makes it difficult, if not impossible, to move beyond not only what has happened but what still occurs.

In addition, as part of the research agenda of the state, inquiries and commissions may memorialize a view of history and reality within what Tuhiwai-Smith (2012) has termed "research 'through imperial eyes' . . . [that] assumes that Western ideas about the most fundamental things are the only ideas possible to hold, certainly the only rational ideas, and the only ideas which can make sense of the world, of reality, of social life and of human beings" (p. 58). They can ossify through memorialization characterizations of the aggrieved as persons as in need of repair, the supremacy of individual human rights over all others, and the temporal placement of such commissions or inquiries as within a period of postviolence. Thus, in their animus and in their operation, inquiries, commissions, and other reparative justice and reconciliation practices may be co-opted as tools for redeeming the colonial state. As Coulthard (2014) and others have argued, they can be used to mend the state rather than simply study it.

Although the emergence of discourses of anticolonialism is often attributed to writers like Fanon, Cabral, Memmi, and Cesaire, anticolonialism in the North American context must be understood through the lens of settler colonialism as a specific kind of structure and practice of domination predicated on the dispossession of Indigenous lands and governance and enabled by the active erasure of Indigenous ways of knowing and thinking about the world (Coulthard, 2014, p. 151). The anecdote then, as Betasamosake Simpson (2004) has noted, must be based in a mobilization of anticolonial strategies that "foster the political mobilization to stop the colonial attack on Indigenous Knowledge and Indigenous Peoples," including remembering through the recovery of Indigenous intellectual traditions and the subsequent recovery of control of lands (p. 181). As such, for societies and nations who have been colonized, remembering languages, practices, laws, and histories that state archives and actors have worked to remove is an important part of knowing who we are as Indigenous people and of finding a path forward. It is an anticolonial act. As Kennedy noted as part of *Reclaiming Power and Place* (National Inquiry, 2019), "Our stories are—oral history tells us, you know, there was other times that we almost lost all of who we were, some of it just all by ourselves. And the spirit loves us so much that they will always find a way to answer our request to find our way back to life" (p. 141). Anchoring this practice within the context of structures that have long sought to position and remember us as victims and as colonial subjects makes this all the more radical.

Finding our way back to life through remembering of who we were and still are is a central tenet of Indigenous feminisms and engages anticolonial principles that I saw enacted firsthand in the stories of survivors and family members who came to the National Inquiry to speak about the violence that Indigenous women, girls, and 2SLGBTQQIA+ people face. There is anger in these spaces, but there is also so much more. Those who spoke about their loved ones were, in very concrete ways, identifying what Arvin et al. (2012) identified as "the intersections of settler colonialism, heteropatriarchy and heteropaternalism" (p. 14) and by privileging "the persistence of Indigenous concepts and epistemologies, or ways of knowing" (p. 21). Challenging the settlers listening to acknowledge, understand, and address these oppressions, those who spoke pushed back against the barriers often imposed by rules of evidence or other inquiry limitations, emphasizing the importance of being "in good relation" (University of Saskatchewan, 2016). Being in good relation, in this context, references the quality, depth, and breadth of relationships that we hold with each other and with the world around us. In addition, it means that whatever antagonisms or conflicts have come to roost among us and among different worldviews can be addressed through respectful relations, including learning to accept and live with one another's differences, to resolve inevitable conflicts, and to demonstrate compassion, empathy, and understanding.

The Legacy Archive

To reflect that what we were hearing from survivors and family members about relationships and to ensure the knowledge being offered was carried forward, the National Inquiry mobilized memorialization and commemoration in unique ways. The Legacy Archive was created as part of the National Inquiry's Truth Gathering Process, as a foundational part of honoring and recognizing relationships. The archive features 433 pieces created by 819 people. It is a diverse collection of digital music, written poetry, canvas paintings, etched art, books, quilts, and various craft pieces. Those who donated their expressions were encouraged to submit an artist statement detailing the inspiration behind their work, as well as conditions for use and care of the expressions beyond the mandate of the Legacy Archive. Importantly, and for the first time in the history of any inquiry or commission, these expressions were considered alongside other forms of evidence in the drafting the final report. They were also centered in educational and outreach events and used to imagine how the stories of family members and survivors might reach a larger audience and live on to do important work beyond the strict confines of the mandate. As such, the Legacy Archive is based on the idea that art is a powerful tool for commemoration, particularly within Indigenous communities. As Travis Hebert explained in his testimony to the National Inquiry (2019), "You know, the way that we live is through art, whether it's carving, painting, dancing, singing, drumming, all of it is there. It's like the foundation of who we are" (p. 59). Material cultural production rooted in Indigenous ancestral knowledge and traditions, and the remembering associated with it, further serves anticolonial purposes. Within the Legacy Archive, various artistic expressions bore witness to injustice, recognized the human dignity of those who are targeted, raised awareness, and inspired action.

The Legacy Archive is also based on the concept of relationality, focused on generating an ethical space between us as an inquiry and those who chose to share their experiences or the experiences of their loved ones. As Cree researcher Willie Ermine (2007) has written, relationships represent an ethical space of engagement within which "two societies, with disparate worldviews, are poised to engage each other" (p.193). This ethical space emphasizes the opportunities that exist to work out the similarities and differences between the various ways of knowing that may be held by those involved. When we consider relationships as spaces of engagement, Ermine explained, we pay attention to words, actions, and behaviors, recognizing that they tell us something about the attitudes, beliefs, and contexts that run below the surface and that function as a "deeper level force" (p. 195) in shaping the ways of knowing and being that may be present in relationships. This reference to relationships with loved ones, featured in nearly all submissions to the Legacy Archive, animates a central feature of the National Inquiry and of the Legacy Archive in particular.

From the outset, the National Inquiry acknowledged the need to properly steward these important expressions, yet it recognized that archives are colonial spaces that have contributed to the erasure of Indigenous voices. As archivists Cook and Schwartz (2002) contended, archival records are traditionally all about "maintaining power, about the power of the present to control what is, and will be, known about the past, about the power of remembering over forgetting" (p. 172). In this context, they can serve to "wield power over the shape and direction of historical scholarship, collective memory, and national identity, over how we know ourselves as individuals, groups, and societies" (p. 173). As Stoler (2009) has argued, archives are a "consequential act of governance;" in other words, they are "sites of the expectant and the conjured" (p. 1). Who controls the archive, what content is allowed in the holdings, and how archivists appraise, select, arrange, describe, and preserve records convey particular values about what and who we remember and about the value of these recollections.

By reimagining the archive through Indigenous relational and decolonizing feminist praxis, the National Inquiry sought to reimagine its composition, role, and structure on the premise that an archive rooted in Indigenous epistemologies and oriented toward active memorialization could, in fact, work differently. Ghaddar and Caswell (2019) argued that effective decolonization requires a radical transformation through a praxis that "centres the oppressed, those wretched of the earth, in the transformation of society, the articulation of new cultural forms, new ways of being, and new ways of ordering the world and its people" (p. 72). It was in this spirit that the National Inquiry created the Legacy Archive, established using Indigenous-centered epistemological guideposts included in the United Nations Declaration on the Rights of Indigenous Peoples (UNDRIP), including the right to self-determination; community participation in decision-making; free, prior, and informed consent; the aim to reset relationships; and the protection of cultural rights. In addition to applying the guiding principles of the UNDRIP, we applied what are known as the Joinet-Orentlicher Principles on the Preservation and Access to Archives Bearing Witness to Human Rights Violations. Their roots lie in a set of principles approved in 1997 by the United Nations Human Rights Commission and recommended by United Nations Special Rapporteur Louis Joinet in his report on the question of impunity for perpetrators of human rights violations, which were updated by lawyer Diane Orentlicher in 2005. As Mnjama (2008) noted, the Joinet-Orentlicher Principles attest to the power of archival records and outline the resulting responsibilities of archivists, including the need to provide avenues for victims to access records about themselves created by state, military, intelligence, and police services (p. 215). In addition, the Legacy Archive also implemented the best practice protocols known as The Protocols for Native American Archival Materials. These protocols establish the importance of building relationships of respect and of understanding the wishes of communities, and they stress the importance of discussions of education for the public and of understanding the issues faced by Indigenous communities.

Given its basis in Indigenous-based principles, rights and responsibilities, and the care with which archival staff worked with community members across the country, the Legacy Archive effectively addressed the challenges of commemorating diverse Indigenous perspectives and cultures in relation to the National Inquiry process. This included making space for various mediums and art outputs, embracing the artists' statements submitted alongside the expressions as important guidance for their present and future care, and welcoming expressions in ceremony where desired by the donor as part of the National Inquiry community hearing process or statement gathering processes. Its role was both simple and complex: to hold community art representing diverse perspectives in a respectful and meaningful way, and, as a historic first for any inquiry or commission in Canada, to provide a process within which family members and survivors could commemorate those lives lost with great respect, ceremony, and purpose in the form and manner that they chose. Importantly, and as cited by many family members, the Legacy Archive underscores the importance of artistic creation for commemoration as a component of healing, as well as of making sure that loved ones are never forgotten. As such, the Legacy Archive serves as a collection of love stories commemorating lives lost, calling forth the best in all of us and pushing against the creation and imposition of Western forms of knowledge.

The Heart in/of Submissions to the Legacy Archive

Many expressions from the Legacy Archive were characterized by anticolonial thinking, working to recover knowledge and to challenge the naturalized colonial frame of the nation by situating Indigenous women, girls, and 2SLGBTQQIA+ people within frameworks of their own, as people who come from nations with their own lands, histories, languages, stories, and ways of knowing. These unique histories and ways of knowing also support a central theme in much of the Legacy Archive's work: the sacred nature of the lives that have been lost. For instance, the paintings *Walk With Us* and *Bella Spirit* were submitted to the Legacy Archive by Nicole Carpenter, a member of the Heiltsuk First Nation from Bella Bella, British Columbia. Nicole attended the National Inquiry's hearing to support another family member, and she describes her work as therapy. Both paintings feature important markers that challenge the colonial frame of nation by depicting the strength that has been passed down from that artist's grandmothers, the importance of intergenerational knowledge transmission, and the cultural dress specifically rooted in Heiltsuk heritage. For instance, in *Walk With Us*, Nicole's mother is depicted in a black and red blanket and holding copper for protection. Her sister is in a brown and purple blanket and holding a feather. Nicole's daughter is in a black and brown blanket, wearing the same headband as Nicole. In *Bella Spirit*, Nicole emphasizes the importance of the water and the landscape of mountains across from the beach where her grandmother lives. She noted in her artist statement that those mountains are the site where her loved ones are buried, and the painting features three red blankets on the mountains to represent Nicole's late sister and grandmothers. The power in this expression, the emphasis on the knowledge and sacred nature of our grandmothers, and the connection to land are all part of a remembering that is set against the backdrop of colonial systems that sought to erase these forms of knowing and being in the world, as well as their relations to each other.

Other expressions also speak to this kind of embedded traditional knowledge and to the importance of identity within an anticolonial frame. Lorraine Richard, who is Red River Métis, donated a pair of beaded booties to the Legacy Archive to honor her mother, Irene, who died in 2001. Irene spoke Saulteaux fluently, practiced and followed traditional medicine (picked, brewed, and consumed), and participated in spiritual ceremonies attached to her culture. The crafted beaded booties that are donated represent a skill Irene mastered early on, based on teachings from her mother. As Lorraine noted in her artist statement, "To me this skill and knowledge are priceless. When my grandmother and mom were teaching me to make these, the moments were special. The connection made with these two strong women came with stories and using our language, which are times I remember with love and calmness." Lorraine's emphasis on good relationships and on the intergenerational connection through the transmission of knowledge is a rebuttal to Western frames of knowledge that would insist on expertise validated by so-called experts and that would place value and significance only on the production of material objects.

As is evident, those who submitted artistic expressions located their identities squarely within their Indigenous histories, languages, and teachings rather than in Canada as a colonial framework. Expressions consistently featured support for the mobilization of Indigenous intellectual traditions that would place women, girls, and 2SLGBTQQIA+ people in a position to reclaim power and place. For instance, *Bear Clan wall mural*, donated by Veronique and Brigitte André (both First Nation from Maliotenam, QC), was created to honor relatives who have passed as well as to honor the spirit of the bear as a symbol of strength. Bear oil is also an important medicine in the community and relates directly to the traditional roles of women in harvesting medicine. In this way, the medicines are also about reclaiming power and place. Our knowledge systems, our medicines, our languages, and our symbols all worked within the Legacy Archive to create an active anticolonial frame within which we could find new solutions to ending violence through Indigenous epistemological frameworks that center good relations and connection.

Another important element carried through many of the pieces submitted to the Legacy Archive was the calling upon the sacred feminine as part of a radical

Indigenous feminist praxis. The sacred is not well centered in Western academic frameworks; for many, anything "sacred" smacks of superstition or eschews a so-called scientific lens. But for the family members and survivors who spoke to us, thinking about the sacred as a component of anticolonial thought was a foundational way to push back against the dehumanization and devaluation of Indigenous women, girls, and 2SLGBTQQIA+ people and was inextricable from their experiences of having their Indigenous roles, rights, and responsibilities violated. As Audrey Siegl, traditional medicine carrier for the National Inquiry and member of the Grandmothers' and Elders' Advisory Circle, explained, "We are sacred because we exist. We are sacred because we have survived" (National Inquiry, 2019, p. 175).

This core teaching of the National Inquiry—that our women, girls, and 2SLGBTQQIA+ people are sacred—was not only part of our projects but was also a way of living and being in an inquiry space and a central component of the project of memorializing the stories we were documenting. As Commissioner Marion Buller noted, "Everywhere we went we did our work in ceremony . . . and that was critical for the focus and the grounding of the work that we did do" (personal communication, 2020). Ceremony included hearing from local elders and knowledge keepers, as well as maintaining and sharing core beliefs from within the National Inquiry that emphasized the recognition of Indigenous power and place. The bundle of sacred objects that traveled with the National Inquiry from hearing to hearing served to ground the community hearings and included a red willow basket, a qulliq (an Inuit women's oil lamp), a copper cup with water, a smudge bowl, and various medicines. Some of these items became part of the Legacy Archive, including the sacred antler donated by Jean St. Onge (Innu from Uashat Mak Mani-utenam, Quebec) at the community hearings in Maliotenam, Quebec, which was placed in the center of the hearing space as a portion of the sacred bundle—a traditional responsibility of women and Two-Spirit people—to witness the truths shared at each hearing.

Other expressions presented as part of ceremony and that upheld the sacred feminine that is inherent to Indigenous epistemologies included a button blanket created by Samantha Pelkey of Namgis First Nation. Chief Commissioner Buller was presented and blanketed with this button blanket at the Vancouver community hearings on behalf of Saa-ust Centre and the Urban Indigenous Advisory Committee for the City of Vancouver. As the artist noted, each part of the blanket has meaning: the black border represents ashes, the white center represents hope, the opening at the top is a smoke hole for all the prayers of families of murdered and missing Indigenous women and girls (MMIWG) and survivors of violence, and the butterfly represents transformation. The button blanket was presented in memory and support of MMIWG and families and traveled with the National Inquiry to every hearing and event to be placed on display, along with several other quilts and blankets donated during the process.

There were expressions of the sacred beyond the hearings and the sacred bundle. For example, *Unspoken Words* by Mikhayla Patterson, in collaboration with the second-year students of the social work program at MacEwan University, is a quilt that represents the memory and legacy of many Missing and Murdered Indigenous Women and Two-Spirit+ (MMIWG2S+) people. Students were provided with a photo and the name of a person who had gone missing or who had been murdered and were encouraged to think about the fact that these people had families and friends who loved, and still love, them. As Mikhayla explained in the artist statement, "I truly think that having the picture in front of them and making the students look into the faces of these people made it real to them. To me, everyone should see that." Upon reflecting on the person assigned to them, each student wrote a letter to the person that would remain private. The letters were then put into envelopes, assembled onto a quilt, and smudged. As Mikhayla detailed, "The idea is that once it is smudged, the letters will go to the spirit world where these women and girls can read them and know that they are loved and cherished and that their memory will be honoured." In this way, the expression emphasized the importance of each person and their sacred nature.

Another donated item by Mylinda Gislason, Métis, is a piece of Red River driftwood that the donor found on a walk along the banks of the Red River. During her walk, and as she expressed in her artist statement, she thought about the power of the water and of the river, and what it may carry beneath. Given that the Red River has been a site where many Indigenous women's and girls' bodies have been recovered, Mylinda felt that the driftwood may hold the spirits of those who have been taken—that the driftwood was now imbued with the sacred nature of the women taken. As she noted in her submission, "May the Creator watch over our loved ones; may we heal a little bit, day by day."

Ultimately, the colonial assault on relationships and its antidote—the centering of the sacred and of relationships within Indigenous ways of knowing—sits at the heart of all of the submissions. As Shawn Wilson (2008) noted, "an Indigenous epistemology has systems of knowledge built upon relationships between things, rather than on the things themselves . . . Indigenous epistemology is our systems of knowledge in their context, or in relationship" (p. 74). These systems are Indigenous cultures, languages, worldviews, histories, spirituality, and ways of understanding our place within the circle of life. In all artistic expressions, the powerful spaces of relationship that loved ones and survivors engaged were not contextual to the story; they were the story.

Some of the above-mentioned artistic expressions and stories were supported by deeply personal recollections on those featured or on the relationships they entailed, such as *Motherly Love* by Dee-Jay Monika Rumbolt, a member of the NunatuKavut Nation. Monika donated *Motherly Love* at the community hearings in Happy Valley-Goose Bay to reflect on her experience of growing up in a single-parent family and show the importance of keeping families together. Her mother worked three jobs to support and provide for Monika and her brother, often not eating herself as she could not afford enough food. In her artwork, Monika reflects on her mother's ability to keep them all together, raise them, and to ensure that they were healthy and happy. *Motherly Love* has three loons representing Monika's family: her mother (right), her brother (middle), and herself (left). Her mother, who is on the outside and has her wings open, as loons do when they are being territorial, represents her mother's role as both a provider and protector to Monika and her brother. Monika's brother is closest to their mother in the painting, as he shares a special connection with her.

In many cases, the artwork supported the public or private testimonies of family members and survivors. For instance, *Community Art Piece*, conceived by Jessica Slater, was realized by MMIWG family members during the Vancouver community hearing. *Community Art Piece* is a mosaic in the style of a star blanket, with each of its 128 tiles painted by survivors and families of MMIWG during the Vancouver community hearings. Each tile features a unique expression of love, support, or relationship. Similarly, *Sisters in Strength*, created by women participating in the 1st Annual Sister in Strength Wellness Retreat at Sta'sailes Healing Lodge in October 2017, is a heart puzzle collage that features several smaller memorials to loved ones. During the retreat, each woman was given a puzzle piece to individualize. As they put their pieces together, they realized that they formed two tear drops in the shape of a heart. As the artist statement explains, this collage represents the broken hearts of MMIWG families and how when they come together and express their sorrows as a group, they build strength. The dyed wool piece was used in a ceremony where the participants all sat in a circle, held their wool pieces, and then channeled their energy and emotions into the heart puzzle collage.

As these expressions have documented, each piece of the Legacy Archive was an anticolonial love story and an important part of restoring the sacred, of extending our roots deep into the earth and into our histories, and of reframing what we remember and how we remember through material objects (see de Alwis, this volume). Through every piece, an experience of a truth was revealed as a way to raise awareness, to heal, and to resist the erasure of colonization through active memorialization processes that engaged those who interacted with them on a much more personal and relational level. Artistic expressions that became part of the Legacy Archive allowed artists to share their voices, experiences, and knowledge and to participate on an emotional level in current and future conversations about MMIWG2S+ people.

The Legacy Archive, and even the National Inquiry's Truth Gathering Process, was not without its limitations, however. From my vantage point, there were many significant bureaucratic obstacles to push back against in order to move forward. But its animus—the ideas of anticolonial remembering and of calling forth the memory of those who no longer walk among us—are inextricably linked to the work we must do to reclaim power and place. The archive's collection also offered opportunities for healing for individuals and communities who engaged in building it or interacted with it at the National Inquiry's closing ceremonies on June 3, 2019, at the Canadian Museum of History in Gatineau, Quebec. The National Inquiry expressed the following hope about the future of the Legacy Archive: "In the future, people worldwide will be able to learn and engage with this art, physically or digitally. The Inquiry hopes the art can be used for outreach, education and research purposes in the hopes that the nation, and globally, people can learn and take action against the injustices against Indigenous women and girls as well as members of the 2SLGBTQQIA+ communities by taking on the recommendations that will be put forward by the National Inquiry." (https://www.mmiwg-ffada.ca /commemoration-art-and-education/legacy-archive/)

Toward the end of the National Inquiry's mandate, a call for expressions of interest for a host for the Legacy Archive was circulated. Despite an acknowledgment within the National Inquiry about the affective value of this work and the monumental body of learning that it represented, no initial expressions of interest were received. Reasons provided, in conversations with the research team, included a lack of institutional capacity, a reticence to take on the heavy responsibility that would be involved in creating a safe space for these expressions, and a general reluctance to take on a collection largely comprised of expressions by nonprofessional artists. Ensuing meetings with the National Inquiry commissioners, the grandmothers, and the elders advisory circle, as well as myself as the director of research, emphasized the need to seek a space to ensure that the expressions would not end up, as some feared, "in a dusty box on a shelf." Those present noted the importance of the work for learning and healing, for commemoration, and for calling forth. Ultimately, the collection was placed, for an initial ten-year term, with the Canadian Museum for Human Rights, which demonstrated what many felt was a good foundation for moving forward: a willingness to acknowledge mistakes and create transformational spaces of engagement by supporting the preservation of the material and creating opportunities for public interaction with the collection as well as access for family members, survivors, and Indigenous groups. In this venue, the collection would not collect dust in a box on a shelf; instead, it could be used to support commemoration that would catalyze concrete actions.

In April 2021, to properly welcome the collection, Indigenous elders and knowledge keepers, family member representatives, and museum leadership attended a ceremony to bless the collection and welcome it in a good way to the museum. As part of the ceremony, elders shared important teachings and prayers, the donated pieces were blessed, and a water ceremony was conducted to emphasize Indigenous women's sacred connection to life. In addition, the items were feasted by participants to close the ceremony and give thanks to the Creator, to ancestors, and to those who donated their expressions. The feasting also included a "spirit bowl," whereby food items were placed in a dish to honor those who are no longer among us.

A short time after the ceremony, selected pieces from the Legacy Archive were put on display at the Canadian Museum for Human Rights in Winnipeg, Manitoba, in a small exhibit intended to highlight the need for action on the MMIWG calls for justice. Although a small exhibit, the way in which the Canadian Museum for Human Rights engaged with the process of creating an ethical space of nurturing relationships and ensuring respect for, and access to, the exhibit was a promising sign of work to come.

Conclusion

This chapter has articulated the importance of reconsidering memorialization and commemoration through Indigenous epistemologies using the example of the Legacy Archive from the National Inquiry. Ultimately, Indigenous survivors and family members participating in the National Inquiry's Truth Gathering Process chose to differently inhabit and navigate colonial memoryscapes and remembrance as an anticolonial act emphasizing the idea that our women, girls, and 2SLGBTQQIA+ people are scared through mediums of art and creative and ceremonial expressions that reflect Indigenous epistemologies and ways of calling forth. The importance of finding our way back to life, and doing so in good relation, is central to remembering as an anticolonial act. The rootedness of Indigenous peoples in ancestral knowledge teaches that good relations include understanding the interconnectedness of our experiences across generations, the importance of memory, and the need to pursue and maintain these good relations based on an acknowledgment of truth and responsibility. The Legacy Archive became part of our responsibility as Indigenous women working for the National Inquiry—a sacred bundle that we needed to care for beyond the end of our mandate.

Understanding, memorializing, and commemorating the lives of those lost means recognizing that the cultural memory generated in the Canadian public with reference to Indigenous people is drawn from a variety of colonial contexts in which Indigenous people are imagined in ways that contribute to their lack of safety, security, and justice. Such realities demand that we memorialize and commemorate through the lens of relationship, understanding violence and our healing from it as formulated through relationality. This approach serves to shift frames of analysis to center Indigenous epistemologies and perspectives and reorients us to Indigenous strength, resilience, and knowledge. The way in which the intergenerational teachings about sacredness and care were embodied had roots in the important relationships that reflect Indigenous feminist praxis and anticolonial thought and in the core theme that animated the final report and all related projects: the idea of reclaiming power and place. In reclaiming power and place, we honor our own gifts and the gifts in others, and in so doing, we recognize the sacred in us all.

5

Transnational Contestations

• •

Remembering Sexual Violence in Postgenocide Guatemala

ALISON CROSBY, IRMA ALICIA
VELÁSQUEZ NIMATUJ, AND
MARÍA DE LOS ÁNGELES AGUILAR

"We are what we remember," we are reminded in *La Luz que Vuelve* (The Light that Returns), a thirty-eight-page educational comic for middle school children in Guatemala (Unión Nacional de Mujeres Guatemaltecas, 2017, p. 16). The comic tells the story of a group of Maya Q'eqchi' women's long struggle for justice for harm suffered at the height of Guatemala's genocidal armed conflict, which lasted from 1960 to 1996. It is structured around a conversation between Lucía, a young Q'eqchi' girl, and her mother Isabel about why Lucía's grandmother has been absent from the home for several days. Isabel explains that she left to go to Guatemala City as one of the fifteen plaintiffs in the Sepur Zarco case. As the comic details, on February 26, 2016, in the High Risk Court "A" in Guatemala City following a month-long trial, two former members of the Guatemalan military were convicted of crimes against humanity in the form of sexual violence and domestic and sexual slavery, the murder of a woman and two girls, and the disappearance of seven men at the Sepur Zarco military outpost in El Estor, Izabal, between 1982 and 1983. Isabel tells Lucía that the women's husbands had organized to have their lands legalized and as a result were disappeared. The women were subsequently taken to the Sepur Zarco outpost where they endured years of forced labor and abuse. "Mama, is this why grandma is always so quiet and sad?" Lucía asks. "Yes, my daughter," Isabel replies. "For many years she has had much pain in her heart and also her body" (Unión Nacional de Mujeres Guatemaltecas, 2017, p. 13).

The comic provides a brief history of the community of Sepur Zarco, including the history of dispossession of Indigenous lands and livelihoods, and the violence brought by the establishment of the military outpost during the war. It describes the trial itself and the reparations ruling designed to ensure that such violence never happens again. It is dialogical in nature—between Lucía and her mother, among Lucía and her peers, and with students themselves. It begins by asking students to situate violence within their everyday lives and to reflect on its meaning, who suffers the most, and why it is ongoing. Students are asked to differentiate between sexual violence and sexual harassment, consider whether they have experienced or perpetrated such violence, and even if not, to think about what this experience might be like: "Let's imagine for a moment that we ourselves have been victims of a sexual violation or sexual assault. The emotions and feelings experienced are many: anger, frustration, feelings of vulnerability, pain, and even guilt" (Unión Nacional de Mujeres Guatemaltecas, 2017, p. 27).

Drawing on the testimonies of the Sepur Zarco plaintiffs, the comic was created by the National Union of Guatemalan Women (UNAMG) with support from the Ministry of Education and funding from the Swedish Embassy. It explicitly centers Mayan women's protagonism, with the army mentioned but not depicted and an overall absence of male-identified figures. As Ada Valenzuela, the executive director of UNAMG, explained, "Our intention was to visibilize the women's courage, break the *machista* [male chauvinist] vision and place them as the protagonists of the story" (Coronado, 2017, para. 6). The comic's very existence is noteworthy, given that the armed conflict is minimally discussed in the postwar national educational curriculum (Oglesby, 2007) despite two high profile and extensive truth-telling reports by the Catholic Church's Recovery of Historical Memory (REMHI) project (Oficina de Derechos Humanos del Arzobispo de Guatemala, 1998) and the United Nations-sponsored Historical Clarification Commission (CEH; Comisión para el Esclarecimiento Histórico, 1999), both of which unraveled a history of extreme racialized inequality, loss, and ruin. The CEH report (1999) *Guatemala: Memoria del Silencio Tz'inil Na'tab'al* (Guatemala: Memory of Silence) found that over two hundred thousand people were killed or disappeared during the war, 83 percent of whom were Maya (vol. 5, p. 21). The report documented 626 massacres attributed to state forces as part of its campaign of extermination (vol. 3, p. 252) and found that acts of genocide were committed against specific Mayan communities at the height of the state's scorched earth policies in the early 1980s (vol. 3, p. 358). The report highlighted 1,465 cases of sexual violence, 88.7 percent of which were perpetrated against Mayan women (vol. 3, p. 23).

Two and a half decades after these truth-tellings, silence and denial about *la violencia* (the violence) is pervasive among Guatemala's political, economic, and military elites who continue to hold power; *no hubo genocidio* (there was no genocide) is a common refrain. *We are what we forget.* There are few state-sponsored memorials to the victims of the war, particularly in the predominantly Indigenous rural areas devastated by the armed conflict. Instead, it has been Indigenous victims' movements, accompanied by organized civil society, that have assumed the arduous tasks of creating and holding space for public remembrance of la violencia, bringing its perpetrators to justice, and demanding reparations. The Sepur Zarco trial was part of an extraordinary but short-lived judicial spring that saw several high-profile prosecutions for genocide and crimes against humanity, including the 2013 trial of the former de facto head of state (1982–83) and army general José Efraín Ríos Montt. These prosecutions, part of the predominant transnational turn to the paradigm of transitional justice as a means to address the aftermath of atrocity (Teitel, 2000; see also chapters by Duhamel, Ratih, and Riaño-Alcalá, this volume), were facilitated by a strengthened and increasingly independent judicial system, supported by international funding.

The Sepur Zarco trial received international attention; it was the first of its kind whereby these specific crimes were prosecuted in-country. Hashtags such as #IAmSepurZarco and #WeAreAllSepurZarco circulated widely, and the verdict was recognized as a rare example of gender justice (Nobel Women's Initiative, 2016). In this chapter, we reflect on the significance of the emergence of a particular and transnational public memory of wartime sexual violence in Guatemala that relies upon Mayan women's testimonial practices. A transnational witnessing "we" are asked to relate to, and even assume the position of, the Indigenous protagonist or survivor. However, remembering and memorializing sexual violence is fraught terrain. It is "poisonous knowledge" (Das, 2007, p. 54) swallowed by survivors as a strategy of survival and resistance yet seeps into everyday life as well as into transnational human rights and feminist discourse. Its transnational seepage creates the spectacle of the "raped woman," a truncated identity category caught within its gendered, racialized, and colonial fault lines that assumes a homogeneous experience of sexual violation and indeed of survivor subjectivity (Mookherjee, 2015). As such, we have to ask, what story gets told and who creates it? As Das (2007) argued, there is a difference between speech and voice, between narration and authorship. As we explore in the chapter, the story of wartime sexual violence in Guatemala is a relational one, forged between Mayan women protagonists and their many interlocutors, ourselves included, and such relationality is imbued with power.

The chapter draws on data from a four-year (2014–18) transnational feminist research project on the memorialization of loss in the aftermath of violence in Guatemala and Sri Lanka led by Crosby and de Alwis (see preface, this volume), including a workshop in Sepur Zarco with the fourteen surviving plaintiffs in August 2017, a year and a half after the trial.[1] It also draws on our respective experience working with fifty-four Mayan women who survived sexual violence and many other forms of racialized gendered violence during the armed conflict, including the plaintiffs in the Sepur Zarco case. Crosby, a white Scottish and Canadian sociologist and gender studies professor, conducted an eight-year feminist participatory action research project from 2009 to 2017 with the fifty-four Mayan women protagonists alongside her colleague, the Unitedstatesian community-cultural psychologist M. Brinton Lykes, and in partnership with UNAMG (Crosby & Lykes, 2019). Velásquez Nimatuj, a Maya K'iche' social anthropologist and journalist, was an expert witness during the trial (Velásquez Nimatuj, 2013), as well its precursor, the 2010 Tribunal of Conscience organized by several civil society organizations to raise public awareness and lay the groundwork for the legal case (Velásquez Nimatuj, 2012; see also Crosby & Lykes, 2011), which is where Velásquez Nimatuj and Crosby first met. De los Ángeles Aguilar is a Maya K'iche' historian who conducted fieldwork for Crosby and de Alwis's aforementioned memorialization project, collecting testimony from Indigenous communities and genocide survivors.

In the following section, we trace the contestations inherent to the formation of sexual harm as a communal, national, and transnational public memory and examine Mayan women's usage of their cosmovision, or worldview, to center the land-body-territory nexus in remembering gendered violence as embedded in colonial violence. We then proceed to examine the particularities of a public memory of wartime sexual violence in Guatemala that emerged through Mayan women's testimonies of trauma, testimonies embedded within transitional justice mechanisms such as the Sepur Zarco trial. Such testimonial practices are shaped by a Western humanitarian frame that assumes that *speaking is healing*, in contrast to the Latin American understanding of *testimonio* as collective and revolutionary. We situate the reenactment of testimony–*testimonio* by Mayan protagonists as a remembrance practice entangled with the Western rights regime but also always exceeding it. We draw on the aforementioned 2017 workshop in Sepur Zarco to highlight the plaintiffs' memory work in the aftermath of the trial, which rejects the essential woundedness in reifications of sexual harm and instead seeks to suture land and body and reconcile the living and the dead.

Sexual Harm as Transnational Public Memory

The prosecution of the Sepur Zarco trial drew upon international jurisprudence to make its case (Impunity Watch and Alliance to Break the Silence and Impunity, 2017). In the 1990s, sexual violence as a weapon of war gained increasing recognition within the transnational human rights regime due in part to sustained advocacy by international feminist activists and legal experts (MacKinnon, 2006). This heightened attention led to the prosecution of cases of sexual violence as genocide and crimes against humanity in the ad hoc tribunals for the former Yugoslavia and Rwanda and to the inclusion of rape and sexual violence as violations in the Rome Statute of the International Criminal Court, which came into effect in 2002. United Nations Security Council resolutions 1325 and 1820 were introduced to address the gendered causes and effects of war, specifically sexual violence, leading to increased activism and funding for projects on the ground. The figure of the "raped woman" became the primary signifier of how war is gendered.

Indigenous, Black, and postcolonial feminist scholars have critiqued the spectacularization and abjection of racialized gendered bodies within colonial discourses and recognition politics, including feminist discourses of violence against women, which continuously (re)center white subjectivity and homogenize gender as a universalized category (Arvin et al., 2013; Grewal, 2005; Hartman, 1997; Jaleel, 2021; Mookherjee, 2015). Survivor subjectivity and agency are often occluded as mediated fragments of broader stories that circulate within national and transnational domains. The survivor occupies a particular liminality at the interstices of invisibility and hypervisibility; as "the raped woman," she is seen but not seen, heard but not heard, and as the narrator of her story but not its (sole) author. Speaking to these tensions, in her study of the *birangonas* (war heroines) who survived sexual violence during the Bangladesh war of independence in 1971, Mookherjee (2015) asked, "What makes the raped woman visible and audible at certain historical junctures? And what makes her invisible and inaudible at that same moment?" (p. 24). As Mookherjee detailed, the birangona seemed to be an exception to the entrenched silence on the issue of wartime sexual violence in so many contexts; indeed, she played a particular visible role in the Bangladeshi national narrative. Yet, Mookherjee argued, drawing on Derrida, she is a spectral, wounded absent-presence: "In the nation's positive conceptual formulation of the raped woman, she can only be exemplified in the absence of her presence, through horrific enactment and representation as a wound, which ensures a greater invocation of her 'trauma'" (p. 25). In analyzing how birangona narratives—including testimonies and visual representations in photographs, books, and newspapers—are shaped by their engagement with the state as well as human rights activists, Mookherjee used the metaphor of combing (Cohen, 1994) to trace how "both the war heroines and the documenters of their history undertake public memory and public secrecy alike" (p. 23). As Mookherjee explained, "The comb represents simultaneously the power to reveal and search for knowledge and attempts to cover and veil knowledge from inspection" (p. 23). In her analysis of human rights activists' documentation of birangonas' narratives, Mookherjee detailed how they "combed (searched for) the *birangonas* horrific wound as well as combed (hid) the intricacies of her life after the rape" (p. 24). In seeking to resist the spectacle of the wound, Mookherjee accompanied the birangonas as they combed over their wound within the complexities, contradictions, and specificities of everyday life (Das, 2007).

These dynamics of combing are also at play in Guatemala. As the Sepur Zarco trial traveled into the trans/national domain, it was celebrated as a victory for women worldwide (Nobel Women's Initiative, 2016). What was combed over was how Indigeneity was central to the experience of violence as well as to the struggle for redress. Mayan women scholars, activists, and survivors have emphasized the connection between the colonization of Indigenous peoples—as historical and current practice—and gendered violence. As Velásquez Nimatuj (2013) argued, "The rapes of q'eqchi' women are an extension of the colonial relations of dependency and exploitation that have prevailed in Guatemala throughout its history" (p. 5), adding that "[Mayan] bodies have not been seen nor addressed with dignity or respect" (p. 50). The experience of structural dispossession of land and livelihoods is gendered and racialized. In Sepur Zarco, the *señoras'* husbands were disappeared because they were organizing to have their lands legalized, and the neighboring landowners called in the army, a connection they made clear in their testimonies to Velásquez Nimatuj for her expert witness report. As Demecia Yat emphasized, "Because we defended the land, they took our husbands" (Velásquez Nimatuj, 2013, p. 30), adding that, "Our crime was to live close to the landowners" (p. 31). Rosa Tiul stated, "When I lived with my husband, we had everything: house, cows, chickens. We saved a little and above all, we did not buy corn or chili, but when they killed him, we could no longer work the earth" (Velásquez Nimatuj, 2013, p. 17). They also identified racism against them as Indigenous women as central to their experiences of harm. Cecilia Caal testified that "the soldiers, the army, did not value us as people, for them we are just indigenous women who can't read or write, we are not worth anything in their eyes, and so they abused us, time and again" (Velásquez Nimatuj, 2013, p. 43).

In their decolonial memory work, Mayan women emphasize how land and bodies are intertwining territories to be defended against ongoing colonial extractivism (Cabnal, 2019; Centro para la Acción Legal en Derechos Humanos [CALDH] & Pérez Sián, 2014; Chirix García, 2019; Velásquez Nimatuj, 2019). As the Maya Kaqchikel scholar Emma Chirix García (2019) articulated, "We are living bodies, peoples in movement who aspire to bodily wellbeing and that of Mother Nature" (p. 139). In the Mayan cosmovision, the land is not an object to be plundered; it has agency and rights, and indeed, it remembers. Identifying as a "community territorial feminist," Maya Xinca activist Lorena Cabnal (2019) described how "being an indigenous woman and defending our ancestral territory means putting on the front line of attack . . . our first territory of defense, the body. To defend the land territory, as women we conduct an impressive, parallel and daily defense in two inseparable dimensions: the defense of our bodily territory and the defense of our land territory . . . we recognize that the body as well as the land are spaces of vital energy that must function reciprocally" (pp. 121–122).

Indigenous women push back against the colonial tendency within non-Indigenous academic research to construct them as always essentially damaged

(Tuck, 2009) and instead assert their agency in forming memories of violence and resilience as a strategy of resistance. As one publication bringing together diverse groups of Mayan women argued, "Reclaiming historical memory through the bodies and territories of [Mayan] women as a central thread that gives meaning to individual experiences is a strategy that enables the identification of violences and their sequelae but also the capacity for resilience that has made possible confronting adverse situations, supporting community resistance/persistence" (Centro para la Acción Legal en Derechos Humanos & Pérez Sián, 2014, p. 172). And Chirix García (2019) emphasized how Mayan ways of thinking and acting, articulated through two key concepts in the cosmovision, *qana'ojib'äl* and *qab'anob'äl*, respectively, "come into being within social relations, in community life, through oral history and in the sacred texts" (p. 147). Mayan bodies are collective (*qach'akul*) as well as individual (*nu ch'akil*) (p. 148) and are in resistance; "not all bodies are docile, submissive, dominated" (p. 149).

The concept of sexual violence does not have direct translation in most Mayan languages. As explained by the linguistic anthropologist Mayra Nineth Barrios Torres in her expert witness report during the Sepur Zarco trial (which is discussed in Crosby & Lykes, 2019), in Q'eqchi' sexual violence is referenced in a number of ways, most commonly as *muxuk*, which in Spanish can be translated as *profanar* (to desecrate or defile), *traspasar* (to transgress or dispose of) and *ensuciar* (to dirty or defile; Crosby & Lykes, 2019, p. 115). Originally muxuk meant *pasar encima* (to pass up, through, or by). It was resignified during the armed conflict to become the root of several ways of describing the violences of that time. The concept of *muxuk chaq'rab* "can refer to forced disappearances, the burning of crops, the loss of belonging, and many other experiences of violation" (Crosby & Lykes, 2019, p. 115). According to Barrios, given the centrality of muxuk within the Q'eqchi' cosmovision, "when women use this word to refer to sexual violence, they are also attaching meaning to having been robbed of their self-respect, as well as the respect of their community" (Crosby & Lykes, 2019, pp. 115–116). The concept of muxuk helps us unravel any assumed linearity or individuality in relation to the experience of violence and points us to other ways of knowing and being that elude the Western frame but at the same time must be explicated within it, as evidenced by the act of translation performed by the expert witnesses during the trial, Velásquez Nimatuj (2012) included. She affirmed the courage of Indigenous women who have decided to testify and demand justice within a racist judicial system "that is incommensurable with their own frameworks, does not recognize their maternal languages, that racializes them as culturally inferior women, and as beings who don't feel, don't suffer, and don't dream" (p. 119). In her expert witness report, Velásquez Nimatuj (2013) addressed the colonial system within which the judicial system is situated. She underlined the heterogeneity of Indigenous and Q'eqchi' communities as well as of the protagonists themselves and warned of the dangers of homogenizing Indigenous peoples and occluding the complexities and specificities of their lived experiences of

Indigenous cultures. She also emphasized the limits of what can be known about Indigenous cultures from the outside.

The meaning of sexual harm against Indigenous women is always in translation yet at the same time unknowable and untranslatable. Chirix García (2019) argued that "it is not possible to understand the Mayan conception of the world from the Western vision, because Eurocentric and ethnocentric knowledge distorts, rationalizes, racializes, subordinates, and violates indigenous knowledges" (p. 147). This raises critical questions regarding how sexual violence is remembered and memorialized transnationally by a multiplicity of actors, including white researchers from the Global North such as Crosby. What can or even should they/we know? As Velásquez Nimatuj and de los Ángeles Aguilar have experienced, the power of whiteness continuously displaces the knowledge of Indigenous researchers who seek to defend their communities from ongoing colonial harm, including knowledge extractivism. Such tensions have been inherent to our work together that has led to this chapter. With these questions of untranslatablity, unknowability, and the incommensurability of Western and Mayan onto-epistemologies lingering as colonial hauntings (Gordon, 2008), in the following section we detail the formation of public remembrance of sexual harm in Guatemala through the mediation of Indigenous women's testimonies in the struggle for redress for harm suffered.

Testimony as Act of Transfer

The creation of a public memory of wartime sexual violence in Guatemala began in 2003 when Mayan women in several regions of the country who were seeking redress for the sexual violence perpetrated against them by military and paramilitary groups during the war began working with the Actors for Change Consortium (UNAMG, the Community Studies and Psychosocial Action Team, or ECAP, and independent feminists). These Mayan protagonists were responding to the gendered gaps and silences in the CEH and REMHI truth-telling reports; it was generally acknowledged that the cases of sexual violence that were documented were but a fraction of the racialized gendered harms experienced by Mayan women during the armed conflict. Protagonists' work with the consortium emerged during the transnational moment of heightened attention to wartime sexual violence detailed above, and international funding was forthcoming. Members of the consortium were active participants in transnational advocacy, participating in UN advocacy spaces and other Tribunals of Conscience such as the Women's International War Crimes Tribunal on Japan's Military Sexual Slavery held in Tokyo in December 2000 (Sakamoto, 2001).

Over a six-year period, fifty-four Q'eqchi', Kaqchikel, Mam, and Chuj protagonists received psychosocial support and participated in women's rights workshops. They gave testimony to a groundbreaking oral history project documenting their experiences of the war (Fulchiron et al., 2009). And, in 2014, fifteen Q'eqchi' protagonists formed the Jalok U (which means transformation in Q'eqchi') Collective to develop and prosecute the Sepur Zarco case, alongside the Breaking the Silence and Impunity Alliance, which includes UNAMG, ECAP, and the feminist lawyers collective Women Transforming the World (MTM; Impunity Watch and Alliance, 2017).

Throughout the long struggle for redress detailed in this brief genealogy, protagonists' testimonies have been the primary "act of transfer" (Connerton, 1989, p. 39) of the memory of *what happened*. Felman and Laub (1992) have argued that only those who have suffered harm can give testimony; no one else can assume this unique positionality. Protagonists are at once the victims of and direct witnesses to such harm. However, testimony is inherently dialogical; it requires a listener, an audience to hear and validate the truth that is being told. As Laub stated, "Testimonies are not monologues, they cannot take place in solitude. The witnesses are talking *to somebody*: to somebody they have been waiting for for a long time [emphasis original]" (Felman & Laub, 1992, p. 71). Protagonists in the Sepur Zarco case gave their testimonies to multiple audiences, including lawyers, judges, expert witnesses, psychologists, activists, human rights practitioners, and researchers, as well as the general (transnational) public. Giving testimony can be liberating, an affirmation that *this happened to me* and that *it was not my fault*, and an excavation of poisonous knowledge that perhaps presents possibilities for healing. However, "one testifies when the truth is in doubt [when it has yet to be decided]" (Ahmed & Stacey, 2001, p. 2); as such, it makes protagonists vulnerable to (yet again) not being believed.

Testimonies are stories of harm retold, exposing protagonists to the pain of repeated remembering. *La Luz que Vuelve* depicts one of the plaintiffs, *q'ana'* Juana, telling an interlocutor during the trial, "I am very tired. My chest hurts. I am remembering yet again what we lived through." She is urged to persist, "to have [her] truth heard" (Unión Nacional de Mujeres Guatemaltecas, 2017, p. 20). Protagonists must bear the burden of remembering in the service of justice and for the greater good, despite the toll it takes, the pain it surfaces. As Felman said, "To testify is thus not merely to narrate but to commit oneself, and to commit the narrative, to others: to *take responsibility*—in speech—for history or the truth of an occurrence, for something which, by definition, goes beyond the personal, in having (nongeneral) validity and consequence [emphasis original]" (Felman & Laub, 1992, p. 204).

The Latin American literary tradition of testimonio (Beverley, 2004; Gelles, 1998) has a different onto-epistemology from the individuated, rational, and linear narrative construction of testimony required to prove harm suffered within Western rights regimes such as truth commissions and war crimes tribunals (Crosby & Lykes, 2019; Henry, 2009; McAllister, 2013). In testimonio, including most famously Menchú's (1984) *I Rigoberta Menchú: An Indian Woman in Guatemala*, the individual is a refraction of the community; the *I* of the narration is implicitly understood to be a collective *we*. As Menchú noted on the first page, "This is my testimony. I didn't learn it from a book and I didn't learn it alone. I'd like to stress that it's not only *my* life, it's also the testimony of my people.... The important thing is that what happened to me has happened to many other people too: my story is the story of all poor Guatemalans [emphasis original]" (p. 1). Testimonios are historical and contextual rather than only event-based, forcing us to account for the structural and systemic dimensions of harm rooted in colonization, and allowing us to see how violence is lived and resisted within the everyday.

Gaining prominence within the rise of guerrilla organizing in Latin America in the 1970s (McAllister, 2013), testimonios are an expression of coming to consciousness, of conscientization (Freire, 2000), a form of political protest against injustice, and a revolutionary call to action that demands a response from its audience. They are a form of "collective autobiographical witnessing" (Gelles, 1998, p. 16) and are mediated by the relationship between the narrator and her interlocutor; *I Rigoberta Menchú* was a dialogical co-construction between Menchú and the anthropologist Elisabeth Burgos-Debray. The attack on the veracity of Menchú's story by the Unitedstatesian anthropologist David Stoll (2008), and the storm of outrage that ensued within Western audiences, reflects an inability to reckon with testimonio's particular onto-epistemology and reveals the orientalist underpinnings of the West's consumption of the stories of the racialized, gendered Other, as well as the precarity of making oneself vulnerable in this way. The extensive discussion of the Stoll controversy (see, for example, Arias, 2001) productively brought to the fore differing meanings, usage, and contextual specificities of testimony within Indigenous and Western worlds.

As McAllister (2013) detailed, in Guatemala, the revolutionary underpinnings of testimonio, what she terms "the call to 'go on'" where the narrative "does not end in suffering" (p. 97), have been occluded by an emphasis on trauma within Guatemala's postwar testimonial truth-tellings, part of the increasing hegemony of the transnational humanitarian human rights regime and the assumption that "speaking is healing." As she argued, "The reiteration of *testimonio* as therapy began to exclude even the memory of its links to revolutionary futurity," with trauma as the only "true event" (p. 97). However, in her research in the Maya K'iche'-speaking hamlet of Chupol in Chichicastenango, McAllister found revolutionary echoes in Chupolenses' ways of resisting, renarrating, and eluding the humanitarian frame of therapeutic testimony, finding multiple meanings in silences, evasions, erasures, and retellings.

Although the humanitarian frame continues to hold power in the Guatemalan postgenocide landscape as a dominant form of truth-telling, how and why it is taken up by protagonists cannot be assumed, and they are certainly not merely acted upon within these processes. In their struggle for redress, the Sepur Zarco protagonists continuously mediated between Western and Mayan onto-epistemologies. They gave testimony within the judicial realm as one means to seek justice and demand accountability, an act of translation that intervened in the site of colonial power, the Guatemalan state. At the same time, they are seeking to recover their Q'eqchi' cosmovision that was fragmented by the war (Velásquez Nimatuj, 2013), rethreading spiritual and community life as they collectively resist the ongoing, unresolved violence of colonial extractivism and land dispossession. In the following section, we return to Sepur Zarco as the protagonists comb through the trial's aftermath and its testimonial traces, invoking testimonio as a reiterated dialogical remembrance practice, an act of transfer that retells memories of harm as a methodology of resistance.

Return to Sepur Zarco: Suturing Land and Body

In August 2017, our research team traveled to Sepur Zarco to conduct a workshop with the fourteen surviving plaintiffs from the trial. Located in northeastern Guatemala, the community is not easily accessible, especially when rains wash out the unpaved road and make the river crossing impossible. As we drove through the numerous African palm plantations that surround the community, which is itself still a private *finca* (landed estate), we were viscerally reminded of the question of land that remains at the heart of protagonists' struggle for redress—an as-yet unfilled component of the trial's reparations ruling. *What does the land remember?* The workshop sought to try to understand what memory, justice, and reparations—key discursive constructs within the transnational paradigm of transitional justice whose meanings remain elusive, contextual, and liminal—signify to the protagonists in the aftermath of the trial.

In the workshop, as in many others that Crosby and Lykes (2019) had facilitated with these protagonists over the preceding decade, we used creative techniques, including drawing and dramatization, to facilitate performances of knowledge and protagonism; we were trying to avoid asking protagonists to retell stories of harm. Creative resources also facilitated and indeed enabled our dialogic encounter given our failure to speak Q'eqchi', for which we were rightly reprimanded at the beginning of the workshop: "You should learn Q'eqchi' so that we can talk." All conversations in the workshop were mediated by translators, moving between Q'eqchi' and Spanish. Once again, the colonial hauntings of untranslatability, unknowability, and incommensurability permeated this hyphenated space of Western and Mayan onto-epistemological encounter.

Participants were happy to engage in our methodological process, creating collective drawings and performing dramatizations to represent the trial's aftermath. In their memory drawings, depictions of trees and flowers infused the concept with their relationship to the land and Mother Earth and indeed were an expression of their sense of agency and connection to the land, as well as the agency of the land itself: "The tree represents us. We have roots and leaves and branches, and we want to bear fruit." However, contrary to our own intentions to avoid such narratives, they also insisted that we bear witness to their testimonios, to dialogically participate in their retelling of their stories of harm, as some of us had done many times before. These retellings again situated the experience of individual bodily harm within the collective fight for the land:

> When the conflict started it was for the land . . . for the land this started. There were some representatives who led a group who gathered like this to fight for the land and so we can't forget that the fight is for the land . . . that they occupied this land and killed much of the community . . . completely disappeared the group . . . this is what we live with here. But all of us here now, not only 14 . . . there have been many, many women that have been made widows, but they went to other villages, other communities far away here because they are afraid. This is what happened to us. What we want now is possession and tenure of the land where we have lived. We won't live longer but our grandchildren and children will be here . . . we don't want this to happen in the future.
>
> I raised eight children and I was in the military encampment for six years, washing the soldiers' clothes, their uniforms. For this I hurt. It is because of this that we demand justice, that they give us reparations, that they restore and return what they destroyed. Still they haven't given reparations to us, like they don't want to give them to us, what we want. This is what we keep demanding, but they haven't give them to us, they haven't listened to us . . . This is why we keep asking for this because we get sick . . . but nothing, like the president and government don't want to hear us . . . Now we live with hope here in Sepur Zarco . . . just a little bit of hope . . . it urges me to fight for the land, God willing they give it to me.

Testimonies—*testimonios*—are stories of harm retold. And, as discussed earlier, the audience for the retelling is an integral part of the testimonial practice. In the transitional justice paradigm, testimonies are retold as evidence to prove harm suffered, *when the truth is in doubt*. The dialogical encounter fails when the audience—in this case, the Guatemalan state—refuses to act. What emerged in our workshop was the enactment of testimonio as a collective remembrance practice—this is what happened to us—continuously performed as a dialogical call to action. And what about us, the workshop audience? Our methodological processes and questions shaped the testimonial practices that emerged during the workshop.

A transnational encounter about forced disappearance had a particularly piercing effect. De Alwis had traveled from Sri Lanka to participate in this workshop and related fieldwork as part of our research project exploring the transnational dimensions of the inhabitance of loss—the travelings between distinct experiences of violence. Toward the beginning of the workshop, following a series of introductions and warm-up exercises, she gave a presentation on the Sri Lankan war. The pervasiveness of forced disappearances in Sri Lanka struck a chord, with many participants responding emotionally to the PowerPoint slide depicting Sri Lankan widows holding photographs of their disappeared loved ones.

Although mass graves were exhumed at Sepur Zarco and the neighboring finca Tinajas in 2012 and these remains displayed during the trial (to the anguish of the plaintiffs; see Crosby & Lykes, 2019 for further discussion), most of the protagonists' disappeared husbands had yet to be identified. Pointing to the slide, one participant noted, "Looking at the photo there, she hasn't found her husband yet." She related it to her own experience, saying, "There are no photos, nothing. It would be much better if I could even find a part of a photograph of my husband, but until now I don't have one." The trial has not resolved their husbands' disappearance: "The people who are responsible are in jail for what they did, but the disappeared ones are still not here." Their husbands' absent-presence as a generational loss permeated their responses to de Alwis' presentation: "When they took my husband, they threw him in the river or we don't know where, and they left him. They left us as widows with children. How sad it is what happened to us and now we are trying to do this for our grandchildren. We are fighting to search for our disappeared ones. Sadly, we haven't found them, but we have faith and hope so we will continue looking until we find them. Maybe we die but we will return, and our children will continue fighting."

Taylor (2019) has shown how, beginning with the Mothers of the Plaza del Mayo in Argentina, the representation of forced disappearances through grieving mothers holding photographs and demanding the return of their loved ones has become a transnational "traumatic meme," instantly recognizable and taken up and adapted across a range of contexts, continuing to "accumulate affective and symbolic power in each new iteration" (p. 117). Indeed, workshop participants immediately knew what the Sri Lankan PowerPoint image depicted; their own lack of the signifier—the photograph of their disappeared loved one—pierced, ruptured, and caused more pain. As Taylor noted, trauma "is never for the first time. It is also known by the nature of its repeats" (p. 117). However, the encounter with de Alwis was also an encounter of transnational solidarity and resistance through the memorialization of absence-presence, with protagonists telling her that she was not alone and encouraging her to keep fighting. They aligned themselves with the struggles of other women, across language and culture.

The loss of land is integrally tied both to the violation of bodies and the absence of bodies. Indeed, at one point during the Sepur Zarco trial, one expert witness talked about the *dismemberment* of the land (Burt, 2016, para. 5)—its body torn apart by the colonial occupiers, in the process dismembering the community itself and the bodies who inhabit it, both living and dead. Das (2007) spoke of the "complex relationship . . . between building a world that the living can inhabit with their loss and building a world in which the dead can find a home" (p. 58). The suturing of land and body as integrated, integral territories who remember and have agency and the reconciliation between the living and the dead are the urgent goals of the protagonists' reiterated remembrance practices.

Conclusion

"We are what we remember," *La Luz que Vuelve* reminded us. The comic drew upon the Sepur Zarco protagonists' testimonios to create a dialogical, intergenerational, and indeed transnational encounter, inviting *us* to participate in the act of transfer of *what happened*. The increasing transnational recognition of wartime sexual violence and sexual harm more broadly within rights regimes can lead to a presumption of universality and knowability that combs over the complexities and indeed incommensurability between differing ontoepistemologies underpinning particular remembrance practices and their meanings.

As differently positioned researchers, we were reminded of the liminality of recognition when, towards the end of the workshop in Sepur Zarco, we asked participants whether there were sometimes things that should perhaps be forgotten: "Are there things that you want to forget? We have talked a lot about the things that we want to remember, but are there things that you want to forget about?" The question provoked tearful outrage. As one protagonist commented, "Even if we want to forget something, we can't. Nothing. It's in our hearts, in our minds, in our physical, in our emotional [being] . . . so it's hard to forget. Us, no. Even though we are happy for a while . . . it's always there. But we will continue to fight." And another participant remonstrated, "It is sure that the military was living here, that here was a military camp. I was enslaved there. I was never paid a cent, and I was washing their things and cooking for them, and they raped me, many times. And it hurts me a lot to remember this, so when we talk about forgetting, every time I have to talk about this it stirs it up again. It's very hard." Underpinning our question was a concern about the traumatic repetition of testimony and the related assumption that speaking is healing. The question also assumed that such a clear-cut choice between remembering and forgetting was possible. Protagonists' outraged responses exposed our limitations and failures of knowledge, of understanding, and indeed of witnessing. We had combed over of the painful dialectics of remembering and forgetting that are repeatedly enacted within ongoing systems of colonial power and dispossession.

Q'eqchi' protagonists' inhabitance of collective remembrance of sexual violence remains largely elusive to the Western/non-Mayan gaze. As we have argued in this chapter, such collective remembrance practices simultaneously utilize, disrupt, comb through, and ultimately always exceed the confines of transnational transitional justice spaces. Protagonists are enacting a tradition of testimonio that resists the fetichized spectacle of the wound, instead claiming a holistic ontoepistemology of land and its memory and a temporality that reconciles the living with the dead. This is protagonists' call to *go on*, whose urgency stems from a concern for the future and for the next generations of the Maya. As they told us during the workshop, "We won't live much longer, but our grandchildren and children will be here." They will persist.

Note

1   We are very grateful to Mujeres Transformando El Mundo for organizing this field trip to Sepur Zarco, and accompanying us there, and to Rosario Tio Garcia for her logistical support. The workshop was designed and facilitated with M. Brinton Lykes, Malathi de Alwis, and Heather Evans; our sincere thanks to them for this collaborative endeavour. The research was funded by a grant from the Social Sciences and Humanities Research Council of Canada. We are immensely grateful to the Mayan women protagonists who invited us into their journey, and we are inspired by their courage and strength.

6

Poetics and Politics of Sound Memory and Social Repair in the Afterlives of Mass Violence

• •

The *Cantadoras* of the Atrato River of Colombia

PILAR RIAÑO-ALCALÁ

On September 27, 2016, national and international dignitaries, personalities, and ordinary Colombians gathered in the city of Cartagena for the signing of the peace accord that sought to put an end to more than five decades of armed conflict between the Armed Revolutionary Forces of Colombia (FARC by its Spanish acronym) and the Colombian state.[1] The "emotive and sober" ceremony, according to the media, featured short speeches by Juan Manuel Santos, the president of Colombia, and Rodrigo Londoño, the chief commander of the FARC, as well as a single performance by a group of Black singers, *cantadoras* of Bojayá, where one of the deadliest massacres in the history of the country took place in 2002. After a minute of silence, the cantadoras were solemnly announced: "a group of women who used to dress in Black, in mourning, to sing the pain of war and now sing to the hope of peace." As the presenter said the word "peace," the voice of Oneida vibrated forcefully through the open-air convention center:

> We feel very happy
> full of happiness
> that the FARC guerrillas will leave their weapons.[2]

The nine other cantadoras who came with Oneida, responded:

> that the FARC guerrillas will leave their weapons.

Standing beside the ocean and facing the 2,500 people in the audience, the ten women dressed in white blouses with violet flowers on their chests and black skirts intoned with vigor and feeling their commitment to peace, calling for non-repetition and urging the government and all Colombians to assume responsibility for the peace process. Meanwhile, "the whole political country was listening to them" (*El Tiempo* Editorial, 2016, para. 3). Following Oneida, Ereiza, *cantadora mayor* and *rezandera* (major singer and prayer), called upon the president:

> Listen, Mr. President
> we come to congratulate
> for your great courage
> to work for Peace.[3]

The group responded with, "for your great courage to work for peace." Ereiza then summoned the historical trajectory of colonialism and violence that grounds the history of dispossession against Black and Indigenous communities and demanded non-repetition:

> And five hundred years
> We suffer this pain
> We ask the violent ones
> No more repetition . . . [4]

The cantadoras, as the Afro-Colombian leader Delis Palacios remembered later, were mindful that on such a historical event, "they were the only voice that the victims had" and that their singing and presence would be represented through racialized discourses that appropriate them as symbols of victimhood and reconciliation.[5] In the five minutes they were given, they adjusted their *alabaos*, the traditional funerary chants sung during the burial and mourning rituals in Black communities in the Pacific region, to ensure they said what they needed to say.

I start from this gendered and layered space of performance and politics to examine the complex intersections of voice, memory, and affect in changing contexts of mass violence and transitional processes of justice, truth telling, and reparation. I explore the trajectory and ways in which this group of Afro-Colombian women from the Pacific Atrato River region have recreated the expressive oral and aural practice of alabaos into a creative form of political action and a caring practice of social repair in the afterlives of mass violence (Clarke, 2009; Friedmann, 2006; Tobón, 2016). The chapter examines how the cantadoras respond to invitations to perform in gendered and racialized "spaces of encounter" and "reconciliation" and how they remember violence and carve an awakened soundscape of social action and plurality of voices. In these practices of sound memory, I argue, they contest their encounters with the State and transitional justice institutions responsible for the implementation of the victims' law[6] and the peace accord[7] through a politics of affect and refusal and a poetics of repairing worlds deeply affected by political violence.

In exploring these practices of sound memory, I document the manners in which the *alabadoras*[8] refuse to be silent and the range of quiet and loud sound practices embedded in the singing and listening of alabaos that regenerate the force of voice. These practices of sound memory permeate the acts of memory and commemoration with affect and refusal as they work to restore the relationship with the ancestors and the territory, reignite rituals in soundscape, and carve autonomous spaces of political action. The chapter introduces voice and the acoustic dimension as part of a resonant web of relations and practices of remembering the world. The sound dimension—voice, listening, the aural, the acoustic, and the sonic frequencies in the everyday—is a feature of reparative rememberance practices (Cavarero et al., 2018; Sedgwick, 2003; see also Ratih, this volume).

My work in the region began in 2009 when I was part of the research team for the Historical Memory Group's report *Bojayá: The war without limits* (Grupo de Memoria Histórica de la Comisión Nacional de Reparación y Reconciliación, 2010). In 2013, after a consultation and agreement for collaborative work with the local community councils and the group of cantadoras, I began research work with the cantadoras about their practices of sound memory. The chapter draws on the fieldwork conducted in the region from 2013 to 2020, during which my research collaborator Ricardo Chaparro and I documented the sounds, lyrics, and process of composing the alabaos, as well as the trajectory of the group, through in-depth interviews, workshops, and meetings with the cantadoras and in visits and conversations at their houses or when accompanying them to the commemoration of the massacre or other performances. The research process and analysis were enriched with ongoing knowledge exchange and learning with the cantadoras, and in four meetings for the analysis and the revision of the materials, we committed to produce with the group a booklet with the lyrics of the alabaos—both the traditional ones and the

90 • Pilar Riaño-Alcalá

compositions—and a timeline of the group's trajectory and critical events in their life as a group.

Translocality and Situated Knowledges

Working with and accompanying the cantadoras has challenged me to interrogate what is involved, ontologically and politically, in listening to the voices of the cantadoras within a complex landscape of armed violence and constant threats to the peoples of the region. The collaborative ethnographic work I have conducted over the last decade has been a journey toward an attentive, emplaced, and reflexive listening to the unique sounds and poetic records that silently germinate under the noise of "war" and "peace," to so-called transitions, and to the situated knowledges they embed. This form of ethnographic attunement to sonic frequencies has been a humbling practice of learning and interrogating the conditions of listening, as well as of being in relationship and in the territory (Campt, 2017).[9]

Listening, Campt (2017) has stated, "requires an attunement to sonic frequencies of affect and impact. It is an ensemble of seeing, feeling, being affected, contacted, and moved beyond the distance of sight and observer" (p. 42). The embodied and relational labor of listening to the unique voices of the cantadoras led me to examine this dialogical form of call and response as a living archive of the voices, knowledge, and histories of the cantadoras. The notion of the living archive (Riaño-Alcalá & Baines, 2011) records how such practices are inscribed in the bodies of the singers and further in the very ecology and reverberant sensation that alabaos produce: singing as a site of meaning creation and a living repository of the force of feelings and memory. It is a living archive curated and embodied in the material and embodied traces of violence where survivors and community members retain and transmit memory in everyday encounters. It is also about the manner in which the cantadoras craft a soundscape of memory and collective refusal to all forms of violence and to the construction of the victim as a gendered, racialized, and disembodied passive and suffering subject. Memory work is anchored here in a memoryscape that archives and activates the individual and social memories that a person or collective may draw upon to enable action and historical consciousness at particular times (Cole, 2001; Riaño-Alcalá, 2015).

The cantadoras, I argue here, stage a collective voice by adapting the lyrics of their compositions to the rhythms of the alabao and by building a sound narrative that expresses both, in the words of Oneida, "the pain we feel" and "the demands we make." By locating affect and feeling as creative forces of memory, composition, and coming to voice, the cantadoras recreate languages and modes of political action. The defense of the territory, the practices of care, and their relationship to the dead ground these forms of sound memory as the critical points in their political action. I refer to these politics of location and emplacement as practices of translocality, practices that situate local concerns and territorially imagined futures within transregional contested spaces of memory politics (see also Ford-Smith & Stephen, this volume). They are practices of being and thought that challenge Western feminism's disregard for the defense of land (Vergara & Arboleda, 2014; Riaño-Alcalá, 2023; see also Crosby et al., this volume).

My approach to the notion of translocality is grounded in these expressions of Afrodiasporic thought and politics (Vergara & Arboleda, 2014). It draws on the work of Latin American and Latina feminists to refer to a politics of location, movement, struggle, and situated knowledges that are firmly emplaced in the land, memoryscapes, and living beings of the Middle Atrato River (Alvarez, 2014; de Lima Costa, 2014). I understand translocality not as an opposed location to the transnational or as its lower micro "end" but as a situated and emplaced way of knowing that is attentive to the workings of social and power relations across geopolitical borders (Alvarez, 2014). This translocal feminist politics grounds racial, gender, and class oppressions in feminist epistemologies of the South and their epistemic struggles (Vergara & Arboleda, 2014; Viveros, 2018; Espinosa et al., 2014). It dialogues with transnational feminist engagements that are critical of Eurocentric tendencies in canonical feminism, decenter the Global North as "default comparative for women's experience" (Briggs & Spencer, 2019, p. 253), and ground feminism in community activism (Nagar & Swarr, 2010) and decolonial thinking (Escobar, 2015; Lugones, 2014; Viveros, 2018). This understanding of translocality engages with Afrodiasporic and Indigenous movements that decenter the nation-state as the interlocutor for recognition and move toward an anticolonial agenda that links issues of gender and race with the defense of their territories and the restoration of harmonious and balanced relations with the environment and sentient beings (Erengezgin, 2021; Viveros, 2018).

The practice of situated and embodied listening in which I place my research work and collaborations are similarly located within these circuits and practices of translocality, as a process that interrogates the geographies and scales of power (local, regional, national, global) and hierarchies of knowledge production and memory work (Nagar & Swarr, 2010). It signals my own situated knowledge and position as a translocal subject who moves back and forth between different localities and borders—as a mestiza woman born in the mountainous Andean central region and capital of Colombia, Bogotá, as a settler immigrant living in the unceded ancestral territory of the Musqueam people in Vancouver, Canada, and as a woman of color—in Canada—and Brown Bogotana mestiza in the Atrato.

Composing and Performing Alabaos

Church of Bellavista Nueva, May 2, 2014, twelfth commemoration of the Bojayá massacre. A group of twenty-one women whose ages range from 16 to 90 sit in the front of the church, waiting for the commemoration to begin. As living crafters of an ingrained tradition, the cantadoras are called upon to sing when government officials and "internationals" arrive in the area. This began in November 2000, with the first anniversary of the murder of priest Jorge Luis Mazo by right-wing paramilitary forces, and then in 2004 when they were invited to sing at the second commemoration of the massacre, a tragedy for which they continue to mourn as mothers, sisters, grandmothers, and relatives of those who lost their lives there.

The town of Bellavista in the municipality of Bojayá, Chocó, is located in a region rich in biodiversity in a mostly humid tropical jungle that borders Panama and the Caribbean and Pacific Oceans.[10] On May 2, 2002, after twelve days of infighting for the territorial control of the middle Atrato region between the left-ist FARC guerrilla and the right-wing United Self-Defence Forces of Colombia (AUC), the FARC seized Bellavista, the town in which the AUC paramilitary had temporarily established their base of operations. As the confrontations intensified, over three hundred residents took refuge in the church. While the paramilitary barricaded themselves behind the church, using the civilians as a human shield, the FARC fired several explosive bomb cylinders, and one of them landed in the church. The cylinder killed eighty-two people, forty-five of them children, and injured more than one hundred. Survivors fled the town en masse as soon as the fighting subsided, hastily burying the dead in a mass grave and unable to perform the rituals with which the Black communities of the Medio Atrato River accompany the transit between the world of life and bodily materiality to the world of the dead and the ancestors.

At the 2014 commemoration, the cantadoras sat next to the figure of the *Cristo Mutilado*, the Christ that used to stand in the altar of the Bojaya's church and that was blown up by the explosion, losing its legs and arms. When the moment of singing alabaos came, the women stood, and Ereiza invoked one of her compositions:

> Forever be *el bendito*
> Eternally praise the lamb
> Without blemish
> Bojayá has been condemned.[11]

The nearly three hundred attendees listened in silence while journalists from various media took photos and recorded. The rest of the cantadoras responded to the invoked stanza with a sorrowful but emphatic tone, and thus their singing unfolded between the grave call of Ereiza and the group's response that resonated with force. The women slowly moved their bodies from one side to the other.

The sung poetic texts of the alabaos are part of a broader and rich literary and musical genre of the romances: verses that narrate the daily life and imaginary of a group of people in a particular historical moment (Tobón, 2016). They combine and recreate archaic popular Catholic practices and language brought with

Spanish colonization and the forced evangelization of Indigenous and Black people in the region; African spiritual repertoires, in this case, Bantu, brought by enslaved ancestors to the Choco region to work in the mines; and a conceptual logic—notions such as *vital force* and the *interdependence* between soul, energy, and body when death is imminent—that is based in shamanic knowledge from the Indigenous Embera groups who have ancestrally inhabited this land (Losonczy, 1991; Tobón, 2016; Valencia, 2009). Through various forms of romances, Black populations appropriated and recreated this genre as resurgent practices of veiled Africanness (Maya, 1996).[12] Historically, through forms such as alabaos, Black people have evoked the exploitation and suffering of slavery and forced labor in the mines and the feelings associated with living in the rough landscape of the rainforest jungle of the Atrato River basin (Leal, 2018; Tobón, 2016).

The group of women—some of them schoolteachers, others health practitioners, healers, and farmers—have close family and community ties, as they are all from the village of Pogue. They have sung at each of the commemorations and important events with government officials, presidents, and international delegations visiting the region. There are several reasons for the presence of official delegates in a remote territory of the country. For one, the massacre of Bojaya was one of the deadliest massacres in the war, and the responsibility of the FARC for this massacre became a rallying point for the conservative government of Andres Pastrana. Bojaya, in the official discourse, was an example of the FARC's atrocity and terrorism. Such a portrayal has been silent about the shared responsibility and involvement of the paramilitary and the armed forces of Colombia and the government's failure to respond to the numerous calls for protection from community and humanitarian organizations. As Vergara (2017) argued, these discourses perpetuate a historical silencing of Black and Indigenous populations.

The cantadoras recreated the practice of alabaos by first forming a group and then elaborating compositions that remember the suffering, pain, and violence in the region, including social and political commentary and lyrics that express their resistance to the armed control of their lives. Such recreation of the alabao locates them as collective workers of memory through practices of caring that seek to address their debt with the dead. Communities and families in the region are deeply disturbed by their inability to conduct proper funeral rituals and burials due to the war and climate of fear, particularly for the victims of the massacre who up until 2019 had not been properly located, identified, or buried.[13] In Afrochocoan ontology of living and dying, the living have responsibilities to care for and accompany the dead with songs and prayers during the nine days of wake. Having been unable to conduct the rituals that facilitate the transition to the world of the ancestors constitutes a debt for the people of Bojaya, haunting them in dreams and daily life (Orjuela, 2020; Millán, 2009; Quiceno, 2016). The cantadoras describe this imbalance as a feeling that tragedy and violence threaten to take away the reparative power of their singing; to counter this, they sing, compose, and perform, drawing on their determination to accompany the suffering of their relatives and neighbors and to sing their refusal to violence. The singing is part of a repertoire of imaginative and everyday practices that locate the cantadoras as embodied witnesses of the terror and suffering experienced in the Atrato and of the creative ways through which they bear witnesses and craft their refusal to violence (Riaño-Alcalá, 2015).

In 2013, Máxima, a cantadora and community leader, explained, in a personal communication, the affective power of this form of repetitive and responsive singing and how its effectiveness depends on being "heard well": "The essence of alabao is to invoke, respond . . . that is, to invoke is [by] a person who is the first to sing and to respond is what we do second, that is the essence so that it can be heard well, it has to be done thus by invoking and responding." The women describe this exercise of "placing" the song as one in which "one voice is preserved" because those who respond must "catch the tone of the [singer] voice." But what particularly motivates the need to respond and catch the tone, the cantadoras insist, is "the tune's feeling," the sentiment that the singer transmits to the point where, according to Rosa, "It is pain itself that places the singing. . . . Sadness gives one the force to place the chant."

The cantadoras learned their craft during childhood, accompanying their grandmothers, mothers, fathers, and aunts to wakes. They remember nights of listening to their parents and others sing alabados and, with time, joining in responding and eventually placing an alabado. This oral tradition in the teaching and transmission of the alabaos is also about learning to sing with emotion, the affective fabric and power of this form of poetic singing. Alabaos impose an aura of respect and are attributed with power and strength. As acoustic and aural practice, the performance of alabaos builds upon a participatory style and bears the aesthetic and symbolic expressions characteristic of the movements of mixture, resurgence, and cultural resistance of the Black communities of the Colombian Pacific (de la Torre, 2003; Tobón, 2009; Valencia, 2009). It constitutes a repertoire of living orality and sound memory in which song and voice "appear simultaneously as a force that constitutes the world and a medium to build knowledge about it" (Ochoa, 2014, p. 3).

The women have seen the invitation to perform traditional mournful chants as an opportunity to subvert the formal, public scenario by composing sound narratives of the "pain we feel" and to convey their demands and truths on the violence and dispossession on their land and in their rivers. Oneida, one of the main composers of the new form of alabados, reflects on how they came to this practice of the alabado: "The massacre was on May 2nd, since May 2 *nos nació un sufrimiento*/we gave birth to a suffering, and through this sorrow we began to gather as a group, to make compositions, *a sentirle al mundo*/to make the world feel that it was hurting us, that they were destroying us, that they did not repair us, that we were displaced people fighting and that day by day things have worsened for us. Since May 2nd, we formed as a group to denounce through songs."[14] The commemorations became a moment in which they enacted a transgressive strategy that challenged reductionist depictions of the victim-women who dressed in Black to sing mournful songs to the dead and instead brought their pain to a singing that "speaks hard and loud." For over eighteen years they have done it amidst the war, displacement, confinement, and armed control of their lives that have plagued the region.

Bad Death, Mourning, and Social Repair

> Our souls do not find peace because we have not been able to truly mourn the angels we lost, the pregnant women, mothers, fathers, brothers, cousins, nephews, grandparents, uncles and aunts who were uprooted from our territory.[15]

The way the alabado is sung by the cantadoras is recognized in the region as unique not only because they became composers of new content but also for the way they sing and perform it with particular "force:" in the words of the women, when they sing, they engender alabado with a sentiment. Their singing is paused and driven by the invocation of the lyrics that narrate the violence or the pain, and in particular by what they see as the transformative force of emotion. This invocation of emotion is for the alabadoras "what shakes through one's body," a deeply felt sense that lies at the core of what they see as the reparative force of being together to accompany pain and mourning and respond to "bad deaths"—that is, sudden violent deaths or those for which they could not do the proper funerary rituals according to their ancestral practices. The recurrence of bad death in the context of the armed violence and humanitarian crisis in the region, particularly since the 1990s, profoundly destabilized the daily worlds of Black populations due to the impossibility of fulfilling the duties of prayer, ritual, and song with which the balance between life and death is restored when someone dies (Asociación Campesina Integral del Atrato, 2002; Quiceno, 2016).

The invocation of emotion is for the singers deeply incarnated and emplaced and summons other survivors into mourning, offering a reparative device for the imbalances generated by bad deaths in war. In its poetic dimension, the felt singing of the alabaos defines the wake rituals. I locate this labor of memory (Jelin, 2002) as a reparative action. The singing restores the cantadoras' strength, and they engender this poetic of affect into a reparative force for mourning and a refusal against silencing. Social repair, according to Aijazi (2018), also deals with how the spiritual, future, and past lives of the dead and the living are reintegrated into a network of relationships.

As Ahmed (2004) noted, emotions work to shape bodies as axes of action and orientation toward others—in this case, that of the singers as caregivers. Caring, in the context of a region in which violence continues, operates as a practice that partially restores relationships and the spaces to mourn and fulfill moral duties toward those who have died and is a way in which the singers assume their responsibility toward their communities (Gutiérrez, 2016). Feeling in this context communicates a gendered emotional and embodied knowledge and grounds forms of production of their own historical memory (Arboleda, 2011; Million, 2009). Black feminist Colombian scholar Aurora Vergara (2017) has argued that these practices embody an Afrodiasporic feminist practice that arises from the everyday experiences of Black women. In sum, these are forms of expressive politics that contest the racist and gendered violence that characterizes the history of dispossession and war in Colombia and their disproportionate impact on Black and Indigenous people.

I emphasize the affective and symbolic dimensions of the alabao, and in particular their recreation in compositions for war and peace, because it provides a path to examine political agency in the day-to-day of war in this region. The reflection is inspired in Campt's (2017) approach to the sensory register—the silent frequencies and their resonances—that is embedded in the composition and singing of the alabados amidst threat and uncertainty. Tracking the audible frequency—the periodic vibration whose frequency is audible to human beings—in images of Black people that have historically been rejected and ignored, Campt's (2017) work brings us closer to sound and sound memory as embodied affective records. It is a methodology of listening to the low musical frequencies, vibrations, tones, accents, and feelings of these vocal practices, the laments, litanies, and prayers that accompany the constant pain for the dead and disappeared who could not be, as expressed to me by Essau in a 2013 personal communication, "adorned with alabados" and also to the "high" frequencies of women in commemorations and events when they sing harshly and "loud" to "the armed men," the politicians, or the State.

Frictions and Interpellations

Performative spaces such as the annual commemoration of the massacre are at the same time politically charged spaces in which the frictions and contradictions of the public official discourse on reparation are enacted. The presence of dignitaries such as the president, some ministers, and the international community in one of the poorest and most marginalized regions of the country has been portrayed in official discourse as proof of the government's commitment to reparation for the victims. Black and Indigenous survivors from the town have been at the center of an official imagery that portrays them as the "victim" par excellence, and this discursive trope is sustained through the creation of an essentialized link between the status of victimhood for the residents of the town and their racialized and class location as Black and Indigenous peoples (Jaramillo, 2014).

In the middle of the peace negotiations in 2014, leaders of Bojayá were invited to La Havana, Cuba, where the negotiations were taking place. The FARC sought to carry out the first recognition of responsibilities for the atrocities committed against the people of Bojayá and to ask for forgiveness. This recognition was decisive to advance the negotiations and demonstrate the will and commitment of the FARC to the peace process, due to the political and symbolic weight that Bojayá has as a paradigmatic war crime in Colombia. Although the community accepted the invitation, the members who traveled to La Havana made it clear to the negotiators that they could not consider the apology without consulting the Indigenous and Afro-Colombian communities of the Medio Atrato affected by these actions.

The delegates from Bojayá listened to the FARC's message, and when they returned to the Middle Atrato, they embarked on a journey to consult with the riverside communities about their conditions for accepting, or not, the FARC's request for forgiveness. Seven months after the visit to La Havana, a FARC delegation led by Félix Antonio Muñoz Lascarro (alias Pastor Alape), until then a member of the FARC secretariat and its spokesperson in the peace negotiations, traveled to Bojayá on December 6, 2015, to formally recognize their responsibility for the crimes committed.

The place of the symbolic act was the ruins of the building adjacent to the church of Bellavista Viejo, where the explosive artefact fell. The representatives of the FARC, the government, international intergovernmental organizations (such as the United Nations), and institutions engaged with the transitional justice process sat in a row of chairs with their backs to the ruins of the building where a large quilt had been placed with the names of the victims. The quilt was woven by the women of the Guayacán group in the years after the massacre. In front, in a semicircle of rows of white chairs, people from the community and some companions sat.

The cantadoras were invited to witness and perform at this critical event. When their turn came in the program, they stood up in front of the FARC representatives, the government representatives, and the national and international delegates. La Negra, the group's leader, standing a few steps ahead of the group, invoked an alabao that they had composed for the fifth anniversary of the massacre and to which they made special arrangements for this act. With emphatic movements and taking a few steps forward and others back, her gaze fixed on the delegation and on Pastor Alape as she rhythmically waved her arms up and firmly made the "no" movement with her hand:

Gentlemen of the armed groups
Don't cause us any more pain.[16]

The group responded:

Gentlemen of the armed groups
Don't cause us any more pain.

Lyrics, movement, and gaze were repeated until the alabao ended. This is a moment of high sound frequency, of "denunciation." Next, Oneida summoned another alabao, and with her gaze fixed on the delegates of the FARC and the government representatives, she slightly lowered her eyes while singing solemnly:

> We are here in the church united through the heart
> and those who did the damage, amen
> they do not feel any pain
> Gentlemen of the armed groups, we ask from the heart
> to repair those damages
> caused in our region.[17]

The sung murmur and sense of pain are registered in this quieter, lower frequency and in the imperative to act that it communicates. It calls for a careful and affective listening because it reveals these compositions and the performance as a situated knowledge and historical memory of the war (Campt, 2017). The singers have taken every opportunity to communicate and make their singing an affirmative practice of refusal, of the lack of meaningful recognition of responsibilities and effective action that materializes in the constant visits and presence of high-ranking officials in the region, and of the impunity and violence that prevail in the Middle Atrato. The alabaos performed at this critical encounter challenged the delegations present into a truthful commitment, while the cantadoras communicated their opposition to empty gestures of forgiveness and reconciliation when the region and their lives continue to be militarized and marked by uncertainty, threats, and the prevalence of fear.

The riverside communities that the Bojayá's Committee for Victims Rights consulted for months about the FARC's request for forgiveness disputed the idea that the necessary gesture was forgiveness. On the contrary, their demands were that each actor—the guerrilla, the paramilitary, and the State—recognizes their responsibility in the violations and crimes committed; that there is a confirmed commitment to nonrepetition; and that the armed actors immediately stop all intimidating actions and threats against the community, including an end to their armed presence in the territories. La Negra recalled, "We put a stanza there that says: the FARC guerrillas today want to apologize, we Colombians ask that no more repetition."[18]

Months later, at the meeting place of the Guayacán women's group in Bellavista, Máxima and La Negra reflected how during the event, they defiantly stood up and looked straight into their visitors' eyes. When Pastor Alape, the top ex-guerrilla commander who issued the apology, asked Máxima if she was afraid to be standing beside him, she replied she had been afraid in the past but that she had lost all fear. In a clear reference to the injuries she has as a result of the violence, she recalled telling him, "I am without knees, I have the column diverted because of you, so what fear I am going to have?" Máxima then explained that it was through singing with the force of sentiment and in the manner they look at them that they communicate their demands: ". . . and she [referring to

La Negra] pointed at him, because she pointed at him with her gaze. . . . 'Do not come back here anymore and do not come back around here.'"[19]

Conclusion

I have tried to map here the movement to possess and control Black bodies in a liberal and racialized transitional justice regime (Riaño-Alcalá & Chaparro, 2020) as the symbol of and for national reconciliation that attempts to stand as proof of a transformed moral and political commitment to build peace on the part of the government and the FARC. More specifically, government officials, the demobilized guerrillas, the transitional justice institutions, and the media sought to appropriate the bodies and voices of the cantadoras as the sites of apology and reconciliation. Bolivian Aymara sociologist Sylvia Rivera Cusicanqui (2012) highlighted how the type of discourses that circulate in these moments may seek to democratize or repair past wrongs against Black and Indigenous nations but that they also carry tacit political and cultural privileges and notions of common sense that render incongruities tolerable or hidden. The cantadoras disrupted these scripts with other movements that place their voices and bodies in an affective ecology that seeks to repair their debts and duties with the dead and to refuse their representation and appropriation as model victims and agreeable subjects of reconciliation. Practices of resistance and refusal of colonial and capitalist formations and discourses operate in these incongruous and awkward spaces, drawing on a historical legacy of disrupting the script, displaying tactical "obedience," and resorting to resourceful practices of transgression (Riaño-Alcalá, 2012; Thomson, 2013).

I have come to understand the creation of this affective and acoustic memoryscape as an ongoing collective process of creating and restoring relationships and the means by which rich and sensory worlds are sustained against the forces of armed violence and liberalist interventions. The group practice of a responsorial singing that demands attunement with emotion and sound and listening with sentiment to their experiential truths reveals a pluriphonic soundscape of refusal and a form of political agency that I characterize as a translocal practice of coming to a collective voice. The tracing of the cantadoras' sound memory practices reveals a politics of location and forms of creative political agency attuned to emotion, embodiment, the uniqueness of voice, and the sentient acoustic territorial worlds of the rainforest, the river, and the land. These practices of remembering violence reveal a narrative and conceptual frame for living and interacting with their social worlds, memorialized landscapes, and the institutional world in the aftermaths of mass atrocity and dispossession. Alabaos, their singing and composing, are part of a rich repertoire of translocal politics of marking territory (Branche, 2015) that reveals the intersecting geographies of power relations in which the memory acts and political action of the cantadoras take place.

Notes

1 In August 2016, the FARC came to an agreement with the government on a bilateral ceasefire as part of a lengthy and difficult negotiation process that had begun informally in 2010 and formally in 2012. After six years of negotiations in which the armed confrontation continued, the parties signed the Final Agreement for the Termination of the Conflict and the Construction of a Stable and Lasting Peace.

2 *Nos sentimos muy contentas*
llenas de felicidad
que la guerrilla de las FARC las armas van a dejar.

3 *Oiga señor Presidente*
venimos a felicitar
por su grande valentía
y a trabajar por la Paz.

4 *Y quinientos años*
Sufrimos este dolor,
Pedimos a los violentos
No más repetición . . .

5 Group session in Bellavista to review the conclusions of research, May 15, 2017.

6 The National Victims and Land Restitution Law was passed in 2011 under the government of President Juan Manuel Santos. It outlines the legal framework to provide redress to the victims of the armed conflict and includes measures for land restitution, financial compensation, symbolic reparation, the right to truth, and collective reparations. There are also a series of associated decrees that complement this law, particularly as it applies to Indigenous and Black peoples.

7 The final peace accord consists of six sections: rural development, political participation, illicit drugs, victims, end of conflict, and ethnicity. In the section on victims, the parties agreed to the creation of the Integral System for Truth, Justice and Reparation that includes three transitional justice institutions and mechanisms: the Special Jurisdiction for Peace, the Truth Commission, and the Special Unit to Search for the Disappeared.

8 Both terms *cantadora* and *alabadora* are used locally and by the women themselves to refer to the singers of alabaos. I use the notion of cantadora and alabadora interchangeably as used in the Middle Atrato and by the cantadoras.

9 Three local leaders and thinkers—Leyner Palacios, Delis Palacios, and Jose de la Cruz Valencia—have been a source of inspiration and constant dialogue in this work, as have fellow researchers in the same region: Natalia Quiceno, Camila Orjuela, Aurora Vergara, and Germán Arango.

10 The Chocó Department has historically been isolated from the central region and government, showing high rates of inequality and social exclusion (Bello et al., 2005). Its population is mostly Afro-Colombian and Indigenous. Its rich biodiversity (second in the world) and strategic location are linked to the presence of mostly extractive industries and the increasing presence of multinational, private, and various other capital and infrastructure, commerce, and integration projects in the region, as well as the drug trade.

11 *Para siempre sea el bendito*
eternamente alabado el cordero
sin mansilla,
Bojayá lo han condenado.

12 Adriana Maya Restrepo (1996) used the notion of the *mimetic permanence* of Africanness among the descendants of African slaves in the Viceroyalty of New Granada (northern South America) to name the web of traces and expressive practices alive in the region that do not explicitly communicate their roots.

13 See https://bojayacuentaexhumaciones.com// for a description of the landscape of fear and death in the Middle Atrato and the exhumation process that took place in 2017.

14 First workshop with the group of cantadoras, Pogue, Bojayá, June 12, 2014.

15 Speech pronounced by social leader and member of the Committee for the Rights of the Victims of Bojayá, Leyner Palacios, during the Act of Recognition of Responsibilities by the Armed Revolutionary Forces of Colombia.

16 *Señores grupos armados*
No nos causen más dolor.

17 *Estamos en la iglesia unidas de corazón*
y los que hicieron el daño, amén,
no sienten el dolor.
Señores de los grupos armados, les pedimos de corazón:
que reparen los daños
causados en nuestra región.

18 Third workshop with the group of cantadoras, Bellavista, Bojayá, May 15, 2017.

19 Third workshop with the group of cantadoras, Bellavista, Bojayá, May 15, 2017.

Part 3

Invoking Revolutionary Present Pasts

● ●

7

Figures of Dissent

• •

Women's Memoirs of Defiance

SHAHRZAD MOJAB

In this chapter, by writing and remembering revolutionary women of the Middle East as figures of dissent, I step out of the dominant memoir-reading practice concerning women in the Middle East and North Africa (MENA), which covers a vast array of individualized life histories, autobiographies, and witness testimonies (see, for example, Ebrahimi, 2019; Grassian, 2013; Naghibi, 2016; Whitlock, 2007). The texts that I will engage are political memoirs, in which there is a dialectical and historical relation between the self and the collective, the particular/local/national and the universal/transnational/global, and the social that is historical. These memoirs are "individual memory projects by women to provide public memories of their lives, their social context and their political struggles" (Reading, 2014, p. 209). I read them as a transnational archive of women's defiance.

Two memoirs, *Sara: My Whole Life Was a Struggle* and *Sara: Prison Memoir of a Kurdish Revolutionary*, represent the defiance of one woman who speaks to a collective dream, to fears but also to hopes and aspirations of a generation (Cansiz, 2018, 2019). Both volumes are autobiographical accounts of a revolutionary Kurdish woman's life history of endurance and her steadfast determination to confront the violence of the Turkish State, to subvert its colonial and patriarchal rule. In *Aziz's Notebook: At the Heart of the Iranian Revolution*,

I read through the anguish of a father and grandfather whose daughters were executed in Iran (Makaremi, 2011; see also Makaremi, this volume), and in *With the Omani Revolutionaries: The Dhofar War Diary*, I explore the life and time of two Iranian revolutionary sisters engaged in an anti-imperialist resistance movement in Oman (Afraz & Afraz, 2015).

The chapter is also my yearning to find an answer to a question arising from my personal quest about how to mourn the defeat of a revolution and how to survive under the mark of a lingering grief but also to think of resistance, hope, and the future. Thus, it aims to speak to silences and absences in the historicization of women's struggles in MENA: where are all the revolutionary women? As such, the chapter is a transnational feminist encounter with the geopolitics of the region; it traverses national and cultural boundaries. As I read the texts, I remember and make my own story matter, too. The more I get to know the storytellers, the more I come to know myself, which is "no simple task" (Hirsch & Smith, 2002, p. 10). I resist being a "passive spectator" of the lives of the women in their memoirs. I write myself into them, "to convert the individual ownership of memory into a collective memory" (Bold et al., 2002, p. 129). Thus, it is not the stories and witnessing that are being judged in these texts; rather, it is about how they become life histories of a generation—my generation—and thus my extended autobiography of a revolution. These texts are my intellectual reflective tools to write *with* and *through*. I excavate them as archival materials of women's resistance movements.

The selected texts narrate three stories with spatial and temporal proximities; they take place during the 1970s and 1980s in Iran, Oman, and Turkey. All the women in these texts and I were born within a few years of each other in the 1950s. The texts speak of failure and transcendence, though as witness narratives, they are deeply personal, perceptive, and reflective. Mostly, they are notes and letters crafted in silence and in secret, in fear of further persecution, a persecution that they spoke to while also fearing the possibility of its future repetition. I do not intend to write a thorough analysis of each text. Instead, I choose to write as an involved witness in these women's struggles in order to tell my story so that we can collectively (re)write a different history of/for/with the women of MENA. The women in these texts, and myself in this chapter, are the forgotten revolutionary generation of the region.[1] Nonetheless, politically speaking, there are many differences among us; the conditions of the world and regional histories connect our writings and memoirs.

Sara: My Whole Life Was a Struggle and Sara: Prison Memoir of a Kurdish Revolutionary

I wrote the following words elsewhere. I repeat them here, for I do not have any better way to express them:

Esmail Khoi, an Iranian poet, has beautifully, meaningfully, and metaphorically captured my experience of participating in the 1979 Revolution in Iran when he writes:

The joy of a raindrop
and the sorrow *of it* in a swamp.

It is me 'joyously watching the life-giving raindrop [revolution], only to abruptly recognize its horrid fall into the abyss' [coming into power of the Islamic Republic in Iran]. (Mojab, 2015, p. 7)

The image lives viscerally in me. I am captivated by the experience of the 1979 Revolution for justice, freedom, and democracy but am equally haunted by its rapid demise. Four decades of battling with my own thoughts and emotions has undoubtedly matured me enough to appreciate continuities/discontinuities, setbacks/achievements, the cautious yet audacious and reformist/revolutionary paths in a century-long struggle of women in the region.

The revolution took me to Rojhelat (the Kurdish region of Iran). It was in the fall of 1979 that I entered this ragged land for the first time. Rojhelat was a place known to me as primitive, tribal, unruly, not modernizable, and traditional. As I was growing up in Iran, the colonial, national chauvinistic, and racist construction of the Kurds simultaneously extolled Iranian national politics, cultural discourse, and consciousness. The 1979 Revolution interrupted the incongruity of Iranian/Persian nationalism and restored the right of national minorities to self-determination and autonomy, albeit for a short period, but long enough for me to find myself in the early 1980s in the mountains of Rojhelat, joining an armed struggle and being among the first cadre of women to go through the armed training.[2]

The newly established Islamic regime consolidated its power through a series of violent attacks on women's rights, symbolized by the enforcement of veiling; military aggression against the Kurds and other national minorities to liquidate their nascent autonomous movements; the suppression of oppositional voices among students, artists, workers, and writers; and the closure of the universities, publishing houses, and the press to suppress freedom of expression. In the first decade of the Islamic regime from 1980 through 1990, we all became witnesses to unparalleled purging, imprisonments, exiles, disappearances, and executions (Mojab, 2007, 2019; Naghibi, 2016; Talebi, 2011; Iran Tribunal, 2012).[3] Between 1979 and 1983, the streets and the Kurdish mountains became spaces of radical politics and resistance for me, before being forced into exile. Since then, I have refused to reside in the "diaspora" so as to maintain my political contestation. There is a stunning pain in the interminable nature of the diaspora, but exile is a conscious reminder of a great wound of expulsion caused by the state.

Sakine Cansiz (political codename: Sara) was brutally assassinated in exile on January 9, 2013, and only in death returned home to Dêrsim, Turkey, to be buried. She and her two women comrades, Fidan Doğan and Leyla Şaylemez, were murdered in Paris. They were political figures and members of the Kurdistan Workers' Party (PKK). Sakine participated in the 1978 founding congress of the PKK and became one of its prominent leaders.[4] She exhibited an intense determination in fighting the atrocities committed by the Turkish State against the Kurds. The Turkish government has been accused of involvement in the assassination of Sakine and her comrades, but the case has not been officially resolved. Sakine wrote her three-volume memoirs in Turkish in the late 1990s while in exile, but the books are still banned in Turkey. They were first translated into German, and the first two volumes are now translated into English (Cansiz, 2018, 2019). The first volume is on Sakine's life from childhood to the time of her becoming a revolutionary, and it ends with her arrest and imprisonment (1958–1979). The second volume covers her twelve years of morbid but inspiring resistance in prison (1979–1991). The third volume has not yet been translated into English; however, it starts on December 26, 1990, as written on the opening page, and ends in 1997.

Sakine was a Kurd from Dêrsim in Turkey, a place of Armenian genocide in 1915, and then of the Kurds between 1938 and 1940, and a space thereafter of perpetual national oppression (van Bruinessen, 1994). Poverty, patriarchy, feudal relations, and Turkish nationalism made her a rebel. Home, school, and the village were spaces for the Turkish State's nationalism in its ideological, cultural, and political forms to be performed and produced. "At home I had to ask for permission, in school I had to follow the rules and in society I had to accept traditions and values," lamented Sakine. And she continued, "Wherever you looked, things tied you down, diminishing you, hindering you. Being a revolutionary required devoting your entire life to the struggle, but I was continually prevented from giving my life, my energy, and my capabilities to it" (Cansiz, 2018, p. 116). While Sakine was growing up, the claim of Kurdishness in language, culture, and politics was forbidden and punishable if exercised, as it remains today.

We both grew up in the context of the rise of nationalist capitalist modernity and a major regional upheaval during which time nationalists, communists, Islamists, and the new social forces that included women, workers, students, journalists, and members of national minorities were struggling for radical change. Our lives were framed by these forces. Unlike Sakine, I was born into a family belonging to the dominant Persian/Iranian nation, an elite, educated, literate urban family in which the social and class expectation for a young woman was to be modern and Western. Sakine fought the State; at that time, I surrendered to its rules and norms. Her childhood was a struggle: working at home and in the fields, going to school, and routinely confronting state and patriarchal violence. "Life was exhausting," said Sakine. "During that intense time, I learned about life, chafed under the strictures of tradition, and rebelled. Some part of me felt connected to conventions and wished to find a satisfying life along those lines. But another part longed for a new, more beautiful way of life. As I look back and think about it, a deep sigh escapes me" (Cansiz, 2018, p. 77).

Throughout the Middle East, a new wave of student movements began in the 1970s. These groups were mostly left-wing, with various Marxist, Leninist, Maoist, or Guevarist tendencies, thus replicating the global trend (Choudry & Vally, 2020).[5] States violently suppressed these movements and banned their activities. Underground reading materials emerged, and what were called reading cells of subversive, political, poetic, and theoretical literature were organized. I joined out of intellectual curiosity and due to my middle-class sense of "justice." Maxim Gorky's *The Mother* (1906) became a popular read. I read it, as did Sakine; she wrote: "Julius Fucik's *Report from the Gallows* was the first book I read, then *The Mother* by Gorky. Both impressed me greatly. We passed books around and read them and got together to discuss important passages, so it was as if we read them several times" (Cansiz, 2018, p. 70). "Some new words appeared in our lives," Sakine wrote, "sensational and dangerous: *communist, leftist, revolutionary* [emphasis original]" (p. 23). Sakine avidly depicted the discussion in a reading group: "He [the reading cell leader] defined the concepts of People and Nation and spoke of Vietnam, Angola, and Cuba. He recounted episodes from current national liberation struggles and quoted Ho Chi Minh, Castro, Cabral, Lenin, and Stalin to support the validity of his words. At times it seemed like he was telling us a fairy tale or reading aloud from a book. It was like a history lesson" (p. 85).

The year is 1978, only a few months before the mass uprising in Iran. I was enrolled at the University of Illinois in the United States and captivated by feminist, student, antiwar, anti-imperialist, and civil rights activism, in particular by an organization, The Confederation of Iranian Students (see Matin-Asgari, 2002). Marxist reading and discussion groups were being organized by different student clubs. Stories of resistance—from Palestine to Algeria, from Latin America to Kurdistan and Iran—were the dominant topics.

I joined the revolutionary surge in Iran in 1979 and became a member of the Union of Iranian Communists. Sakine was arrested. I arrived in Rojhelat. Sakine was imprisoned. I joined the resistance movement of the Kurds for autonomy. Sakine initiated the prison resistance movement in Turkey. She became a legend. She endured torture, months of solitary confinement and the inhumane condition of the prisons, and she organized several hunger strikes, all while remaining conscious of her political commitment to the PKK and the liberation of the Kurds. "I braced myself with my new determined attitude: *I won't say anything more. If they ask questions, I'll refuse to answer*," Sakine remembered, and added: "Thereafter, when I was interrogated, I limited myself to making propaganda for the party, knowing that a political defense disconcerted them. 'Would you really say that to the court?' they said. 'That you want an independent Kurdistan?' Then you really will be executed.' The next day, they came to finalize my statement. They wrote down exactly what I said. If they altered any wording, I objected. Their last line was interesting. Without consulting me, they wrote: 'She shows no remorse.' This sentence delighted me, even if in their eyes it counted against me and would increase the punishment [emphasis original]" (Cansiz, 2019, p. 33).

The Islamic State of Iran attacked the Kurds in August 1979, only a few months after coming to power. This military operation was followed by mass arrests of activists and the summary executions of hundreds of Kurds. People were mobilized to resist. I arrived in the city of Sanandaj in Rojhelat, also known as Sine, in early 1980. It was a liberated area, like what we read about concerning Vietnam or Cuba. Revolutionary Councils were established to run the city; teachers, nurses, workers, and even high school students created their own councils (Cabi, 2022). The city was mobilized from below; it became a zone of participatory democracy. Public spaces such as mosques were turned into a *benkeh*, a safe house or a gathering place. I screened *Salt of the Earth*[6] in a benkeh to discuss resistance and organizing with women as the government forces were closing in on the city to dismantle its revolutionary self-governance. I fled the city with other resistant forces when it fell onto the hands of the State military. Tens of thousands of people were killed. Political parties pulled out their forces to avoid further destruction and deaths at the hand of the State. The resistance lasted for twenty-four days, and it has been registered in the annals of political history in Iran as The 24 Days of Resistance in Sine, when the city was renamed Red Sine or the Brave Sine by the people (Mojab, 2024).

War is more than a physical displacement. It displaces one's sense of time, place, and being. It has a profoundly disorienting effect; even peace is not a consolation. It injures the soul as the body tries to cope with the pain. War—with its bombings, destruction, the killing of civilians, and the cries of children—became too real for me to make the sounds and colors of fireworks or airshows tolerable in exile, even after almost forty years.

On September 12, 1980, there was a military coup in Turkey, and September 22, 1980, marked the beginning of an eight-year-long bloody war between Iran and Iraq. For Sakine, September 12, 1980, was a "turning point" (Cansiz, 2019, p. 96). "On the morning of September 12, 1980, we awoke to the sound of racist, fascist marches and generals giving speeches over the radio and TV" (p. 96). "The military coup had extreme effects in the prisons," Sakine stated. "The junta issued a decree: 'Every prisoner is a soldier!' . . . And prisons now had to adopt military discipline" (p. 97).

The States in Iran and Turkey began a brutal suppression of dissidents. A new round of mass arrests, imprisonments, and executions began in Iran and lasted for a decade, marked by two massacres of political prisoners in 1981 and then in 1988. Women's resistance history is vigorously delineated in prison memoirs from this time (Mohajer, 2020). The memoirs archive the political and ideological tensions, the sexual violence including rape, the desires, the complex thought processes of being in captivity and dreaming freedom, and the fragility of the human mind and body. If the Islamic regime aimed to turn prisoners into an "obedient Muslim," a pious "Muslim woman," the Turkish State's intention was to exterminate Kurdishness in prisoners. Prisoners were forced to "acknowledge Turkishness and the indivisibility of the fatherland" (Cansiz, 2019, p. 111). Esat Oktay Yildiran, known as the butcher of the notorious Diyarbakir Prison, asked Sakine, "Are you Turkish?" She replied, "No. I'm a revolutionary. In the revolution, one's ancestry plays no great role, but I'm a Kurd" (p. 103). "Then he clubbed my feet. I mentally counted the blows . . . 1, 2 . . . 15 . . . 20 . . . The policewoman turned her back to us while Esat beat me. She clearly couldn't stand to watch—her face was twisted in pain, as if she could feel the clubbing herself" (p. 103). Sakine defied rules: "In court, we decided to make our statements and defend ourselves in Kurdish. Use of the Kurdish language had been one of our demands, since many families couldn't speak Turkish. In the time of torture, when it [the Kurdish language] was banned, we could hardly talk without it, and a visit without a conversation was hard to endure" (p. 238).

Defeated, we were forced to leave the mountains of Kurdistan in the summer of 1981. Sakine remained in prison for another decade, dreaming of return to the mountains of Kurdistan: "On my last night in prison, people talked about their thoughts and feelings and gave me advice. . . . It was such a painful farewell. Leaving comrades behind in jail rips your heart apart—you leave your heart with them. 'See you on the outside,' I said, 'in the mountains! We'll see each other there'" (Cansiz, 2019, p. 331).

A pregnant fugitive living in the shadow of political suppression, I literally went underground. I lived in a basement close to my parents, awaiting the birth of my son and contemplating the death of a revolutionary dream. Sakine led a major hunger strike in prison, writing, "[W]e decided to start a hunger strike right away. 'It should be a death fast,' I said, 'not a hunger strike'" (p. 178). She described the conditions: "We women were taken to the top floor of the hospital, the men to a lower floor. . . . We women were put in the birthing station. Almost every night there was a birth—the cries of newborns and their mothers woke us up at night. We were on a death fast, while these babies were starting new lives. Later, when they grew up, they could say, 'I was born in a hospital where prisoners were on a death fast under armed guard'" (p. 184).

My son can say that he was born on December 12, 1981, in a hospital in Shiraz, which was a designated facility at the service of the Iran–Iraq war. The city was under the occupation of the Pasdaran, the Army of the Guardians of the Islamic Revolution, and this made life even more difficult for known activists like me. It was under these conditions that I entered the hospital to give birth to my first child. The hospital rooms were packed with wounded soldiers, their relatives, and security forces. Pasdaran were monitoring the emotional reaction of family members. Even while mourning the death of loved ones, no one was allowed to criticize the War and the State. A small corner of the hospital was left for emergencies unrelated to the war, such as giving birth. No supplies were provided. Patients were asked to bring their own and extra supplies as their contribution to the war. As I waited, I could hear the nurses yelling at birthing women to hurry up so that they could attend to the soldiers. I heard a nurse scolding an anguished woman for the immorality of giving birth at a time of war. I was scared of the unknown of giving birth. I was terrified of the Pasdaran, of being identified, and of being arrested. From down the corridor, I heard the moaning of a mother who had lost her wounded son. I held tightly onto mine.

Aziz's Notebook: At the Heart of the Iranian Revolution

On December 11, 1981, a day before the birth of my son, a young woman committed suicide by blowing up herself and the notorious Friday Imam, the appointed official of the Islamic State, in Shiraz. That young woman was 21-year-old Gowhar Adab Avaz. She left behind a suicide note vowing that the people will avenge the misery that the Islamic State had inflicted upon them. When I read the suicide note, I felt something inside me break loose. Early the next morning, I admitted myself to the hospital.

Aziz Zarei recalled the suicide incident in his *Notebook*: "This attack was later attributed to a young girl," and he continued: "Let us move on from these facts. . . . [M]y task is to set down my memories of these seven years and six months and to recount what happened, during this period, to my daughters who were sacrificed too early in the regime's court of injustice" (Makaremi, 2011, p. 40). Aziz was writing about his beloved daughters Fatemeh (December 22, 1950–June 15, 1988) and Fataneh (December 1, 1954–October 7, 1982). Both were executed. Fatemeh had two children when she was arrested, a six-month-old daughter and a three-year-old son. She was executed after serving seven years and six months. Fataneh was executed when eight months pregnant after a brief period of imprisonment. Aziz's sorrowful rage takes us into the depth of the culture of the State's revenge of oppositional forces and the refusal of his daughters to submit, to surrender, and to repent.

Aziz's Notebook (Makaremi, 2011, 2013) is a sorrowful testimony of a father and a grandfather of the Islamic State's atrocities. Chowra Makaremi (see chapter 8, this volume) is Fatemeh's daughter, one of the grandchildren for whom Aziz was writing: "My sorrow weighs heavily on my heart and I know there is no escape from this endless pain. To keep myself occupied and to calm my mind I decided to bring the adored beings who are no more, Fatemeh and Fataneh, back to life in a notebook intended for my beloved grandchildren. They know nothing of this story, or are unaware of its details, particularly the flesh of Fatemeh's flesh" (Makaremi, 2011, p. 1). Makaremi came across her grandfather's notebook in 2004, ten years after he passed away. She found it "at the back of a wardrobe," adding, "I translated it into French and added letters from him, my mother and my aunt, written between 1978 and 1992" (p. xiv). She wrote:

> The notebook opens with the evocation of Aziz's project: to tell his daughters' story and to leave a record for his grandchildren. He writes to bequeath us a memory that interweaves the family's genealogy with the country's history. "Fatemeh's children certainly want to know who their mother was and why she was executed." And yet, reading his account, there is no doubt, this voice reaches far beyond the family. There is an urgency in the power contained within it and in the fascination it exercises over the reader. It is his "inner voice" that shouts; "Write down what you saw, what you heard and what you endured." (p. xi)

Listening to Aziz, I wonder, as did de Alwis (see this volume) when she wrote, "How do people continue to have a 'life after atrocity?' How do they cope with waking up day after day to ambiguous absence and lacerating loss . . . another day rife with memories of forgetting, of waiting?" I hear Aziz. I read his words with the intonation of a calm rage. I am following him, he is passing me by; I am certain we have crossed each other but never looked at each other out of fear. In our clandestine life in Shiraz between 1981 and 1983, we left home to visit family members only occasionally. Some resided in the neighborhood of the Zareis. Aziz wrote, and I remember: "[H]undreds of cars filled with pasdars . . . began to patrol the streets of Shiraz, day and night. Constantly storming houses and places of work, to arrest the Mujahedin. People were in such a state of terror that they were even frightened of their shadows" (Makaremi, 2011, pp. 16–17). A cousin remembers the family that was suddenly shunned in the neighborhood out of fear for their security. Their home was marked as the house of Mujahed. "In addition to the suffering and the difficulties we had to face, not one of our close friends or acquaintances dared even walk past our door or speak to us on the telephone," added Aziz (p. 17). Aziz's words refresh the fear and terror that were cast over our lives. Our days began with reading about the number of arrests of "anti-revolutionaries" in the press and ended at night with watching the forced confessions of our comrades on the national television channel.[7] These were women and men who we admired, whose ideas we keenly followed, had political wranglings with, laughed with, shared meals with, and danced and sang political songs with. They were on our TV screen confessing that *our* Revolution was defeated and the Islamic Revolution was the victorious one. We slept tearfully, waking up in anticipation of another horrid day. The forced confessions worked as a technique of fear; it was a warning. We got it. We knew that our names were given to security forces.

On September 5, 1983, I escaped Iran with my husband and son through Pakistan and Afghanistan. "Be happy," yelled the young, bony-looking man. "You are safe now, you are free; we passed the Iranian border." I felt deranged in sadness. My body folded into itself. To soothe my husband and my crying eighteen-month-old son, I swallowed my tears and faked the joy of *freedom*. I wrote in a notebook, of which only a few pages survived the escape. Sakine is in prison. Fatemeh is in prison. Hundreds of our closest comrades are in prison. Thousands are executed. We live a speculative life—a mode of suspension in which death is too close and real. We are told to leave soon. I am troubled by thinking about the way I survived state persecution. It is a sense of enraged guilt. I am incapable of reconciling with this bitter awareness. Those whose lives were cut brutally short by the State were the most brilliant, radical young women and men who had an immeasurable longing for freedom. Aziz wrote ponderingly about his daughter: "Whoever she had been and whatever she had done, she and thousands of other young people like her had placed their lives in the service of their ideals, shone at dawn and were nipped in the bud before they had time to flower. Why? For what crime? By whom?" (Makaremi, 2011, p. 37).

Aziz used palpably endearing words to remember his beloved daughters: caring, smart, learned, kind, independent, with strong wills and convictions. Concerning Fatemeh, he wrote that she "had a strong character but she was also helpful and had good taste. She knew how to unravel our problems and she always gave other people's comfort and peace of mind precedence over her own" (p. 18). Of Fataneh, he said, "She was generous and compassionate; another of her qualities was that she constantly had a smile on her lips. Every day a number of friends she had increased, so much so that she was called the 'rallying pigeon,' in reference to the bird that gathers the other pigeons together in flight" (p. 36).

With the Omani Revolutionaries: The Dhofar War Diary

With the Omani Revolutionaries is a collection of letters written by two Iranian sisters, Mahboubeh and Rafat Afraz, who joined a radical Marxist-Leninist group called Paykar (The Struggle) in 1973 (Shamshiri, 2023). Paykar is an abbreviated version of Organization of Struggle for the Emancipation of the Working Class. It was a radical secular splinter group from the People's Mujahedin Organization of Iran, the group that Fatemeh and Fataneh joined. I came to know one of the founding members, Pouran Bazargan (1927–2007), in the early years of the post-1979 Revolution period when she was a teacher and school principal. She was among one of the first women who joined the armed struggle in Iran. I met her in exile; she was a thoughtful legend with a determined will for justice. In the last days of her life, she talked about her past. "I began activism in 1960s," she wrote:

> I served in the Palestinian Red Crescent Hospital in Damascus. As such, during the 1970s civil war in Lebanon I moved to the Palestinian hospital in Sabra refugee camp near Beirut. One of the best times of my life was living with the oppressed but resisting people of these regions. Later on, I was assigned to move to Turkey where our organization had established a

communication logistics base. I lived underground and worked in clothing sweat-shops and as a hotel worker in order to earn my living; meanwhile I participated in carrying arms from one country to another towards Iran. . . . I also spent time in Libya, where our organization (the Mujahedin) had an office, as well in Aden in cooperation with the revolutionary movement of Oman. Our cooperation with movements of other nations showed the international dimensions of our struggle. Our small organization had sent a physician and a nurse to Dhofar. Mahbubeh Afraz, a physician, and her sister Rafat Afraz, a nurse, both served in Dhofar, along with the revolutionaries in the region. . . . As always, I stood along with the Palestinian people's struggle and I'm happy that in the last weeks of my illness, I was able to send some money for the education of my two adopted children in Palestine. I was relieved when I knew the funds had been received. (Bazargan, n.d.)

Eight years after Pouran wrote these words and mentioned Mahbubeh and Rafat, Paykar published their letters for the first time in a new book in Persian titled *With the Omani Revolutionaries: The Dhofar War Diary* in 2015 (Mojab, 2022). The sisters came from a working-class family and moved from the small town of Jahroom, in the southern province of Fars, to Shiraz and then later to Tehran to study and work. Rafat became a teacher, and Mahboubeh was a physician. Rafat, like other radical women in the region, went to Damascus and Palestine to receive military training. Soon after, both sisters went to Oman and were stationed in a hospital in Al Ghaydeh, on the border of Yemen and Oman during the Dhofar Rebellion (1962–76). Their letters describe a strong sense of international comradery, as the hospital was mostly run by Cuban doctors. They detail the functioning of the hospital, its shortcomings, and challenges; they report on the ideological and political wrangling among the international staff. As they write letters to the leadership of Peykar, they also strategize on how to build an anti-imperialist front in their fight against the Shah's regime; they dream of a future in which the people of the region are free from the yoke of feudalism, religion, capitalism, and imperialism.

Raftat died in 1973 in Oman at the age of 40 as a result of a malaria infection. She received a military burial and was honored by the international revolutionaries. After the defeat of the Dhofar Rebellion in 1975, Mahboubeh moved to Aden in Yemen and worked in a Farsi-speaking revolutionary radio program. The radio program broadcast anti-imperialist and anti-Shah messages to the budding mass uprising in Iran. She left Aden for Paris as the news about the uprising in Iran became widespread. But she became mentally ill in exile and finally took her own life in Paris in 1978. As she was living with a group of undocumented refugees, none of them dared to call the police to report her suicide; instead, they contacted the landlord and asked her to call the police.

There are many ideas in these letters that beg critical interrogation as we read them today. Most significantly, the letters open the possibility of looking deeper at the Left, its theoretical weaknesses, and its practice in the context of transnationalism in both the region and globally. In the letters, we can trace the pervasive nature of a patriarchal ideology of the Left. However, these letters, like *Aziz's Notebook* and Sakine's memoirs, are evidence of decades of radical resistance throughout the region. My intention is not to uncritically glorify this past; in fact, I argue that part of the region's continuous and intensified experience of poverty and the rise of authoritarianism and fundamentalism are interrelated with the failure of resistance movements to think through the analytical and strategic mistakes of the past in order to renew themselves for the challenges of our time. The question is how to employ these texts as our evidence and archival record of the past for an understanding of contemporary State atrocities and in deliberating about a range of possibilities for rebuilding a revolutionary transnational feminist resistance. The three texts used in this chapter illustrate this potential, which I know I have not yet explored fully.

Figures of Dissent: Echoes of Revolution

Sakine, Fatemeh, Fataneh, Mahbobeh, and Rafat are gone, as are thousands of other women revolutionary figures of dissent throughout the Middle East and the Arab world. I inserted moments of my life into theirs, for I could not resist the temptation of speaking back dialogically. I agree with Olick et al. (2011) that "studying memory . . . is a matter not of reflecting philosophically on inherent properties of the subjective mind but of identifying its shifting frames" to see "memory as a topic that extends far beyond the bounds of the individual mind" (pp. 10, 11). This chapter is the narrative of a journey that has not yet reached its destination, neither for me nor for those who fought with their lives while imagining a different world. They all are gone, in body but not in their revolutionary spirit. The echo of their revolutionary dreams ring in my head. Mina Assadi captured this echo in words when she said, "I've saved the unworn floral dress, for return"; this is an anticipation, a dreaming of another revolution.[8]

I was formed by the 1979 Revolution, though not frozen in it. I am an embodiment of its defeat, displaced from the megacity of Tehran to the snowy mountains of Kurdistan to the desert terrains of Pakistan and Afghanistan, to Europe, the United States, and eventually to exile in Canada. Exile is a new chapter, one that is continuously *becoming*. I escaped arrest and imprisonment but remained captive in the destiny of my comrades in prison, their life after prison onto exile, their dispersal throughout the world, and their settling into unsettling conditions prevalent for most émigré populations.

I have agonized in academia when a certain frame of analysis having to do with women in the Middle East becomes *off limits*, in particular in analysis of Left movements, class, internationalism, and secularism. In such frames of analysis, these are considered relics of the past; one can certainly address neoliberalism, globalization, or the authenticity of cultures as long as they are *culturized* within Islam and are delinked from the long history of struggle against colonialism, orientalism, capitalism, and imperialism. It is in the context of this historiographical account that women in the region were reified as "Muslim" women belonging to "Muslim" societies. In the span of a decade between 1970 and 1980, women in the region who had previously been categorized as "Third World," as Arab women, and as women of the Middle East all became "Muslim" women and their movement renamed "Islamic Feminism." The three memoirs reflected upon and written within this chapter represent a small record of women's struggles, ranging from Islamic Left to Marxist, Leninist, and Maoist. I engaged with these texts in a dialogical manner. I felt visceral sensations as I read through them and witnessed the enormous human similarities in enduring violence, in fighting against violence, and in dreaming freedom and love. I was in love, a personal love that concurred and deepened with the rise of revolutionary surge. As was Sakine in the 80s, I hear her heart pacing when she contemplates her personal and revolutionary love: "Love is not a quiet feeling. It is an active attitude. It creates values. It is to be judged by how it aligns people with their ideals and empowers them" (Cansiz, 2019, p. 242).

I agree that "transnational studies of feminist memory also disrupt national paradigms, showing the interconnections and movements by feminist activists around the world" (Reading, 2014, p. 209). Nonetheless, to engage in transnational feminist analysis, other *borders* should be crossed. Without overcoming language barriers, feminist transnationalism—in theory and practice—remains partial. In the context of the Middle East, for instance, with my knowledge of Persian and Kurdish, not knowing Turkish and Arabic is limiting in accessing knowledges that are produced to capture the experiences of revolutionary women. This body of knowledge only becomes available to us through translation, mostly English. Furthermore, knowledge production is strictly controlled and surveilled by the state censorship apparatus. In this process, manuscripts, letters, artwork, and films are confiscated or do not receive permission for publication, exhibition, or screening. Thus, they never enter the domain of oppositional knowledge production and circulation. We need to reach out, to dig out, to unpack, and to explore materials that help us archive women's resistance as a radical feminist project within the frame of feminist transnational analysis.

Notes

I want to recognize the inspiring work of Alison Crosby, Malathi de Alwis, Heather Evans, and Honor Ford-Smith, which gave me the courage to write this chapter. I also want to thank Sara Carpenter, Susan Benson-Sokmen, and Chandni Desai for their insightful comments.

1   In the extensive and growing body of literature on women in the MENA region, there is a dearth of research in English on women in socialist and communist movements. Some exceptions are Abdo (2014), Botman (1988), and Moghissi (1994).

2 Fatemeh Karimi at the École des hautes études en sciences sociales (School of Advanced Studies in the Social Sciences) is the first researcher to write a dissertation on this movement ("Les rapports sociaux de sexe dans les forces politiques kurdes en Iran entre 1979 et 1991: le Komala," doctoral thesis in sociology, EHESS, Paris, 2020). However, some Kurdish women have recently published their memoirs of this period in Kurdish, Persian, and English (see Ghobadi 2015; Hasanpour, 2012; Kakabaveh & Ohlson2021; Kamangar, 2016; Nammi, 2020; Vafaei, 2018). For an analysis of these memoirs see Mojab (2024).

3 For memoirs written on these atrocities, see the website that I have created to archive a vast body of scholarship and artwork: The Art of Resistance in the Middle East at http://www.womenpoliticalprisoners.com.

4 On the history of the Kurdistan Workers' Party, see Akkaya (2016), Aydin & Emernce (2015), and Çağlayan (2019).

5 The rich history of student movements in the Middle East is yet to be written; Salih's (2018) memoir is a welcome new addition.

6 *Salt of the Earth* is a 1954 American film written by Michael Wilson, directed by Herbert J. Biberman, and produced by Paul Jarrico, three Hollywood artists black-listed during the McCarthy era due to their alleged involvement in communist politics. The film is based on the 1951 New Mexican miners' strike and is one of the first feminist dramatizations of women's roles in the resistance of a community in support of strikers. The film covers such topics as gender oppression, racism, and state repression of the labor movement.

7 The Islamic State has created an "Oral History" project and regularly broadcasts these confessions on a YouTube channel.

8 Mina Assadi (b. 1943) is a well-known exiled feminist poet and writer living in Stockholm, Sweden. This line is taken from her 1994 poem titled, *A Dream in Awakening*.

8

Filming Disappearance

•••••••••••••••••••••••

An Account of a Visual Battle

CHOWRA MAKAREMI

How is state violence remembered when it is not memorialized? This question triggered my film *Hitch: An Iranian Story* (2019), which documents a family history of political disappearance and executions in Iran in the 1980s. The film is the latest outcome of a multilayered project that uses witness testimonies, film, and auto-fiction to look at mass violence through the imbrication of intimate and political spheres. In this chapter, I reflect on the making of the documentary and the extreme difficulty of researching the past in so far as it made me confront an actualization of political violence that impacted the project and turned it into a visual battle—a battle I did not lose but did not win either.

State of Denial

In the first decade after the 1979 Revolution in Iran, tens of thousands of political opponents to the newly established Islamic Republic, as well as members of subaltern groups, were killed and tortured en masse. Prison massacres took place in 1981, 1984, and 1988. Two leading perpetrators of the 1988 massacres, which killed several thousand in a few weeks, have been appointed respectively Minister of Justice and Chief of Justice of the President Rohani between 2005 and 2019.[1] One of them, Ebrahim Raissi, was elected as Iran's President of the Republic in 2021. These appointments provoked neither public debate nor scandal, showing the depth of denial at the state and societal levels about postrevolution Iran's founding history of violence. Today, hardly a trace of this violence remains; bodies have disappeared, and individual and mass graves have been destroyed. These orchestrated actions have resulted in a multitemporal economy of silence, a diffused state terror; they have organized a government of the living through the management of the dead (Makaremi, 2014).

In Iran, the memory of this violent genesis, entwined in a politics of denial, has evolved from an initial phase of silence and prohibition from the 1990s until the 2010s into a new phase of state denial and a rewriting of the past through multiple mediums such as digital archives, oral history projects, block-buster movies, and museums. This new memory politic came in reaction to extensive efforts by the Iranian community abroad to record and remember state violence through testimony (Mojab, 2007; Mohajer, 2020; Talebi, 2011; see also Mojab, this volume), legal fora such as the People's Tribunals (Nice et al., 2019; Talebi 2019), and fact-finding reports establishing crimes against humanity (Robertson, 2010).

In 2004, when the silence around the 1980s in Iran was not quite yet broken, I received a notebook written by my grandfather, Aziz Zarei, a few months before his death, now decades ago. It was a written testimony destined for my brother and me that recalled our family story after the 1979 Revolution. My grandfather's exhaustive and honest narrative put events, names, and dates to the blurred memories of my childhood years, which I spent in Iran with him and my grandmother: "I have a small scar on the back of my right hand: it is not a line (the mark left by an incision) but a delimited zone where the injured skin reproduces—with a different roughness and scale—miniscule scaly diamonds that form its texture. From close up the scar is invisible: all one can see is a certain asperity. The memory my grandfather's sentences created in my mind was like that" (Makaremi, 2013, p. 99). The notebook was a founding layer and a prehistory to this diasporic film project. Here is the story that it told.

Fatemeh and Fataneh Zarei

My mother, Fatemeh Zarei, was a high school teacher of physics and a Mojahedin-e Khalq party candidate in the town of Shiraz in the first legislative elections after the Iranian Revolution of 1979. She was an opponent of Khomeini's fundamentalist project, a revolutionary who did not want the revolution to turn into a totalitarian Islamic state. She was the head of a women's grassroots association linked to the Mojahedin and fought for the equal presence of men and women in the public and political spheres. She also organized extracurricular, anticolonial readings for her students. In her letters, she described herself as an educator. She was what we would call today a dedicated grassroots community leader. Her political career did not last more than one year, however, because she was arrested right after the 1981 legislative elections. At that time, I was eight months old.

The Mojahedin-e khalq organization was created in the mid-1960s as a guerrilla group inspired by nonaligned movements. Their ideology was based on socialism and anticlerical shi'ia Islam, through the claim that shi'ia Islam was in essence a socialist religion (Shariati, 2003). During the Shah regime, the Mojahedin was repressed and most of its members detained and executed. After the revolution, the party initially supported Khomeini, but it soon opposed his project of an Islamic republic. Mojahedin-e khalq became one of the main opposition parties, with hundreds of thousands of followers. Right after the 1981 legislative elections, the party was declared illegal and its followers persecuted. In the summer of that same year, the party leaders went underground and declared armed struggle, claiming several terror attacks. The hundreds of thousands of followers who supported the Mojahedin's program but were not involved in the armed struggle were imprisoned, tortured, and killed. Most of them were teenagers or young people in their early twenties. My mother was arrested for participating in a demonstration on June 15, 1981, at which many were arrested and injured. She was charged by a revolutionary court with "threat to the security of the state." Because my mother was arrested before the party went into armed struggle, she was sentenced to fifteen years in prison. Activists who were arrested after the Mojahedin began the armed struggle were systematically sentenced to death. This was the case of one of my mother's four sisters, my aunt Fataneh.

Fataneh Zarei was also a candidate for the Mojahedin party in the legislative elections in the oil city of Gashsaran. She and her husband, Ali-Mohmmad Qambari, escaped a first arrest attempt after the elections and went into hiding in the port of Bandar-Abbas in the Persian Gulf. This is where they were arrested in March 1982. Ali-Mohammad was killed on the spot in front of their house, and Fatemeh was arrested the same night at a checkpoint while on a bus from Bandar-Abbas to Shiraz. After a few months of detention, she was "executed by a *tavvab* [a repenting fellow prisoner]," as the newspaper *Keyhan* reported on October 17, 1982, and she was buried in Bandar-Abbas. Fatemeh was pregnant at the time of her arrest and during her detention. We still do not know if she was carrying her baby when she was killed or if she gave birth prematurely before her death.

My mother learned about her sister's execution while in prison and told her parents during a prison visit the night of Fataneh's killing. Two guards kept her in an office the entire night, hitting her if they saw signs of tears or sorrow. My mother endured five more years of prison and torture. Meanwhile, my older brother and I left Iran in 1986 to live with our father, who had escaped and found refuge in France, where I grew up. My mother's sentence was finally revised, and she was set to be freed in March 1989. But at the end of the war with Iraq, in the summer of 1988, prisoners were suddenly isolated from the outside world. My mother was killed in the following months, along with thousands of political prisoners throughout the country in what is now known as the 1988 massacres. Her remains were not given back to our family. Instead, the authorities indicated a grave as the site of her burial—an old grave belonging to a woman deceased decades ago, covered up with fresh cement. Did they bury the prisoners in pits already containing other dead? Did they simply place tombstones while the bodies were buried in mass graves, as the families in Shiraz believe?

Tracing Countermemories of Violence

A difficulty of working on state violence in the Iranian 1980s lies in a methodological double-bind: there is a need to establish the (concealed) facts, but adopting an evidence-based approach shifts the burden of proof onto the survivors, which seems particularly perverse. This is the reason why my project was not about investigating the crimes. I used an investigative approach but one that subverted and distorted the fact-finding episteme by presenting as "evidence" what is usually considered irrelevant or way below the threshold of acceptability in the establishment of truth: dreams and their threatening epiphanies, silences, and the fingerprints of the victims. The counterinvestigation focused on the production and sealing of silence itself as a cognitive and emotional experience. The film explored an attempt to be liberated from the grip of denial; it both documented this process and was its concrete outcome. As such, it was an act of memorialization itself. This search started from the traces left behind in an effort to conduct a cartographic study of silence through what resisted it: family secrets, objects, names, affinities, testimonies, and places. It retraced the path I followed to understand why and when my mother died, how she lived, who she was, and what happened to all of us.

How can we find a face that has been forgotten, the face in our memory and not in the photos? I have no memory of my mother. The work through texts and films that I have engaged over the past fifteen years represents many attempts to approach the problem—the secret—of this image missing from my memory. This secret resonates in a much larger collective memory, infused with a violence that is busy erasing its contours. This is why the investigation is constantly shifting from one dimension to another: from the disappearance of my mother as a personal matter to disappearance as a broader tool for controlling a society turned amnesic to a disappearance, whose memory is the fragile, haunted, and besieged place of a demand for justice.

Can a memory lapse be reconstructed? The film explores this question. In doing so, it produces a set of images and sounds that fills the lapse. It follows the recollection of a family story that is also a collective history by revealing the footage, photos, and private archives into which I dig to put images where there were none—on missing memories, forgotten faces, and absences that have not been explained. How can we give a visual account of the work of memory and its accidents from an intimate and perceptive experience of historical violence? The question brings out a reality that unfolds outside of the closed spheres of family and silences of history. One has to find the conditions for the film's opening to the world, yet at the same time doing justice to the texture of the *secret* that binds together private and collective experiences of violence and their long-term social and political effects. Taussig's (2010) reading of Walter Benjamin has clearly formulated this concern: "Nietzsche pleads in vain for historians who can write histories equal to the events they relate. We need to do the same with our dead. Benjamin says something similar where he cautions that truth is not a matter of exposure that destroys the secret but a revelation that does justice to it. He was referring to the work of truth in the passage of love from the body to the soul in Plato's Symposium. Death poses the same issue. Exactly" (p. 7). Because the secret is so fragile in its texture that the slightest exposure destroys it, a light too raw reduces it to powder, we can only grasp sight of it through almost anodyne imprint: the traces. A trace is simultaneously the imprint preserved from the passage of time—the witness of this time that has passed—and the fragile attempt to track the evidence (*to document* would be an exaggeration). So, I gave my project the working title of Archaeology of a Silence in Twelve Traces (see Figure 8.1).

FIGURE 8.1 Archaeology of a Silence in Twelve Trace: A film synopsis in twelve chapters.

Unburial

There was no image for trace number twelve because I did not have one yet. This stone slab had been laid in 2014 on a boulevard in the city of Bandar-Abbas. A newly constructed road had covered about fifty graves on the edge of the town's cemetery, which belonged to political opponents executed in the 1980s. The families of the executed opponents mobilized at the city hall to ensure that the graves would not be buried under asphalt, successfully securing the construction of a median in the middle of the boulevard at the exact location of the section where the executed lay. Among these graves are that of my aunt, Fataneh Zarei, and her husband, Ali-Mohammad Qambari. On the lawn on the median, the families had arranged for small commemorative stele to be placed at the site of the graves, now covered with dirt. However, the municipal employee who had placed those of my aunt Fataneh and her husband had, on his own initiative, added poem verses that are significant for those who knew their history (see Figure 8.2). Intrigued, I carried out my investigation in order to get in touch with this municipal employee, this relay-witness who, by his presence and his action, had reinstated the family secret in the public space. Unfortunately, we lost track of him.

Our last contact with him was on December 20, 2017. That evening, he called a relative in Shiraz to warn him that bulldozers were in place; the boulevard was going to be razed. On whose orders? This is information that I still have not been able to obtain. The families had not been warned of this destruction. In the following weeks, the map of the boulevard was modified, and it now passes over the cemetery of the executed, of which no trace remains.

While we were living this unprecedented experience, this transformation of a deceased relative into a disappeared person, we also realized that the memory of these crimes was not completely buried. For those who had deemed it necessary to raze the steles and terrorize the families once again revealed the memory with their actions (see Figure 8.3).

This development impacted my filmmaking. My investigation in Bandar-Abbas was falling apart, but beyond that, a relative whose testimony I had filmed at length had become afraid—and rightly so—and wanted to withdraw. This testimony was all the more precious because it came from a person still living in Iran; I had made it the backbone of my film, and it accompanied the story from beginning to end. Indeed, starting from the "twelve traces" to find the purpose of the film and to define exactly the content of the counterinvestigation was only an initial stage of the research process. I then had to find a narrative form that would transform my research through images into a film with a plot and a progression based on the present-tense of this narration. One of my characters, not the least important one, disappeared at the same time as traces—also important ones—disappeared under the asphalt. And with these traces, which were dear to us, also disappeared the energy, the desire to continue, the creativity, the optimism . . .

FIGURE 8.2 "This sorrow that I carry in my heart, I try to contain it, but my chest says to me: 'shout it, I'm suffocating.'"

FIGURE 8.3 Satellite map of the cemetery section of those executed, Bandar-Abbas 2005–2017.

At this stage, a large part of the film had already been edited, so with the editor, we had to unravel the plot and undo the images whose lifespans were shorter than the film's manufacturing time. The political question of denial, which was the starting point of the film, caught up with us by corroding the images and the narrative. We were facing two difficulties: on the one hand, how could we not let the images be impoverished by this constraint? To blur the image, to change the voice of the testimonies, to proceed to the formal destruction of the film ... would it not sanction the victory of denial? On the other hand, how could we, within the film, make sensible and visible this process of endangerment that accurately recounted the extent and nature of the denial that I was trying to define?

There was no simple answer but a series of adjustments, some cropping, and the fabrication of false-bottomed images that both replaced and suggested the lack of these other images, which had belatedly disappeared. In particular, I replayed part of the interviews filmed around a table over images from the same empty table. The empty chairs were filmed in precisely the same frame as the shot they replaced (see Figure 8.4).

On the one hand, I wanted these images to be haunting for the viewer, as they were for me. I did not know how else to go about it than through a reconstruction that appeals to the spirit of this lost sequence. On the other hand, I kept open the possibility of, perhaps one day, reintegrating the disappeared images into my film and to tell, through this staging, the story of their erasure and

FIGURE 8.4 The story of the graves in Bandar-Abbas. First (above) and final (below) edits.

restitution. The film became a film that was not yet closed, to be reopened, completed, and transformed. The only difference between the two frames, one alive and the other empty, was the light. We refilmed during twilight, at a time when, in my childhood memories, adults absorbed in their thoughts, busy skimming courts and prisons, tired, or preoccupied would forget to turn on the light to welcome the evening.

A final twist in the making of the movie proved me right to look back into my childhood perceptions to find a way to complete the project. I had decided to keep the sound of the interview while anonymizing the image, but I started second-guessing this choice as we approached the very end of the editing and as the witness in Iran and I both felt the palpable risk of releasing her testimony, albeit in diminished form. We consulted with human rights advocates who thought there would be interrogations and intimidations, but nothing more serious. The decision was very difficult for both of us. On a Thursday, she finally agreed to take this risk. I was relieved that this last obstacle was settled and happy for my movie (these twists were difficult to explain and justify to the French film crew, the producers, and the editor).

However, that very evening, my back started to ache. The morning after, I could hardly move the top of my body. By Friday evening, I could not breath at all if I lay down and had to sleep seated. I went to the emergency room on Saturday morning. By that time, the pain had moved from my back to my chest and was very difficult to locate or describe. The tests showed I was in perfect shape and health. I "didn't have anything," as the doctors said, but I still could hardly breathe, eat, drink, or walk when I left the hospital. I was lucky to find an immediate appointment with an osteopath and went straight there. As he performed his massage, I was traversed by waves of pain that resembled lung spasms, if such a thing is possible. "In Chinese medicine, they say that lungs are the siege of sadness and fear," he told me. "What is causing you such sadness?" I think that it was actually more fear than sadness. I was the little girl in the twilight of our Shiraz house. The fear—and maybe sadness—embedded in this chest thirty years ago was coming out. After the session, I was relieved from my back and chest pain, and my decision was crystal clear: we would cut the oral testimony from the movie. The story of my aunt Fataneh's death and burial would not be told. My witness in Iran would not be exposed. The movie was reaching its final cut and so was my journey, in ways that I could not have foreseen. I believed when I started making *Hitch* that all the work of coming to terms with my past and my inheritance was way behind me, having been done in the first decade following the discovery of the notebook. For days, I tried to keep the memory of the strange throbbing pain in my lungs—my most personal truth, which filled me with amazement.

FIGURE 8.5 Fataneh and Fatemeh Zarei, pictures on the wall, Shiraz, Iran.

My film project turned into a visual battle as the traces I was filming in Iran were being destroyed and the main character in the movie withdrawing her testimony. Because of the very politics of denial I wanted to unravel, the images I produced were disappearing before I could turn them into a movie. Something is lying there, covered with dust, ancient and unimportant. It belongs to a past long gone, and there is no point in touching it. But if you do, then the frames of reality shiver in a threatening way, and destruction growls at your ears, reminding you that things are not what they seem, but also reminding you to keep it a secret. State massacres and disappearance perpetuate violence through the open-endedness of memory and mourning. This I knew for a long time, but through making the film, I realized how the process is being actualized each time one touches upon this memory of violence. The problem is not the traumatic nature of memory but rather the way in which this contagious open-endedness targets political agency and subjectivity, and to this serious problem the notion of trauma and its healing offer no solution. In this context, the act of simply completing the work became an unexpected political and artistic challenge in response to the violence of the open.

Note

1 Mostafa Pour-Mohammadi was the minister of interior from 2005 to 2008 and minister of justice from 2013 until 2017. Ebrahim Raisi was the conservative presidential candidate in 2017 and became the chief justice of Iran in 2019.

9

Dialita Choir

• •

Women Survivors Reclaiming
History in Indonesia

AYU RATIH

Indonesia was once a leading force in the transnational anti-imperialist movement. It hosted the historic Asia-Africa Conference in Bandung, West Java in 1955, at which twenty-nine countries committed themselves to ending a world dominated by European imperialist powers. The Bandung Conference, as it has become known, expressed the ethos of the postcolonial era, when many newly independent countries wished to avoid war, remain neutral in the Cold War, develop their own national economies, and stand on equal footing with all other nation-states (Eslava et al., 2017). For feminists in Indonesia at that time, the conference became a key reference point. They could see that the goals of the Indonesian nationalist movement were shared by nationalists in many other countries. The largest women's organization, Gerwani (*Gerakan Wanita Indonesia*, or the Indonesian Women's Movement), began to promote cross-border solidarity with their Afro-Asian sisters and challenge the imperial nature of Western feminism (McGregor, 2012). However, these initiatives collapsed in late 1965 when the U.S.-backed Indonesian army under General Suharto organized a nationwide military operation to violently destroy the Communist Party of Indonesia (*Partai Komunis Indonesia*; PKI) and its affiliated organizations, including Gerwani. Suharto refused to continue Indonesia's support for the Asia-Africa movement and firmly sided with the U.S.-led Western bloc.

As an Indonesian who was born after 1965 and grew up under Suharto's authoritarian rule, I had no knowledge of Indonesia's left-wing past. It was not until I engaged with the pro-democracy movement in the 1990s that I became aware of the hidden history of the PKI and the massacres of 1965–66. My graduate studies in the United States also exposed me to historical work that was forbidden in Indonesia. But it was my encounters with surviving men and women of the anticommunist violence that occurred following the collapse of Suharto dictatorship in 1998 that prompted me to gather stories about their experiences. I will call these survivors the Bandung people. They were key actors in the anticolonial nationalist movement who at the same time proudly supported other anticolonial movements around the world. From former Gerwani leaders and activists, I learned about the roots of Indonesian feminism and their connections to the international feminist movement. As a feminist historian and human rights activist, I feel responsible for amplifying the survivors' voices and revealing the richness of the historical period in which they lived.

Beginning in 2000, with my colleagues at the Indonesian Institute of Social History, I co-organized an oral history project and a series of women's truthtelling sessions to gather stories from the survivors of anticommunist state violence. Through these projects, I came to know the female ex-political prisoners and their daughters who formed the Dialita choir. Between 2015 and 2019, I attended some of Dialita's practice sessions and performances and regularly talked with the founders and members of the choir. I found Dialita's performances intriguing. Before 1965, choirs were very popular among left-wing youth groups in Indonesia. They were central to developing the youth's sense of civic responsibility and solidarity with the oppressed around the world. Many groups founded choirs that performed at union meetings, party conferences, and public concerts (Yuliantri, 2012). Then, after 1965, political choirs with progressive overtones were nonexistent. The Dialita choir harkens back to that earlier period, especially when they sing songs from the era such as those about transnational Asia-Africa solidarity that have not been heard since. Yet the context for their performances is completely different; they are elderly women performing for younger generations, not to mobilize them for the anti-imperialist campaigns of Sukarno's time but rather to invite them to understand more about the history of the nation during the time immediately preceded the mass violence.

Unlike many other survivors of the 1965–66 violence, the women of the Dialita choir avoid presenting testimonies about the violence and the suffering of the victims. They do not clearly posit claims to truth and justice. Instead, they appear as a collective body that offers a glimpse of the forgotten world of the persecuted revolutionaries. On stage, they focus more on constructing ephemeral sites of memorialization where they can celebrate the suppressed history of anti-imperialist nationalism and the determination of the female political prisoners to survive the miserable conditions of their incarceration. In so doing, they pay tribute to the silenced heroines of the nation, those they respectfully refer to as "our mothers."

Dialita's moving away from the practice of telling individual testimonies is, I wish to argue, a courageous and creative act of memorialization that challenges both the state's official forms of memorialization and the typical style of human rights advocacy in Indonesia that positions the women mainly as victims of violence instead of as political agents. Following Taylor's (2003) assertion that performance suggests "a process, a praxis, an episteme, a mode of transmission, an accomplishment, and a means of intervening in the world" (p. 15), I see Dialita's performances as a mnemonic praxis that challenges the militaristic and zealously anticommunist state memorialization practices, which perpetuate Cold War politics and distort Indonesians' sense of history. Their presence in public as surviving female bodies singing what they call "muzzled songs" (*lagu-lagu yang dibungkam*) contests the state's official history that demonizes women who are political activists and erases the significant role of left-wing activists in the anti-imperialist nationalist movement.

Dialita's enactment of the women's "cultural memory" (Sturken, 1997, pp. 3–7; see also Connerton, 2006; Hirsch & Smith, 2002, pp. 5–6) also poses a critique of the dominant mode of human rights advocacy in Indonesia that relies heavily on the testimony of individual victims in public truth-telling sessions. This truth-seeking practice, tied to the reliance on transitional justice mechanisms for dealing with past state abuses, was introduced by transnational organizations and funding agencies (Hayner, 2002; Minow, 1998) and became very popular among human rights groups (Wahyuningroem, 2013). In choosing collective singing to transmit a more diverse range of memories, the women of the choir want to assert a more complex agency than that defined by victims' abilities to render their sufferings in public. If we contemplate Sturken's (1997) suggestion about how cultural memory and history can at times be entangled (p. 5), Dialita's act of memorialization, which is dense with historical tropes, presents the singers as both survivors of the mass violence and as historical agents.

In this chapter, I investigate how Dialita engages with Indonesia's controversial past in ways that are different from state memorializations and NGO truth-seeking practices. Dialita performances convey a variety of messages: they represent a nostalgic remembrance of the internationalist political culture of the pre-1965 period, a reassertion of their courage to survive repression, a reconstruction of transnational solidarity, and a tribute to condemned heroines. How did they come up with this gamut of expressions? What kind of gendered "repertoire" do they want to build and pass on through their acts of memorialization across spatial and generational boundaries (Taylor, 2003, p. 26)? I examine how Dialita's performances have disrupted hegemonic memorializing practices, contributed to the struggle for justice, and promoted "alternative feminist circuits of connectivity" (Hirsch, 2019, p. 4).

Years of oral history practice have informed my use of the interviews with Dialita women as the primary sources for this study. I draw on the interviews to bridge the gap between my role as an academic intellectual and the women as sources/subjects of knowledge and to avoid the creation of the "hierarchy of knowledge production" (Nagar & Swarr, 2010, p. 6). Such an approach enables me to open the women's "muted channel of subjectivity" (Anderson & Jack, 2015, p. 180) so that we can see the multifaceted layers of feelings these women often conceal in adjusting to their militarized, male-dominated environment. Guided by previous studies on memorialization as an act of transmission of cultural memory through artwork and performances (Altinay et al., 2019; Hirsch & Smith, 2002; Milton, 2014; Taylor, 2003), I analyze three attributes of Dialita's mnemonic praxis: the choir as the mode of transmission, the thematic songs to memorialize survival and assert historical agency, and the legacy of internationalist nationalism. I focus on two performances to analyze how these attributes work in the context of encounters with spectators and the people who assist the choir. As a historian, I view their performances from a historical perspective. I place Dialita's commemorative acts within the trajectory of feminist transnational practices of solidarity—from nation-state-based socialist models of internationalism to people-based, feminist-inspired transnationalism (Grewal & Kaplan, 2000).

The chapter is divided into four sections. In the next section I provide a brief overview of the historical context. I focus on the transnational and gendered dimensions of the anticommunist mass violence that occurred between 1965 and 1966. Then, in the third section, I describe the formation of the choir, its growth in terms of membership and scope of outreach, and the accomplishments that the women consider important. The fourth section analyzes two performances where Dialita's embodied practices of memorialization exemplify the group's gendered strategies to maneuver the complicated field of transitional justice and national history. I conclude with a reflection on the efficacy of Dialita's strategic intervention in the arena of competing memorialization practices.

Anticommunist Mass Violence

The army-organized anticommunist violence of 1965–66 in Indonesia happened during a relatively peaceful time. The country was not in the middle of a war (although Sukarno was threatening a war with Malaysia), and no one expected that the tension among different political groups would lead to one-sided genocidal violence.[1] The triggering event for the violence was a mutiny organized by a group of left-leaning, middle-ranking officers. They abducted and killed six army generals and one lieutenant in the capital city of Jakarta on October 1, 1965. The officers, who dubbed their action Gerakan 30 September (September 30th Movement; G30S), claimed that they carried out the action to protect President Sukarno from a CIA-backed coup planned by a so-called Council of

Generals. The remaining leadership of the army, under the command of Major General Suharto, quelled the mutiny within twenty-four hours. Afterward, Suharto claimed that what had appeared to be a mutiny was actually a coup attempt by the PKI. They further claimed that the PKI and its organizations had started a massive, nationwide social revolt to slaughter the anticommunists and establish a one-party state. Suharto's army called upon people to "crush the PKI down to its roots" (Robinson, 2017, p. 475).

The army used the G30S incident as a pretext to organize the mass killing of PKI supporters who were, in fact, engaged in neither a coup attempt nor a social revolt (Roosa, 2006). With the help of anticommunist civilian militias, the army raided houses and arrested without warrant hundreds of thousands of suspected members and sympathizers of the PKI and its affiliated organizations all over Indonesia. At prisons and makeshift detention camps, they tortured the detainees to force them into revealing information about the nonexistent revolt. The interrogations of the women included sexual assault and rape. Between October 1965 and March 1966, around five hundred thousand people were killed. Many of these were defenseless detainees who had been taken out by the truckload, massacred, and buried in unmarked mass graves. Hundreds of thousands of others who were spared death spent at least a decade in prisons or forced labor camps (Robinson, 2018; Roosa, 2020).

Women activists were targeted by the army. Through the army-controlled mass media, the army spread false, misogynic stories about Gerwani members participating in orgiastic rites before killing the six abducted army generals. These "immoral" and "savage" women were said to have castrated the generals, gouged out their eyes, and sliced their bodies with razors, all while dancing half-naked. Women who were once celebrated as freedom fighters and patriots were suddenly condemned as traitors to the nation, deserving to be raped and killed (Budiardjo, 1996). As Wieringa (2002) has argued, the army used sexual politics to justify the mass murder and the banning of PKI and every organization associated with the party. The name Gerwani itself became a label used to demonize any woman who was strong-willed, independent, and eager to participate in politics.

The U.S. government and its allies were pleased with the massacres and immediately provided support for the army. The anticommunist purge eventually targeted President Sukarno, a staunch nationalist and anti-imperialist, and his loyal supporters. Sukarno—with the full cooperation of PKI, the second largest communist party in the region—had constantly posed a significant challenge to U.S. imperial power in Southeast Asia (Simpson, 2008). The army organized the violence partly to prove itself worthy of receiving vast amounts of foreign aid and investment from the United States and its allies. The violence restructured Indonesia's political economy, allowing it to become integrated into the U.S.-led international economy (Kammen & McGregor, 2012; Farid, 2005). The Indonesian army's success in achieving the complete and permanent destruction of the PKI became a model for other anticommunist militaries around the world, such as those in Guatemala, Chile, and Brazil (Bevins, 2020).[2]

Under the thirty-two years of Suharto's dictatorship, Indonesia was in a permanent state of emergency due to what it identified as the ever-present "latent communist danger" (Honna, 2000, p. 59). The official history books never revealed the inhuman violence involved in this "operation to restore order and security" (Roosa, 2006, p. 12), to use the army's euphemism, and never humanized the people who had been victimized (Notosusanto & Saleh, 1968). The public was prevented from talking about the mass violence of 1965, but they were, nonetheless, obliged to be haunted by a discourse of never-ending danger. The regime built a large museum complex with an imposing monument to honor the officers killed by the G30S and to demonize the PKI. In the center of the bas-relief stretching across the monument at eye level is a scene of women dancing naked and stuffing the officers' bodies down a well. The monument remains a site of annual official commemorations of the so-called "treason of the PKI" (Roosa, 2006, p.10). The consecration of selective loss and "grievability" (Butler, 2004, p. 34) was incorporated into the Suharto regime's acts of nation-building.[3]

The survivors were under pervasive nationwide surveillance, even after they were released from prisons and labor camps in the late 1970s. The government stamped *Eks Tapol* (ex-political prisoner) on their identity cards and implemented a "clean environment" screening policy to ensure that children and relatives of survivors would not be employed in government offices and state-owned companies. The "simulacral spectre" of communist threat continues to haunt Indonesian political life even today (Heryanto, 1999, p. 160).

The Birth of Dialita

The Suharto regime came to an end in 1998 after being challenged by a massive popular mobilization led by university students. A new period called *reformasi* began. Human rights groups introduced the word "victim" into the political arena and demanded state responsibility for the crimes committed during Suharto's rule. Survivors of the 1965–66 violence at long last came out and gave public testimonies about their suffering. They proposed various mechanisms for dealing with the past, including an independent investigative commission, a human rights court, and a Truth and Reconciliation Commission like the one in South Africa. State officials wishing to protect the legacy of the outgoing regime insisted on treating these survivors as the people responsible for atrocities such as the killing of the generals.

In this battle over memory, women's voices were rarely heard. Advocacy for victims focused more on the experience of male political prisoners. Victims' organizations were dominated by men, and even the one organization led by a woman did not highlight women's experiences. One group of women survivors decided to stay away from the campaign and hold its own gatherings. The members of this group were former leaders and members of Gerwani or other PKI-affiliated organizations and the wives and widows of male political prisoners. Accompanying them at their gatherings were their daughters, most of whom had never met before. The gatherings primarily served as a reunion for the ex-political prisoners and activists who had not able to meet for decades due to the Suharto regime's surveillance and terror. Soon, the gatherings became sites of learning for the daughters and younger activists who knew very little about their elders and their activities. In a true Gerwani spirit of collective mothering, the former Gerwani leaders treated all these younger females as "daughters of history" (Uchikowati, personal communication, July 20, 2020). These leaders encouraged the daughters to continue Gerwani's unfinished work to address contemporary women's problems.[4]

Under the leadership of Uchikowati Fauzia (Uchi), whose father and mother were once imprisoned, these daughters took up the task of establishing a small women's organization that focused on the welfare of 1965 survivors, particularly the wives of male ex-political prisoners who had to bear the hardships of keeping their families alive. One activity that became crucial both for fundraising and expanding their social network was selling secondhand goods. It allowed them to be in contact with children of survivors who did not want to appear in public but who were willing to participate in this kind of humanitarian assistance. During the process of gathering and sorting used goods, some of them who happened to be members of a prominent choir group of the Sukarno era, Gembira, reminisced about their past activities and started to sing songs that represented the spirit of their youthful era. Uchi recalled a crucial moment in 2012:

> Here, as we did the sorting, we also sang songs, had a good time, until we came to the idea to establish a choir, or a vocal group, or whatever its name. The goal at that time was very simple: with a singing group we can do a kind of busking. Our goal was to raise funds so that we can help our elders because when we make them happy, we also feel happy. When we visit them, they also feel delighted, and we hear their stories. But the choir has to have a name. What should it be? So, sister Tuti said, "Just name it Dialita." (Uchikowati, personal communication, July 20, 2020)

In the midst of this nostalgic act of remembering emerged Utati, a former youth activist who was incarcerated for eleven years. She introduced the prison songs that were composed by Gerwani leaders to enliven the spirit of demoralized younger inmates. Because prisoners were not allowed to take notes, she strived over her years in prison to rewrite the songs by relying on her memory and that of other prisoners. It had always been her "dream," she said, that someday these songs would be sung to memorialize their victimization and to affirm their sisterhood while surviving repression.

They agreed to name the choir Dialita, an abbreviation of *Di Atas LIma puluh TAhun*, meaning above fifty in Indonesian, as in the beginning the members of the choir were all over 50 years old. Within a span of eight years, Dialita, consisting of a small group of women who mostly appeared at NGO events with limited audiences, gained a surprising popularity. Their performances were met with enthusiastic responses from the younger generation who knew nothing about the 1965–66 mass violence and did not experience living under the dictatorship. Young people crowded their concerts, wrote about them, sang their songs, and created plays based upon their experiences. People from different backgrounds were eager to collaborate with them and help polish their recitals, from vocal trainers, conductors, singers, and musicians to make-up artists and costume designers. Their first album, *Dunia Milik Kita* (The World is Ours), was hailed as one of the ten best albums of the year by the Indonesian version of *Rolling Stone* magazine (Vice Staff, 2017; KBI Telegraf, 2017).

Enthusiastic responses to Dialita's performances boosted the women's confidence and changed the nature of the group. From an exclusive assembly of "daughters of history" carrying out social work, Dialita became a more open and dynamic hub of women, men, and transgender survivors and activists committed to memorialization and transgenerational transmission of memory. The women gradually came to treat a choral performance as a mnemonic praxis that allows them to cultivate a critical sense of history among the youth. Maternal lineage—of the mother-daughter relationship—still serves as an inspiration for Dialita women, but their encounters with present-day artists and activists opened new possibilities for them to enrich their repertoire.

In 2019, Dialita received a Special Award for Gwangju Prize for Human Rights for its role in "showing the path to reconciliation and healing through music" (The May 18 Memorial Foundation, 2020). The award was given by The May 18 Memorial Foundation, a South Korean-based organization formed by survivors of the 1980 Gwangju Massacre. The representative of the foundation made special mention of Dialita's significance in educating the younger generation about Indonesia's forgotten past (Dipa, 2019). In her acceptance speech on behalf of the group, Uchi stated, "This prize is not only for the choir but also for all who struggle for democracy, peace, and human rights. We will continue singing to bring these values to this world" (The May 18 Memorial Foundation, 2019, para. 4). She also extended a message of solidarity with the victims of the Easter bombing attacks in Colombo, Sri Lanka, which happened just a few weeks before the ceremonial presentation of the award.

Uchi's experience in South Korea introduced Dialita women to a different mode of progressive international connectivity. They learned about the power of a strong survivors' organizations like The May 18 Memorial Foundation to lend solidarity for survivors of state atrocities in other countries. If in the Sukarno era the state played a major role in endorsing nation-based international solidarity movements, the Dialita women are now part of a people-to-people transnational struggle to promote peace and justice for survivors.

Connecting with Transnationalist Cultural Practices

The Dialita choir's exposure to transnational activism did not begin in South Korea. In 2015, Dialita was invited to perform at the opening night of Jogja Biennale art exhibition in the city of Jogjakarta, Central Java. Established in 2011 by a group of Jogja artists, this hugely popular biannual art exhibition event has carried on the theme of South-South solidarity in their collaborative work with artists from countries in the equatorial region. It aims to challenge the dominance of the metropole in producing global discourses on art and culture. Every two years, the biennale invites artists from countries in the Southern Hemisphere to have joint exhibitions with local artists. In 2015, the biennale invited eleven artists from Nigeria to show how the exploitation of natural resources like oil and gold has bred conflicts. Carrying the theme of "hacking conflict," the exhibition intended to show how communities in Indonesia and Nigeria dealt with various forms of conflicts through experimental art expressions (Biennale Foundation, 2015).

Dialita women often identify this first open-stage performance as their most memorable one. Indeed, the timing of the performance could not have been more evocative. The year marked the sixtieth anniversary of the Bandung Conference and the fiftieth of the 1965–66 massacres. Older Dialita members immediately connected the transnational spirit of this event with their memory of Asia-Africa solidarity and anti-imperialism campaigns during Sukarno's rule. They picked old songs that had been composed to celebrate this spirit: *Padi untuk India* (Rice for India), *Viva Ganefo* (Viva games of the new emerging forces), and *Asia Afrika Bersatu* (Asia Africa united).

On an open stage with elaborate lighting and audio equipment, Dialita was set to perform last after the other bands played their experimental music. Upon seeing that the majority of the audience was as young as their grandchildren and upon listening to the loud music of the other bands, the women were rather anxious. They were unsure if the audience would stay to watch their performance.

To Dialita's surprise, the audience of around five hundred mostly young people was astounded. A choral performance was not a musical form with which they were familiar; it had become associated with church activities or the boring ceremonies of the state. They never thought a choir could be political. But that night they were clapping boisterously after each song, demanding the women to sing more. As the curator of the event, Wok the Rock, recalled, many of them, including him, were crying: "We were touched, we were trembling. Those women were roaring and huge. [...] The show was magical, the old songs were like rising from the grave!" (Wok the Rock, personal communication, July 29, 2020).

Dialita women used the choral performance to become "retrospective witness[es]" (Hirsch & Smith, 2002, p. 2; see also Riaño-Alcalá, this volume) who, in the act of transferring their memory of their past cultural activities, suggested a historical link between the anti-imperialist tradition of their generation and the contemporary transnational art activism. There was a semblance of nostalgia in this mnemonic practice. But it was not necessarily a chauvinist longing for an idealized past or a lost homeland. A "retrospective nostalgia" can mediate "narratives and rituals that evolve out of gendered historical experiences" (Hirsch & Smith, 2002, p. 9; Boym, 2011). The choir had been a means for the women to assuage their traumatic feelings of loss and develop a sense of camaraderie among the survivors. But once they started performing for larger audiences, it became a way for them to memorialize the Gembira choir of the pre-1965 period. They made other Indonesians aware of the prominent conductor of the choir and the composers who had been persecuted in 1965 and 1966. Likewise, resurrecting the solidarity songs represented a challenge to the state's destruction of an earlier anti-imperialist culture.

The Dialita women may have simply wanted to provide historical roots to the spirit behind the exhibition by singing old songs, but the choir offered an ensemble of complex visuals that reflected the tension between conflicting memories. Even though the songs were sung in a joyful and high-spirited manner, the audience saw that the elderly women's voices and bodies bore "traces of horror" (Milton, 2014, p. 18). An audience that barely knew anything about the genocide and never experienced authoritarianism was confronted with human beings who had survived massacres and years of terror, not the faceless, mythical monsters in the army's misogynic atrocity tales about Gerwani that they had learned from school textbooks. In defiance of the official stigmatism and demonization that they had lived under for decades, the women asserted their humanity. A feminist in the audience who helped to manage Dialita practices recalled: "These women, through their songs, through dialog, through their stories, gently called these young people to return, to read their history, the nation's history, their family history. And many of them, I heard, after attending Dialita concert they began to investigate their family" (Ira, personal communication, July 31, 2020). For the women of Dialita, the warm and enthusiastic response transformed the way they saw themselves and sharpened their vision to turn the choir into an open space for the intergenerational exchange of knowledge and experience. "We were so well taken care of by those young people that we felt more accepted. In the past, as victims we felt alone. But there [in Jogja], we gradually felt a bit of change" (Uchikowati, personal communication, July 20, 2020). The women were relieved that after years of propaganda, there was a section of the youth who did not believe in the specter of communism (Heryanto, 2006). This encounter attracted renowned Jogja artists to collaborate with Dialita to produce an album of songs that the women had archived.

Countermemorializing Act

Almost a year after the historic performance in Jogja Biennale, Dialita held another performance in Jogja to launch their first album, *Dunia Milik Kita* [The world is ours], which was the result of the collaboration mentioned above. I attended the concert at the invitation of Dialita because they wanted me to be a facilitator for their postperformance workshop. From the date and site chosen to the number and diversity of individuals and groups participating in the production of the performance, it was clear that Dialita and its collaborators were determined to challenge the state's hegemonic memorializations. They promised an antithesis to the uniformed, militaristic, and anticommunist state commemorative rituals.

They chose October 1 as the day of the performance. Throughout Suharto's rule, every year on October 1, the state held a commemorative ritual to honor the slain officers, to acknowledge Suharto and the army as the saviors of the nation from PKI's "treachery," and to remind Indonesians of the danger of communism. This ritual was meant to establish the historical narrative Suharto used to legitimize its repressive rule (Roosa, 2006, pp. 7–13). This process of selective remembrance was accompanied by what Bold et al. (2002) would call "active forgetting" (p. 127), whereby the state forced people to ignore, forget, and then naturalize the state-organized violence against those considered as PKI. As I will show below, I see this performance as significant because it incorporated various mnemonic devices, including gendered bodily interpretation, in its "cultural countermemorializing" act (Bold et al., 2002, p. 126).

The site for the night's performance was Taman Beringin Sukarno (Sukarno Banyan Tree Park) in the middle of Sanata Dharma Catholic University.[5] The choice for the site signified that part of Dialita's repertoire came from the anti-imperialist tradition of the Sukarno years. Besides the historic relevance, it reflected the protection offered by one of the organizing participants of the event, the University's Center for the Study of Democracy and Human Rights. All victims of the 1965–66 violence, the Dialita women included, were vulnerable to being attacked by anticommunist paramilitaries.

A brightly lit stage was erected right under the shelter of the historic banyan tree. The performance started with the sound of a piano played by a young female musician as Dialita women came single file up to the stage. They were clad in dark brown Javanese *batik sarongs* and teal and red tie-dyed cotton blouses called *kebaya*.[6] Some of the elderly ones had to be assisted in climbing the steps. They were smiling and waving at the audience who were clapping clamorously. I noticed that two of the choir members were victims of sexual assaults in detention. The rest were daughters and granddaughters of survivors who grew up being discriminated against because their parents were considered communists.

Dialita sang ten songs that had been rearranged by young musicians. Three of them were the songs of international solidarity that they sang at the Jogja

Biennale, and the rest were the prison songs composed by women political prisoners. During one of the breaks, Uchi explained to the audience that it was exhilarating for Dialita to be able to perform and record the "muzzled songs" (Yes No Wave Music, 2016, 3:06) that had been forbidden during the Suharto era with young musicians: "Something that had never happened—three generations, with different histories, different times, met in one album" (Yes No Wave Music, 2016, 3:28). The reinterpretation of the songs in one sense called into question Dialita's ownership of them but at the same time represented the women's reconstitution of themselves as traumatized survivors of mass violence capable of producing historical knowledge.

There were two moments that night when Dialita as "an agent of memorial transmission" (Hirsch & Smith, 2002, p. 2) exhibited shifting bodily practices that signified the women's engagements with traumatic memory and the reminiscence of past performance rituals. When the soloist began to sing the first line of Dialita's classic prison song, *Ujian* (Trial), "From behind the iron bars my heart is tested, whether I'm pure gold or imitation," the rest of the choir stood by solemnly, waiting for their turn to respond in unison. I witnessed two rows of women's bodies bearing painful family histories yet with clear and strong voices testifying that imprisonment did not break their mothers' spirits. And when they sang the last line in ritardando, "Yet with conviction and certainty, the future will come, we will surely return," they tilted their heads and smiled warmly at the audience, and I heard sobbing amid the applause.

The peak of the performance was when Dialita sang the march *Viva Ganefo* in Spanish[7] and danced animatedly during the instrumental part before they repeated the verses. The audience started clapping, following the rhythm. Then the women ended it with a loud "Viva!" as they raised their right fists. This final act I presume came from the bodily repertoire of pre-1965 performances where singers were encouraged to appear proud as Indonesian women and stand up straight to face imperialist challenges. For decades after 1965, these women had been forced to forego these subversive "bodily practices" (Connerton, 1989, p. 88). They were coerced to cower before Suharto military regime. They were considered sinful and dirty because of their association with allegedly communist organizations or parents. Under strict state surveillance, their movement was restricted, and their behavior was constantly judged with reference to PKI, Gerwani, or communism. They had to hide their identities and act measuredly so that they would not go against dominant societal norms. That night, the Dialita women refused to cower, act demure, or be submissive. Through the interactive performance Dialita opened a space where the audience could become the participants and "co-owner of the traumatic event" (Taylor, 2003, p. 167), as well as agents in restoring an erased history.

The idea of a maternal lineage was central to Dialita's mnemonic praxis. Singing the prison songs was their way to acknowledge the suffering and survival of their mothers. The demonization of Gerwani women had ruined many relationships between mothers and their children because the children perceived the mothers' political activities as the source of their sufferings. Dialita's nonconfrontational act of memorialization stemmed from their desire for historical reconstruction and reconciliation to counter the state's continuous attempt to maintain a barrier between the PKI and non-PKI people. The title of the first album they produced in collaboration with the young artists reflects this desire to overcome this transhistorical barrier: *Dunia Milik Kita* is Dialita's way of envisioning a just and peaceful Indonesia with historical connection to its revolutionary past.

Conclusion

The Dialita choir emerged when the proposals for transitional justice, including the plan to establish a truth and reconciliation commission, had all failed and the anticommunists were on a renewed offensive. As they were exploring ways to maneuver within this treacherous territory, they discerned the limitations of the existing truth-telling model espoused by human rights organizations and transnational funding agencies. They wanted to go beyond truth-telling to tap into their cultural memory about the period before the mass violence happened. Initially, the women used the choir more as a way to reminisce about their joyful past and to raise funds for the welfare of the mothers. But the enthusiastic response from the younger generation emboldened them to turn the choral performance into a medium for memorializing the perseverance of women prisoners and for reconstructing the suppressed history of the left movement. By singing prison songs and engaging openly with their audience, Dialita has provided an amicable access to the forbidden history and allowed nonsurvivors to participate in the women's act of remembrance. For the youth, they consider it a privilege to be part of a project with such an organized group that represents a revolutionary force of the past.

Using a cultural approach, Dialita has offered a women-centered alternative model of dealing with a violent past that goes beyond the boundaries of legal approaches. Dialita has contested the existing paradigm of human rights advocacy and the "depoliticization" tendency of transitional justice practices, which often "fail to acknowledge the complexities of suffering and agency" (Leebaw, 2011, pp. 2–3, 17; see also chapters by Crosby et al. and Riaño-Alcalá, this volume). They want to involve people who are not bracketed by victim-perpetrator dichotomy and invite them to bear witness to the legacy of traumatic violence and abuse. The choir has made collaborative work possible as they have expanded their repertoire and built an archive to be transmitted to the next generation. In reminiscing about their past, Dialita women have placed the memory of violence within the history of anti-imperialist nationalist movement in Indonesia. The women of Dialita have creatively presented their vision of a more all-inclusive and peaceful Indonesia.

Notes

1. Some historians have defined the 1965–66 mass killing as genocide. The definition of genocide in 1948 UN convention does not include political groups as the target of destruction. See Roosa (2020) for a brief discussion of this issue.
2. Bevins (2020) shows that Indonesia's mass disappearance as a tactic of state terror was the model for the disappearances in Guatemala in 1966 (pp. 164–65). The armies in Brazil and Chile disseminated ominous messages such as, "Operação Jacarta" (Operation Jakarta) or "Yakarta Viene" (Jakarta is coming) before they started attacking left-wing activists (Bevins, 2020, p. 199).
3. I borrow the concept of "grievability" from Butler's (2004) discussion of how the U.S. government under George W. Bush manipulated public grief following the September 11, 2001, terrorist attacks to justify the war against Iraq (see particularly Butler's chapter, Violence, Mourning, Politics, pp. 30–34).
4. Unless otherwise noted, the account about the birth of Dialita is based on personal communications with the founders: Uchikowati, July 20, 2020, and August 2, 2020; Utati, August 6, 2020; Irina, August 19, 2020; Elly, August 14, 2020; Hartinah, August 11, 2020.
5. Sukarno came to inaugurate the establishment of the university in 1961 and planted a banyan tree there.
6. *Kebaya* and *batik sarong* are classic Javanese female attire.
7. This song was an official march for the celebration of the international sport competition Games of the New Emerging Forces (Ganefo), held in Jakarta in 1963. Fifty-one states from Asia, Africa, Latin America, and Europe participated in the games. The event was meant to respond to the International Olympic Committee's suspension of Indonesia's participation in the Olympics because Indonesia refused entry to Taiwan and Israel for political reasons when it held the Asian Games the year before.

Part 4

Care in/as Collective Mourning

• •

10

Ceremonies of Mourning, Remembrance, and Care in the Context of Violence

• •

A Conversation about Performing *Song for the Beloved*

HONOR FORD-SMITH AND
JUANITA STEPHEN

> What is strange is not violence, but conversation and ways of publicly reckoning with the trauma and incoherence that terror leaves in its wake across the archipelago, imposing limits on what can be said, offering the illusion of safety in silence.
> —D. Alissa Trotz (2014, p. 289)

Song for the Beloved, developed and directed by Honor Ford-Smith in collaboration with visual artists such as Anique Jordan, Kara Springer, and Camille Turner (see Turner et al., this volume) and community members from Hannah

Town, is a performance installation that facilitates an encounter with memories of violence and the very profound labor of mourning within the context of a ceremonial performance. Participants commemorate a loved one who has died as a result of racial violence and work their way through a series of performative interactions with symbolic objects and a soundscape superimposed on images of the ocean. Collectively, they form a memory tableau comprised of writings, images, light, sand, and stone. Guiding performers witness and support the participants as they encounter and reflect on and in this liminal space and then prepare them collectively through dance, chant, and music to reintegrate these experiences into the wider world upon leaving the performance. *Song* has been performed wherever there has been interest in the questions of commemoration and/or overcoming racial violence and human disposability: Kingston, Jamaica; Toronto, Canada; Bogota, Colombia; Santiago de Chile, Chile; and New York State and Madison, Wisconsin, in the United States. [1]

Juanita Stephen participated in a performance of *Song* in Toronto in 2018. Subsequently, she developed *Son*—a multimedia installation of sound, photograph, and moving images—as her final project for Ford-Smith's graduate-level performance class in 2019. *Son* is Stephen's performed response to the threat of racial violence from the perspective of a Black mother parenting a Black son. The piece is a meditation on the caring work of parenting in the context of racial violence.

In June 2021, as part of a virtual three-day workshop that brought together the contributors to this edited volume, Stephen interviewed Ford-Smith about the ideas upon which *Song* is based, and the two then brought their respective performances into dialogue to think about survival, care, mourning, and memory across time and space. What follows is an edited version of this conversation.

* * *

JUANITA I'm excited to speak with you about *Song for the Beloved* after having the chance to attend the Toronto performance in 2018. I've since learned that *Song* has had several different iterations over time and in different locations. Could you talk a little bit about how it began and how it has changed?

HONOR I started the work that *Song* emerged from in 2006. I was working between Toronto and Jamaica, with community-based groups, students, and activists (Ford-Smith, 2011; 2014). It developed in the global context of the so-called War on Terror, about three years after the invasion of Iraq and Afghanistan and in the midst of the ongoing situation in Palestine. It was before the public visibility of BLM [Black Lives Matter] in North America. Alissa Trotz has pointed out that with the possible exception of Haiti and the prison camp at Guantanamo, the Caribbean and its diaspora is not included in debates about terror as it was defined after 9/11. I wanted to center what was happening in the Caribbean in relation to all this global violence and to think about it through the lens of racial violence. I wanted to draw public attention to the different forms of racialized terror spawned by neoliberalism, its internalization by the people most affected, and its human cost. There are different ways in which this violent present drew on deep patterns from the colonial past of genocide, enslavement, and indenture, while also boldly reconstituting them in new ways in the contemporary order. I also wanted to make the point that racialized violence is part and parcel of "enjoying neo-liberalism," as Jodi Dean (2008) puts it—the one depends on the other.

I also wanted to argue that the informal violence of armed strongmen in the Caribbean, which is usually represented as criminal, is a deeply political response to the social violence of neoliberalism, which systemically enshrines unbarred profit-making and extraction in spite of the consequences. So, the performances began at the point where over one thousand young men were dying every year in community violence; uncounted women were enduring domestic violence, being treated as booty; and children were also suffering. We began stimulating a discussion about what violence of all kinds has led to and whether the current iterations of violence are new ways of entrenching the age-old structures of racial violence in society. We found in the communities of Kingston that violence and love exist side by side. Even in the midst of loss, folks find love and joy. That is the most significant thing. If that is so—if it is that you have something terrible, and right alongside it you also have something beautiful, generous, and loving and based on intensely enriching, enduring bonds—then how can we mobilize what is enriching to do the work of making justice happen in the living present? Can we draw on our memories of earlier forms of violence to envision something different? What has led to the current situation? Who is most injured by it? Where do we begin to find alternatives to it? How do we find alternatives in the midst of the present that we are now living? Is it possible to mobilize these memories in the service of an alternative? What secrets does the past hold about what these alternatives might look like? Can we find ways to make those solutions collectively shared?

So, to begin, we had to invite those who are feeling alienation, grief, sadness, and rage as a result of violence to bring their situated knowledge and their memory into the performance to be made material, to be spoken, and to be witnessed. Only then can it be transformed. Lorna Goodison, a Jamaican poet, has a poem called "Mother the Great Stones Got to Move" (1992) and she writes:

> Mother, one stone is wedged across the hole in our history
> and, sealed with blood wax.
> In this hole, is our side of the story, exact figures,
> head counts, burial artifacts, documents, lists, maps
> showing our way up through the stars; lockets of brass
> Containing all textures of hair clippings.
> It is the half that has never been told, some of us must tell it. (p. 138)

So that knowledge, that *half*, was channeled slowly, piece by piece, into *Letters from the Dead*. In 2006, our team began by organizing processions, or walks, in

Toronto with a few folks from Caribbean, Indigenous, African, and Asian communities. In the first performance, we carried a coffin covered with repeating media images of mug shots of those who had died in gun violence in Toronto in the first decade of the millennia into the middle of the center of consumption in Toronto—the Eaton Centre shopping mall. By repeating this image over and over again, we denaturalized it, bringing those who are not wanted into the glamour and glitz of a major shopping center. The performers wrote the names of the dead in chalk on the ground while a triptych of women mourned. Those who carried the coffin asked audience members to read letters from the dead that elaborated how they wanted to be remembered—their dreams and their disappointments. The idea was to make visible what the carnival of commodities conceals; to perform the connection between the bling and death; and to bring into the center of commodification the excluded, the differentiated, the racialized Black and Indigenous voices. To reveal what the shiny surface covers up.

When we retreated, all the names remained chalked on the ground. The pedestrians and shoppers encountered them and either let them remain or rubbed out the fragile chalk marks with their steps. The event in Toronto hinted at the transnational or global links between the deaths of Black youth here and the violence that was taking place around the world, to make clear the scale of the relationships that produce the violence here. In other words, how is the death of someone who is shot by the police in Toronto connected to other events elsewhere that have to happen for that person to die? To make that more explicit, we linked this early work here in Toronto to that of organizations fighting for peace on the ground in Kingston, Jamaica. Horace Levy, a Jamaican elder and activist from the Peace Management Initiative, together with Sistren Theatre Collective, which I worked with for many years, and activists like Joan French, as well as students from York and Edna Manley College in Jamaica, facilitated these efforts.

Working with them, we organized a walk across Kingston, weaving the city together in an act of remembering and commemorating the youth who had been killed over the last ten or so years. This march to remember the dead was led by women from different communities. We didn't intend for it to be led by women, but one of the things that became quickly visible was that the work around mourning and remembering are heavily gendered processes. Community in this context essentially means women, the elderly, and gender nonconforming people. It is they who do the work of remembering and the work of caring for those who are shattered by loss. This invites us to think about the relationship between gender, justice, and care.

We developed a play called *Vigil for Roxy*, loosely based on the stories uncovered while developing the march. It is the story of a woman who's trying to come to terms with the murder of her son by police. Played by actress Carol Lawes, and directed and cocreated by Eugene Williams and Amber Chevannes, the performance reflected the contradictory feelings about violence in the society—an ambivalence that is itself produced by layers of violence. On the one hand, folks want it to stop, but on the other hand, folks find themselves turning it inward against each other, calling for recrimination or revenge, hating themselves for being caught in such a situation, and ultimately accepting hostility and mistrust as natural in spite of loving and caring for each other. *Vigil* also reflects on this in the context of the moment just after independence and neoliberal inauguration in the Caribbean, asking as Langston Hughes does, "What happens to a dream deferred" (Hughes, 1994, p. 426)? What happens to those who are left when the effort to decolonize and to create a society that can care for itself and its people is defeated?

Song is the last iteration. It came out of those many different phases and out of the discussions, the research, and the responses received. It did not offer a solution. It is not didactic. It just allowed the participants to sit with the questions provoked by the process, to grieve, to commemorate their loved ones at their own pace, to sit with the complexity of what they and we are all are faced with, and to think about how this might implicate us. It attempted to recognize and channel feelings and provoke our imaginations. At first that was all it was. But the reaction to it was profound, and some folks had trouble finding closure and reentering the outside world. So, then Alissa [Trotz] suggested we add something that allowed folks to recall activists who had tried to change things. We added a wake space, a room with a deejay chanting and music playing, which allowed folks to celebrate those activists and artists who have tried to change things past and present. In that room, folks could share a simple meal of red peas soup and laugh, sing, and dance.

JUANITA There are a lot of different pieces that have come together to bring *Song* to where it is now. So, I'm curious about your choice of space. The earlier iterations—*Letters from the Dead*, the marches—were quite public. They were in your face, giving you a sort of directive about the connections that should be made. But *Song* is different in terms of space and format—it is less public, less instructive. What does the latest format of the performance allow for in terms of mourning, in terms of memory, in terms of memorialization, and in terms of any of the other intentions that you had for *Song*?

HONOR You're right on Juanita, thank you so much for that. The first two iterations were protest performances in many ways. We walked across town to the commercial center or to the mayor's office and read letters to and from the dead and called for violence to stop. We used familiar images of the dead and the disappeared, carrying enlarged photos of their faces, what Diana Taylor (2019) calls "traumatic memes" (see also Crosby et al., this volume). *Song* was different to that but it synthesized the learnings that these [earlier] pieces allowed for. One of the things that emerged was the need to create a space for people to have their pain acknowledged and to do their own inner work of mourning and memory at their own pace (see Figure 10.1).

FIGURE 10.1 Memorial table, *Song for the Beloved*, at Liberty Hall: The Legacy of Marcus Garvey Museum, Kingston, Jamaica. The card reads, "I want that they stop to kill our children. Omer has died. Liberty Hall Child." Photo by Nicosia Shakes.

From this, they can build a personal narrative from the shards of memory, and when they look at the collective result of that laid out on the long central table of memory, that is at the heart of *Song*; they can see it as a shared, collective pain that has been made and can perhaps be unmade. And this perhaps provokes in them the desire to make material an alternative going forward.

Song allows for a confrontation with the unrepresentable element of grief, and then it asks that this unrepresentable thing be embodied in matter. There is a part of grief that can never be reduced to a singular contained act or symbol. It always kind of bursts through the skin that tries to contain it. *Song* allows for a space where that excess can be present, but not in a spectacular or violent way, in a gentle way that is both personal and collective and that allows for a connection between this and older, deeper memories—the Middle Passage, past struggles for justice, sacred ceremonies of survival. The participants create from their memories, but there is a space between them—a kind of stillness, the repetitive sound of the sea—that allows people to be there with what they feel in that moment.

The first room is fairly dark. You don't enter the first room unless you accept to enter it. At the beginning, there's someone—often artist Camille [Turner]—who explains the context for the performance and warns you as to what's likely to happen in the room. Some people don't go in. Some go straight to the other room downstairs or just go as far as the first door and then leave. People have to decide whether they're willing to do the work that is demanded of them in this room. It's a choice. It's not forced on them, because going through that room is hard work. Remembering and making images of memory is painful and difficult work. That is why folks forget. And so, if they choose to move through, if they choose to remember, they move through at their own pace and in their own space, supported by attendants and witnesses. But if you think you cannot cope with the work demanded by the performance, or if for another reason you don't feel ready to enter, then it may not be time for you to undertake that journey. It may not be safe for you to do that. So, *Song* allows for that.

All of the iterations of the performances are based on the idea that remembering the past holds valuable resources for imagining the future and that this is because the emotional labor of remembering can be a powerful prompt to get us to act in the present. If you don't work through the pain of loss, psychologists tell us, it resurfaces in unhelpful ways in the present. But if you only process the memory and do not find a way to join this work to a collective experience and way of acting together on the material present, then the process becomes a limited one which, like the states of emergency imposed in Jamaica, do not change anything but simply reflects what is.

The word *Sankofa* in Twi, the Akan language, one of the founding languages and cultures of Jamaica, means to go back and take from the past what is needed for the present. In a very different context, in his discussion of Walter Benjamin, Terry Eagleton (2009) reminds us "that what drives men and women to revolt against injustice" collectively is less the "dreams of liberated grandchildren" than it is the "memories of enslaved ancestors" (pp. 44–45). As he continues, "It is by turning our gaze to the horrors of the past in the hope that we will not thereby be turned to stone" (p. 45) that we are then compelled to move, to act. The important thing here is the *we*, the collective encounter with the past that has been silenced.

JUANITA I'm reading care all through here.

HONOR I'm indebted to Heather [Evans] and of course Paul Connerton (2011) for helping me to articulate the idea that memory is a labor of care. Caring for the past and for those who have suffered from the violence of racism, class, and gender is a way of committing oneself to making sure that that trouble does not continue to repeat itself in the present. Care is both a key principle of justice and a political principle. It affirms the reciprocity and the reliance on others that is required to dismantle violence in its myriad forms, and it draws attention to what is still needed if all relationships between humans and their environments are to be based on care. So, one of the key principles that emerged from our first labor in Hannah Town with the walk across Kingston was that commemoration is an act of care. This is a principle of justice because by commemorating the ignored and overlooked dead, we ask what our responsibility is to them and what we might do to realize in the everyday present what they could not in their own lives.

African American feminist Aisha Finch (2020) argues that by focusing on women's embodied performance and caring labor in ceremony (and here "women" doesn't have to be cis women; women can be an expansive term), we can reappraise the meaning of the political as it comes down to us in Western liberalism and also in secular modern states. She proposes that in the context of enslavement, care and its relationship to embodied actions in ritual draws attention to the ways in which the material depends on the immaterial work done by something more than hardship and the drear of oppression. Her work on gender and the uprisings of the enslaved in Cuba and Haiti asks us to consider the work done by sacred ceremonies in the context of these uprisings, and she suggests that this immaterial caring work is a place where knowledge transfer can happen through embodied acts that illuminate the full dimension of transformation.

I like to think that *Song* is such an immaterial labor and that it asks of us what we can do to realize in our collectives lives what has been suppressed and destroyed in the past. In *Song*, to be able to make sense of what has happened in the past, we use the principle that repurposing the shards of violation in acts of caring work and renarrating them can be a way forward out of all those intersecting hierarchies that hold up racial capitalism. And in that principle, we are indebted to Veena Das (2007), whose work enables us to see that we cannot understand those who survive extreme violence entirely through the notion of trauma—a term that I think has become so banalized. What Das argues is that folks who have to continue to live in contexts where their lives and social relations have been violated need to find a space in that everyday context in which they live to occupy, repurpose, and renarrate what happens.

Mourning, Remembrance, and Care • 155

So, I think those were some of the principles that influenced the work of *Song*. It tried to allow for a reflection into the materiality of ceremony in the context of gendered practices of care and the way in which that can clear a space to spark the deferred desire to reimagine some other form of possibility. So, that's a lot.

JUANITA It is, it is a lot. And it's because *Song* does so much. It allows for so much. Like you said, *Song* is built on these principles of care as it attempts to offer a liminal space that is outside of the everyday. Even though it is a more private (or a less public) space, it lives in that in between of public and private; of personal mourning and collective mourning; of remembering together in a space that is curated to always insist that the violences responsible for our respective losses are connected. Can you talk about the projected video that plays on a loop in the first room?

HONOR It's a projection of a montage created by Kara Springer. The soundscape that Ravi Naimpally and I developed is water with the sounds of the city and the music of the city breaking through. The sound of the sea is there because the sound of the sea also evokes the profound memory of the Middle Passage and survival of it. So, there are projections of images of the sea as a way of projecting the layered, atemporal way in which this profound experience of violence continues to break through into today. So, we don't say, "This is the middle passage," but there are underwater shots of the sea water. We show that the water is deep, the water is a space of threat and terror, but it is also a space of life and of re-creation because nothing alive can live without water and all life comes from the sea. So, it's about always trying to hold these two things together, trying to hold ambivalence in the hand. So water, stone, earth, fire, food, and flowers. Those things are the key symbols.

When you enter the room, the first thing that happens is you have your hands washed. It's a very intimate experience, and that is your break with everyday life—that is the washing off of the everyday. And it's the first reference to the revival spiritual imagery that's going through the performance. The water is important because in the revival tradition, ancestral energies can come through water. The washing of the hands, the pouring of water over the stones . . . all of these are important acts. So then the participants work with a stone, and the stone is this site of transference—it's the portal. The stone becomes your portal to remembrance and possibility. There's a whole lot of poetry about stones in Caribbean literature, and *Song* references that. It did not happen consciously. It came from the unconscious, my unconscious, where these poetic images were stored. It came out in a workshop in which I was exploring the persona I play. It was in the studio that I found the work I had to do with the stone, the encounter with the stone.

JUANITA I think the subconscious nature of the development and these symbols has also facilitated a similar sort of subconscious connection that you're making between your own personal mourning, the symbols, and the other people that are in the room. You're asked to write the name of the person that you're remembering on the stone and place it on the table. And it is placed beside the stones with the names of other people who are being remembered from other contexts and other manifestations of violence in places all around the world. And those are brought into very close proximity to each other. And it's that encounter that you've mentioned . . . it really facilitates opportunities for encounter. And the stones are the first place that happens.

HONOR Dennis Scott's (1982) poem says "that the children be enduring as stones with the names of the dead cut into them" (p. 19). I didn't realize that what I was doing was actually dramatizing that quote in a way. I am the performer who washes the stones that participants write on. The washing of the stones, the cleaning of the stones, is in a way such a Sisyphean task, but in the repetition of it, in the doing of it, you find that moment of transforming that which has been discarded. So, people look at this old woman washing these stones and think, "What the hell is she doing?" Then they pick one of these stones, and they write the name of someone they want to remember on it. That is the act where that moment of transition can happen. It doesn't always happen, but it can. I think that the work of survival can only be sustained with care, with the opportunity to work deeply with signs, sounds, and movements in ways that transform that place of devastation, that allow you to imagine and pay attention to meaning-making in a context that is specially prepared for this. So, that's what *Song* tries to do. The labor of survival and caring remembrance of those who have died cannot be sustained without having a space in which we can listen deeply, think and feel deeply, and gather strength. My uncle used to always talk about "gathering strength" to work, and I think it is a key concept—the idea that you have to gather strength to articulate anything, to do anything. "Gathering strength" doesn't just mean getting strong; it literally means *gathering* strength, pulling it in from the collective bits of strength all around you to enable you to act.

Connerton (2011) says that "to care" comes from the same root as "to mourn" (p. 4). So to care, in this profound sense, means to confront what has disappeared in death. Never, ever, ever again is met with the re-creation of what has been blown apart by centuries of profound violation, and to care literally means working to put the fragments together. "Break a vase," Derek Walcott (1992) famously says, "and the love that assembles the fragments is greater than that love which took its symmetry for granted when it was whole" (para. 11).

The love, or the care, here means to pay attention, to feel concern, to mind, to repair, to keep safe, to give importance to what might pass unobserved, walk good, to live, to walk with, to feed, to clean, to bathe, to wipe away shit, to sweep, to dust, to listen, to love, to tend to. This makes me think of your project *Son*. Can you speak to the everydayness of care in this work?

JUANITA Yes, absolutely. *Son* was an exploration of how racial violence can condition the context for care. So, *Son* puts an open letter that I wrote to my own child in conversation with other parents of Black boys. The letter is about him turning 16 and being a Black boy in this geographic, political, and temporal context and about a kind of ongoing, underlying fear or concern that I have because of living under the constant threat of state violence that only increases as he gets older. So, what you hear is a sort of chorus of voices, including my own, reading the letter, and the other parents speaking to their own fears, hopes, and joys that emerge within the context of violence. And as you listen and watch the video projections that go with the sound, all around you on the walls are pictures of the everyday domestic environment—the images of care. It's laundry, shoes everywhere. It's the bed, grocery shopping, the washing machine. Toilet paper. [Laughs]. That's my favorite, 'cause it's just so "every day." But these are the things that go on in the background, that must keep on, and which are also conditioned by living under the threat of violence. And it is a particularly contextualized violence; I am speaking specifically about the gendered nature of institutional violence that Black boys are subject to in a particular place with a particular history.

And so that Walcott quote gives me the bridge between *Song for the Beloved* and *Son*, though they are thinking about this context in very different ways.

HONOR In *Son*, you have this big projection of family videos that you splice together. Could you say a bit about that? And could you also say a bit about the letter? Because another overlap is this idea of the letter, this idea of writing and reflecting on memory through letters.

JUANITA So, the letter to my son was written first and, really, the rest of the installation grew from that. The letter was written in response to James Baldwin's famous *A Letter to My Nephew, "My Dungeon Shook"* (1962). In that letter he asks his nephew not to allow the racism that permeates American society to destroy his soul. My letter asks something similar of my son in the context of Canada. The written letter is projected on the wall at one end of the room, and you hear my voice reading the letter. As it plays, the words on the page are redacted several times to reveal another message to my son. Each of the redactions pull out the different emotions that underlie and live alongside fear. There's fear, yes, but there's also love, there's also joy, there's also celebration, and mourning. All of these things happen at the same time when you are living under the threat of violence, or when you're experiencing violence.

When the letter video ends, on the opposite wall, another video begins. This is a compilation of family photos and videos. You see these images of my son and other Black boys who are experiencing joy and the fullness of childhood and being afforded the opportunity to do that. And those images are set against the audio of excerpts from conversations that I had with the parents of Black boys whom I asked: what is your greatest joy, what is your greatest fear, and what is your greatest hope about raising a Black son? It was important for me that fear not be the only feeling present, because joy and hope and anger and love and connection and care are how we survive. So, they needed to be as visible as the fear. On the two remaining walls, you have the images of the everyday, the materials of some of the caring labor that must continue despite the threat, because of the threat, and to soften or buffer it.

And so, it opened up a conversation for people to think about how all of those things live together. I think that *Song* does that similarly and allows people to bring things together. For me, it's a project about proximity, and care is a project of proximity as well, and so what our works both do in different ways is bring things close enough together for us to start to see how they're connected.

HONOR I think in your case, you used the very famous letter from Baldwin to his nephew. It is a letter from one older Black man to another younger man. And you created a letter from a mom to a young man. And so, there was this space between parental protection and gendered maturity, between the desire to do and the inability to control. *Song for the Beloved* of course references Toni Morrison's book *Beloved,* which itself references the resurgence of memories of violence, care, and the refusal of systemic violence. *Song* references all those who experience the complexity of violence and care simultaneously.

In the case of *Son*, you also reference care and violence, and what was also really interesting was what happened when young Black students went through the exhibition that you created. They responded to it from the point of view of being daughters or sons. It was very much told from the parents' point of view. Students went in and broke down crying and then expressed what it meant to be confronted with all the labor of their parents, which of course, every kid in the world thinks is just . . . well . . . part of the furniture. And at the same time, to understand the limits of their parental commitment in the context of white supremacy. So, it was interesting to see how moved they were and how they suddenly understood the danger that was all around them, and consequently understood love—not as an attempt to stymie their freedom but as an act of protection. It provoked profound reflections.

JUANITA That was unexpected for me, too. I had a particular perspective that I brought to the conversation, and I also had my son's reaction to that perspective as I developed the work. But I didn't consider my experiences of being a sister of three Black boys—now Black men raising their own Black sons—who I watched live through that same violence. So, I was somewhat surprised by how it landed for people who are not parents but who love and live life alongside Black boys in the same context from which I am thinking and creating.

And I think that this is also, perhaps, what happened with *Song.* It went into the world, and there were the responses that you didn't necessarily anticipate. And then what you have done with that is manage to fold those responses into each iteration, so you get this performance that reflects the different places that it has been shown, and the folks who have come through, and the ways that they are grieving and mourning. It also reflects a reckoning with the language that we use to describe these processes and encounters. I remember you talking about the fact that the term "reparations" didn't sit everywhere in the same way, and so we are left with questions such as, what does "repair" mean? What does "reconciliation" mean?

What does that language hold for people in different places, under different violences, who are trying to find their way through mourning, through memory, through proximity, and all of these different things that *Song* facilitates? I think these are the questions that I'll be sitting with for a while.

Note

1   A performance of *Song* in Bogota, Colombia, can found at https://vimeo.com /185023771.

11

Maternal Activism and the Politics of Memorialization in the Mothers of the Movement

• •

A Black Feminist Reading

ERICA S. LAWSON AND OLA OSMAN

Memorializing practices for deceased children are central to Black women's maternal activism and expressions of political subjectivity. This is evident in the antiracist social justice work undertaken by the Mothers of the Movement (also referred to as "the Movement" in this chapter) in the United States. The Movement was established in 2013 by a group of bereaved Black mothers that includes Sybrina Fulton (Trayvon Martin), Geneva Reed-Veal (Sandra Bland), Gwen Carr (Eric Garner), Lezley McSpadden (Michael Brown), Cleopatra Pendleton-Cowley (Hadiya Pendleton), Maria Hamilton (Dontre Hamilton), and Lucy McBath (Jordan Davis). Its stated purpose is to press the state to prioritize criminal justice reforms to improve the historically violent policing of Black and racialized communities. Arguably, the Mothers of the Movement serves a dual purpose. First, through political organizing and advocacy, it pushes for reforms. Second, the Movement provides a platform for bereaved mothers to grieve and remember their deceased children within an intersubjective community of mourners who have a shared history of Black motherhood in the American racial state.

This chapter examines the memorializing dimensions of the political activities that the Mothers of the Movement engages in to remember their deceased children within the context of broader initiatives to address racial harms and advance a social justice agenda. Our examination of such activities is based on critical readings of the mothers' political actions as they are covered in select media. The mothers, who supported Hillary Clinton's 2016 presidential campaign, were prominently featured at the Democratic National Convention (DNC) in that year and were of interest to much of the media ecosystem. As well, after the murder of George Floyd in 2020, some of the mothers in the Movement were interviewed on the news and current affairs program *Good Morning America* about the deaths of their children, about why they keep their memories alive, and about what they hope to accomplish through their activism. Drawing on media coverage of the mothers at the DNC and their appearance on *Good Morning America*, we foreground and analyze the public memorializing practices that the women engage in, with attention to how they remember their children in the present and how they attempt to ensure that their names and the meanings of their lives are carried into the future.

Our focus on memorialization among bereaved mothers stems from our scholarly interests in the politics of grief among diasporic Black mothers and our locations as Black feminist scholars. We build on the insights that Black feminism generates about the particularities of maternal grief, or what Williams (2016) described as "Black maternal grief as analytic." Williams used this framework to examine the contestations in Black mothers' maternal activism at the nexus of grief and grievance, a space that we argue is occupied by organizations such as Mothers of the Movement, whose members work through trauma and simultaneously make claims on the state for the reparation of racial harms. We locate the Mothers of the Movement within a transnational Black feminist praxis that is concerned with Black liberation and, importantly, solidarity building (Hall, 2016). We do so mindful of the pitfalls of privileging a U.S.-centered organization that, seemingly, does not grapple with the politics of diasporic solidarity-building across borders. However, we can locate the Mothers of the Movement in the transnational struggle for Black liberation; as well, it provides a platform for Black women whose experiences are largely marginalized in public culture worldwide.

We think about memory in relation to the afterlife of slavery, as articulated by Saidiya Hartman, and through questions she raised about time and structural violence in Black life. In her book *Lose Your Mother: A Journey along the Atlantic Slave Route,* Hartman (2007) wrote: "If slavery persists as an issue in the political life of black America, it is not because of an antiquarian obsession with bygone days or the burden of too-long memory but because black lives are still imperilled and devalued by a racial calculus and a political arithmetic that were entrenched centuries ago. This is the afterlife of slavery—skewed life chances, limited access to health and education, premature death, incarceration, and impoverishment" (p. 6). What then, might the *idea* of memory and memory *practices* look like for people, who, according to Sharpe (2016), live "in the wake?" That is, "[Black people] occupy [and are] occupied by the continuing and changing presence of slavery's as yet unresolved unfolding" (pp. 13–14). Wake work is that movement toward Black social consciousness engaging with ghosts, the "disremembered and unaccounted for" (Morrison, 2010, p. 324), but is primarily a recognition that the anti-Black logics of the middle passage animate contemporary life (see also Turner et al., this volume). Wake work is memory work in organizations such as the Mothers of the Movement, whose members insist on publicly remembering their dead who, we argue, are connected to the memories of those who died in the hold of the ship; of those who were jettisoned from the *Zong* so that insurance money could be claimed (Philip, 2011); and of those who jumped to escape a fate they surmised would be worse than death. Put differently, we view the Mothers of the Movement as a contemporary iteration of Black women's long history, rooted in the plantation economy, of advocating to save their children or to keep their memories alive after they are sold as property or after they die in violent circumstances. We argue that the ways in which the women in the Mothers of the Movement remember their children are connected to the practices of cultural memory in diasporic Black life in ways that bridge the past and present and create different kinds of futures where, despite their physical absence, their children will continue to be memorialized.

We begin this chapter by arguing how such mobilizations of Black maternal grief offer theoretical insights into memorialization that uniquely emerge from Black feminist thought and praxis. We provide an overview of the wider literature on maternal activism, demonstrating how the Mothers of the Movement is inherently transnational. We then address memorializing practices in the Mothers of the Movement by analyzing select media coverage that, more or less, provides a firsthand account of how the mothers talk about grief and the memories of their children. The media coverage we analyzed demonstrate the affective dimensions of grief in relation to memory. That is, some of the mothers talked about the bodily reactions to grief (e.g., "your heart hurts," "your head hurts"), thus capturing the complex and shifting ways that memory work through activism coexists with bodily pain. We then briefly comment on the limits of iconic practices of memorializing deceased children to the extent that this approach can silence those who grieve in private, thereby privileging a particular type of maternal grief over other, less visible forms. We conclude by emphasizing how the Mothers of the Movement is transnational in its insistence on remembrance as resistance.

Black Feminist Theory of Memorialization in Maternal Activism

Within the lived experience of slavery and its afterlife, we think of Black women's activist movements focused on memory and countermemory as radical sites of resistance in the transnational Black feminist tradition. As articulated by Woodly

(2019), "In this sense [these movements] mobilize the memory of trauma and dehumanization for change" (p. 223) within social movements such as Black Lives Matter and Black feminist organizations. Indeed, deploying memories of children is central to bereaved justice-seeking mothers in anti-Black states, and counter-memory is a strategy used by these mothers to reclaim the character of their dead children who are often publicly criminalized to justify their demise. Black feminist epistemologies emerge as counternarratives about Black life wherein people reclaim their humanity against the anti-Black racial tropes that are prevalent in racial states.

Such counternarratives and memorializing are captured in certain cultural productions and initiatives. This includes what Nash and Pinto (2020) have described as a subgenre of "black maternal memoir," referencing in particular two books by bereaved mothers and a father: Fulton and Martin's (2017) *Rest in Power: The Enduring Life of Trayvon Martin* and McSpadden's (2016) *Tell the Truth and Shame the Devil: The Life, Legacy, and Love of my Son Michael Brown*. We add to this subgenre list *And Still I Rise: A Mother's Search for Justice*, written by Doreen Lawrence (2007) to memorialize her son, slain teenager Stephen Lawrence, and his legacy. Memorialization, broadly understood, also includes the establishment of foundations by bereaved mothers and their families that not only keep their children's memories alive but also aim to have a social impact. Kiatou Diallo, the mother of Amadou Diallo, who was executed by police officers in New York in 1999, established the Amadou Diallo Foundation with the mission to "advocate for racial equity and promote education, particularly for students of African descent" (Amadou Diallo Foundation, n.d.). Additionally, the Lawrence family established the Stephen Lawrence Charitable Trust in the aftermath of his death, and Fulton and Martin set up the Trayvon Martin Foundation and the Circle of Mothers, which helps grieving mothers heal, and the Circle of Fathers, which mentors young fathers. Martin's parents have also chronicled his life in a six-part documentary series. These memorializing activities are not unique in form but they are significant in an anti-Black world where murdered Black people usually only permeate public consciousness through the violent nature of their deaths and the political reckonings they provoke.

Black women's work and organizing at multiple sites of remembrance signal what Cooper (2015) described as Black feminist "visionary pragmatism" (p. 19) utilized to fashion solutions to pressing problems that could mean the difference between life and death. Indeed, Hall (2016, quoting bell hooks) argued that a transnational Black feminist framework signposts "a liberatory process" (p. 90); this is explained, argued Hall by quoting bell hooks, as the emergence of "critical thinking and critical consciousness as one invents new, alternative habits of being, and resists from that marginal space of difference inwardly defined" (pp. 90–91). Black mothers who seek justice for deceased children are often forced to grapple with structures of domination that lead to death in anti-Black worlds, and foregrounding the memories of their children is central to visionary pragmatism and liberatory praxis that situates women in a longer history of pro-test for Black liberation.

This is the case with the Mothers of the Movement, whose children were mur-dered by police agents or white private citizens and who find themselves pushed into a political landscape fraught with a history of problematic racial tropes that seek both to define and contest Black motherhood (Williams, 2016). By way of Cheng (2001), we understand that the Mothers of the Movement has translated grief into grievance, defined as "speaking out against injury" (p. 19) perpetrated by the state and as pressing for accountability and restitution vis-à-vis the memories of their children. The remembrance practices they engage in their activism center pictures, public talks, political involvement, and other interventions that are all meant to change the conditions that led to the deaths of their children and to imagine and build different types of futures.

The above-mentioned memorializing practices are mediated through the politics of difference and located within the larger context of a shared cultural memory of Black life. Our understanding of cultural memory at the site of maternal activism is informed by Lowe's (1996) argument that "culture is the terrain through which the individual speaks as a member of the contemporary national collectivity, but culture is also a mediation of history, the site through which the past returns and is remembered, however fragmented, imperfect, and disavowed" (p. x). Cultural memory is anchored in a living and embodied trans-historical archive to the extent that bereaved activist mothers have always constituted Black life in the African diaspora, and the knowledge that they acquired about Black survivability remains dynamic and regenerative at the site of Black feminist praxis.

The experiences of these seemingly disparate groups of mothers and families at different historical moments intersect along the lines of gendered, re/productive global racial capitalism and a shared experience of disposability that, iteratively, have demarcated Black life. Today, as was the case in the epoch of racial slavery, anti-Black violence continues to take Black lives, lives that remain entangled in the political economy of (neo)colonial practices that are remade in the present with material consequences. Through their protests and advocacy, and specifi-cally how they talk about their children, the Mothers of the Movement illumi-nate and challenge their biopolitical management in and by the state. As such, women's maternal activism through shared and fragmented cultural memory is a point of resistance against Black people's disposability.

In this chapter, we argue that distinct forms of memorialization undertaken by bereaved mothers in connection to shared Black cultural memory contribute to the field of feminist theorizing in memory studies. We make no claims that activism writ large is memorialization or that Black maternal activism itself constitutes an exclusive site of cultural memory. Instead, we locate memorial-ization as a praxis within the larger context of cultural memory to argue for its saliency in how women (re)claim themselves and their children as humans within an intersubjective community. This approach to understanding memorialization taken by some groups of descendants of enslaved peoples is distinct from how other oppressed groups may deploy memory as a site of reckoning and reclamation. This is especially so if the roots and routes of their abjection are not tied to their right to be human or to the vestiges of being property (Walcott, 2021). Memorializing for Black people has come to be a praxis of humanization, or a way to "endow ontology to precisely that which has been systemically deprived of the privilege of ontology" (Meijer and Prins, 1998, p. 280, quoting Judith Butler).

How groups grapple with memory as a means of reclamation, sense-making, and belonging is a particular site for examining collective trauma. This reality is poignantly reflected in how Hirsch (2008) took up postmemory in relation to the descendants of people who perished in the Jewish Holocaust. Hirsch explained that "postmemory describes the relationship that the generation after those who witnessed cultural or collective trauma bears to the experiences of those who came before, experiences they 'remember' only by means of the stories, images, and behaviors among which they grew up" (p. 106). But if slavery is a structure rather than an event, then the relevance of *postmemory* to the descendants of enslaved peoples remains an open question.

Cartographies of Memorialization in a Transnational Historical Context

We can locate the deployment of memorializing practices in the Mothers of the Movement within the cartographies and temporalities of slavery. We can trace the ways in which mothers held the memories of sold-off children as a motivating factor to find them long after emancipation. An advertisement placed by Nancy Jones in 1886, years after the American Civil War, captured this sentiment: "Information wanted of my son Allen Jones. He left me before the war, in Mississippi. He wrote me a letter in 1853, in which letter he said that he was sold to the highest bidder, a gentleman in Charleston, S. C. Nancy Jones, his mother, would like to know the whereabouts of the above-named person. Any information may be sent to Rev. J. W. Turner, pastor of A. M. E Church, Kansas, Ottawa" (Shapiro and Pao, 2017, para. 1). Given that Mississippi declared secession from the United States on January 9, 1861, Allen Jones had been sold almost ten years before the start of the war, and his mother lived with the absent presence of her disappeared son well into the years after the war.

In the Sri Lankan context, de Alwis (2009; see also de Alwis, this volume), explained "absent presence" as the psychological and emotional state of precarity that consumed the lives of mothers and other family members whose loved ones disappeared during the civil war. Family members, and mothers in particular, live in the liminal space of not knowing, which results in hauntings, heightened memories, and emotional breakdowns at the sight of objects that remind them of those who are missing. Here, de Alwis's explanation of "absent presence" expresses grief that is unique to the maternal subject. She wrote: "Indeed, the mother's lament . . . while invoking her endless tracings and re-tracings through both natural and manmade scapes in her quest for her disappeared, simultaneously articulates a subtle layering of temporalities through the trace of the disappeared—his face—which appears to her wherever she goes, at whatever she looks. It is as if the very absent presence/present absence of the disappeared is what holds death in check; he is everywhere, always" (p. 242).

This is also what Toni Morrison conceived of as "rememory" (Morrison, 2010, p. 43), described as "the experience of the circularity of time, space, and body, as past places and things are erected through the presence of one's body/mind" (Powell, 2016, p. 259). Long after the end of the American Civil War and into the turn of the twentieth century, African Americans continued to place ads in newspapers across the country in search of any news about their loved ones who were sold away. They likely did this in the context of faded memories of their beloveds, as few, if any, would have had access to photographs, a quintessential signifier of absent presence (de Alwis, 2009, p. 242). To be sure, the women Mothers of the Movement do not live in a state of absent presence; they know where their children are buried. Importantly, they do not live in the liminal space of not knowing that, although anxiety-inducing, holds out hope that their children may still be alive. However, mothers like Nancy Jones, as with some Black mothers today, live(d) with the unique precarity and disposability of Black life such that we can attend to the distinct memorializing practices that resultantly emerged. Moreover, we can locate memorialization in a shared Black/African feminist standpoint in a transnational context in which grief is translated into grievance. Therefore, although this chapter does not directly address how Black women organize against gendered racial violence across borders and the role of memory in doing this, we argue that a Black feminist transnational and maternal consciousness is evident in women's insistence on centering their children, dead or alive, in their struggle for justice.

Mothers of the Movement as Situated in Transnational Maternal Activism

The Mothers of the Movement is indicative of the transnational phenomenon of maternal activist organizing that both constrains and opens up possibilities for women's political participation. Throughout the Americas, mothers have formed organizations for justice and accountability. They engage in initiatives to prevent future murders and disappearances of children and youth, and they mobilize their maternal positions to press for social change. These organizations are also sites of memorialization for deceased or missing children, such that how they function depends on activities that explicitly remember these children. Among the more prominent mothers' organizations for justice and memorialization are the Mothers of the Plaza de Mayo and the Caravan of Mothers of Missing Migrants. Some forty years since they began marching in the Plaza de Mayo to press the Argentinian military junta to reveal the whereabouts of their children, the Mothers—now advanced in age—continue to march with pictures of their children, still searching for answers and keeping their memories alive. The Caravan of Mothers for Missing Migrants travels the Mexico-U.S. border with pictures of their children and other missing loved ones, seeking information on their whereabouts (McLean, 2020). Such organizations underpinned by maternal activism also form cross-border alliances in their efforts for justice, to bear witness to shared pain and to keep the memories of children alive through stories and photographs (Ashika, 2019, p. 140). In their examination of the Saturday Night Mothers in Turkey, Ashika (2019) detailed how bereaved mothers of the Plaza de Mayo traveled from Argentina to Turkey to support the Saturday Night Mothers and share the knowledge and strategies that they acquired over long years of seeking justice. These cross-border collaborations spotlight transnational feminist organizing on common ground, albeit within the reality that "although there are some similarities every society has its particular problems" (p. 141). Arguably, almost all cultures share, to varying degrees, a respect for motherhood that facilitates maternal political organizing, which itself is contested on the basis of intersectional factors such as race, religion, class, and sexuality, and managed by the limits of public empathy for mothers insomuch as they remain within the confines of normative femininity. These, of course, are more complicated positions for African American mothers whose reproductive capacities have been commodified, regulated, and disciplined (Roberts, 1997) and for whom motherhood does not evoke a great deal of empathy in the American public.

Today, the Mothers of the Movement is one of many examples of Black women's continued resistance to empire. We recognize Black mothers as engaged in the complex expression of politicized mourning within a shared community of bereaved people. These are people whose lives have been permanently altered by a unique but all too common tragedy—the murders of their children. By refusing to grieve privately, these Black mothers "animate grief or grievance for racial justice" (Williams 2016, p. 21) through public memorialization.

Mothers of the Movement at the Democratic National Convention

On July 26, 2016, nine members of the Mothers of the Movement took the stage at the DNC in Philadelphia to support the presidential nominee, Hillary Clinton. Eight of the women were dressed in black, and all wore a big, red rose pinned on their lapel. Some of the mothers, clearly designated as spokespersons for the group, spoke in support of Clinton as the right candidate to implement gun reform laws and as a compassionate person in her understanding of their grief. As one of the mothers, Lucia McBath, put it, "Hillary Clinton isn't afraid to say Black Lives Matter. She isn't afraid to sit at the table with a group of grieving mothers and bear the full force of our anguish. She doesn't build walls around her heart" (CNN, 2016, 4:36). Hillary Clinton herself has drawn on her maternal status, cowriting a children's book with her daughter, Chelsea Clinton, titled *Grandma's Garden* and discussing the importance of grand-motherhood to her evolving view of the world.

As previously argued, the Mothers of the Movement remember their dead children within an intersubjective community of bereaved mothers, extended family members, and fictive kin. They use social media and other public forums to reach wide audiences and explain why their children's lives cannot be lost in vain. They extend their personal loss to include a public recognition of the dead. In speaking about the nightmare experienced from watching her daughter, Sandra Bland, lowered into the ground, Geneva Reed-Veal used the DNC platform to call out the names of the women who died in custody in the same month as her Sandra. In memoriam, she called the names of Kindra Chapman, Alexis McGovern, Sarah Lee Circle Bear, Raynette Turner, Ralkina Jones, and Joyce Curnell. We understand this act as akin to acknowledging the ancestors in some African diaspora religions (e.g., Murrell, 2010).

The women at the DNC further spoke about how they continued to see themselves as mothers and how they continued to parent, even though their children were no longer physically present: "You don't stop being a mom when your child dies, you don't stop being a parent. I am still Jordan Davis's mother. His life ended the day that he was shot and killed for playing loud music, but my job as his mother didn't. I still wake up every day thinking about his legacy, how to ensure that his death doesn't overshadow his life" (Lucia McBath, as cited in CNN, 2016, 3:00; see also Drabold, 2016).

Indeed, for the Mothers of the Movement, the memory of their dead children lives on in the political practices of mothering, though of a different sort from how this is typically understood. This is a type of mothering for justice that ostensibly responds to the question "Are you still a mother if your child is dead?" When Michelle Kenney, mother of slain teenager Antwon Rose II[1] was asked "What gets you up and what keeps you going?" she replied: "Be his mom. And even in death, everyday, I don't even have to remind myself, I know that is my son. And nobody is going to fight harder for him than me . . . I've been doing it all my life. [That's] all I know" (Good Morning America, 2020, 7:00). Kenney's desire to continue mothering points both to holding on to and transforming her maternal identity for political purpose. In the physical absence of her son, she has re-created a present and a future where the memory of him will live on through her political work, with the hope that others will continue her activism when she dies.

In addition to sharing stories about their deceased children, some of the mothers displayed pictures of their children to a public audience, which we understand as a specific commemorative strategy meant to bring them to life. For example, when Sybrina Fulton took the mic at the DNC in support of Clinton, a picture of her son, Trayvon, appeared briefly on the screen behind her. This is an iconic black and white image of Trayvon dressed in a hoodie with his face filling the frame. This is also the picture that appears on hoodies worn at protest rallies across the country to commemorate Trayvon while advocating for racial justice. Indeed, similar pictures of the young man with his mother and younger brother were also part of a counternarrative to honor his memory. In her brief speech at the DNC, Fulton told the audience that "this isn't about being politically correct, this is about saving our children. That's why we're here tonight with Hillary Clinton, and that's why in memory of our children, we are imploring you to vote this election day" (CNN, 2016, 7:47). Here, we see a stark example of a straight line between children's deaths and the deployment of their memories as a conduit for political and legal reform. As well, Fulton located her faith in Clinton in her embodied understanding of being a mother, noting, "Hillary is one mother who can ensure our movement will succeed" (CNN, 2016, 8:20).

Bereaved Mothers on *Good Morning America*

Following the death of George Floyd on May 25, 2020, seven Black mothers of murdered children participated in an interview on *Good Morning America* on July 13, 2020. The group included mothers who cofounded the Movement (e.g., Fulton and Carr), as well as mothers whose children had been more recently murdered (Tamika Palmer and Wanda Cooper-Jones).[2] The mothers gathered on Zoom to speak with Deborah Roberts, the journalist who interviewed them, with a focus on remembering their children—to talk about their feelings of grief and discuss how they continue to memorialize their children through their activism. The mothers who had lost children more recently addressed the importance of having a community to help them navigate a strange and painful world, marked by a trauma only another bereaved mother could understand.

Several of the mothers—in particular, Samaria Rice (Tamir Rice), Fulton, and Kenney (Antwon Rose)—held America responsible for the deaths of their, and other Black, children, thus illuminating the role of racial violence that is central to the formation of the United States. Fulton captured this sentiment of state involvement in the murders of Black people by articulating her complicated feelings that led to her decision to attend George Floyd's funeral: "I was okay with being at the George Floyd funeral, but then once I saw the body, I was like, America did this to him. This is the result of the ugliness in America. And it hurt so bad. And it took me a while to get it together because I just, I kept asking God why, why did this have to happen? Why am I looking at a man in this casket who should have just been arrested instead of being killed?" (Good Morning America, 2020, 27:40).

In Fulton's assessment, the U.S. racial state and the centrality of anti-Black violence within it is instrumental in the deaths of African Americans. This assessment stems from a history of racial violence against African Americans that frames shared cultural memories among this group. Notably, as she spoke, Fulton's background was organized with pictures of her son, prompting the reporter to ask: "I'm looking at those pictures of Trayvon behind you. Is there a day that goes by that you don't think about him?" (Good Morning America, 2020, 49:04). Fulton spoke most strongly and forcefully about the importance of remembering her son and the steps she took to reclaim his image so that she could manage her exposure to pain. She stated: "When I first started out, the hoodie would make me sad. Now, when I see a hoodie, I smile about it because I've tried and reprogrammed myself to say, that's a memory of my son. So, you just have to think that in memory of your son . . . or daughter . . . I still cry eight years later, and I don't apologize for crying. Those are my tears. That was my son. And so, when I cry, I know that a brighter day is coming" (Good Morning America, 2020, 5:12).

The mothers in this interview also spoke of the emotional toll of working to keep their children's memories alive, with Fulton likening her feelings to post-traumatic stress disorder. Specifically, Allison Jean, whose son Botham Jean was killed by a police officer in his own home, addressed the complications of pain and memory in advocating for social change: "I am so sorry. Sorry for all these families because we all suffer the pain. Birthdays are no longer the same. Anniversaries are no longer the same. . . . I didn't want to see other people happy. I was so sad that if somebody, a random person at a mall or in a supermarket would laugh, I would feel like holding them and beating them up. I didn't want to see people laughing because I lost a son who did not deserve to die in the way that he did" (Good Morning America, 2020, 18:59). This particular reference to birthdays and anniversaries encapsulates the profound loss of celebratory milestones that create memories in the moment, as well as for the future. Mothers who experience this loss must find ways to preserve memories that mark important milestones and to create new ones by registering their children's existences in the public archives through their activist work.

However, the memorializing practices to which the women refer in these media interviews are not without problems. Remembering a deceased child whose body is the iconic symbol of violence in the racial state complicates their grief and memories. Some women address the ways in which they reclaim or contain public use of images that undermine their own memories of their children in the social justice landscape. Lezley McSpadden explained that this is, in part, one of the reasons she wrote *Tell the Truth and Shame the Devil* (2015). According to McSpadden, "I wrote the book because I wanted everyone to know who Michael Brown was. They had no idea who Michael Brown was and he was being judged and his character was being diminished" (Viera, 2016, para. 7). Concerned that social movements were using her son's name and image without consulting the family, McSpadden explained that she began to keep a journal to track false representations, to correct them, and to preserve the memory of her son in the process: "Anytime I saw something that was just false, things making him look bad, I would write in my book the truth: who he really was, things he really did, aspirations that he had, things he said to his brothers and sisters, how he was with them, and how he made me a mother" (Viera, 2016, para. 7). McSpadden's experience illuminates the contested terrain of memory preservation within the complicated landscape of public grief, racial justice, and the manipulation of the images of deceased children that no longer belong to just their families. This means that, in the depths of grief, bereaved mothers and their families must also reclaim, preserve, or share memories of their children within a public culture where these memories engender multiple meanings that are not always in the interest of the deceased person and those who are left to grieve. This is part of the work that Mothers of the Movement must do so that their children are remembered in the fullness of their humanity rather than being reduced to racial tropes.

Conclusion

The types of remembrance practices engaged by bereaved Black mothers outlined in this chapter are not unique. However, within worlds of racial violence that devalue Black lives, memorializing deceased children in intersubjective communities with the aim of challenging such violence engenders unique meanings. Memorializing practices such as public talks, pictures, interviews, books, and establishing trusts and foundations in the name of murdered Black children are part of our shared cultural memory. In the context of the afterlife of slavery, it is difficult to think about these remembrance practices outside of the shared epistemologies of cultural memory. Differently stated, acts of remembrance among bereaved Black mothers shows us that death, although biologically final, continues to perpetuate its own unequal relations of power that must be confronted long after the deceased person is buried. This, we argue, is the type of work that bereaved maternal activists continue to do "in the wake," as Sharpe (2006) described.

Although the Mothers of the Movement is a social movement, it is also clear that they represent a bereaved community that supports other Black families in the aftermath of other lives tragically taken. The women in this Movement have emerged as public figures in American life and share similar objectives for reshaping the American state. Although we focus here on remembrance practices for social change, Williams (2016) has reminded us of the "ubiquitous presence of grief in the lives of Black women" (p. 22). The vast majority of Black women grieve privately for children and grandchildren whose names never make the agendas of political parties or social movements. This is a reminder of the need to honor all of the ways that Black women and their families grieve their children, and of the importance of attending to the limits of iconic representations of grief centered on remembering lives taken, against the forgetting of other children's lives.

Finally, we locate the Mothers of the Movement in a transnational network of social and biological mothers who deploy maternal activism for environmental and economic justice, reproductive rights, democratic participation, and an end to patriarchal, militarized violence. As anti-Black violence embedded in racial capitalism is a global phenomenon, possibilities exist for the Mothers of the Movement to expand or develop collaborative networks with transnational social justice organizations beyond the borders of the United States. Such a move would facilitate more critical pathways to challenging anti-Black violence, in which the United States is foundationally implicated. The particularities of these types of concerns are threaded together across borders by women's engagement of strategies that memorialize deceased children. As such, memorialization and remembrance practices are forms of resistance against state violence that hold untapped possibilities for expanded transnational collaborations among bereaved mothers.

Notes

1 Antwon Rose II was murdered by a police officer in Pittsburgh on June 19, 2018.
2 Although Mothers of the Movement reached out to support Tamika Palmer, Wanda Cooper-Jones, and Allison Jean, whose children were killed in recent years, we do not know if these particular women are members of the Movement.

12

The Embroidering for Peace Initiative

• •

Crafting Feminist Politics and
Memorializing Resistance to the
"War on Drugs" in Mexico

CORDELIA RIZZO

This chapter narrates the history of the Embroidering for Peace Initiative, a transnational network of activists and embroidery-based protest founded in 2011 that continues to challenge militarization in Mexico, and surveys the experiences of participants who embroidered in public spaces during the last year of Felipe Calderon's presidency in 2012. I mobilize a transnational feminist framework to argue that embroidery as political praxis offers a uniquely effective medium through which to confront state violence and to hold collective space to know, acknowledge, and feel the absence of loved ones lost as a result of political violence. I contend that the tactility of absence rendered possible through embroidery frames the quarrel with the state and its attack on freedom of thought and feeling to dissuade further political opposition. I argue that using touch to communicate politically is necessary to cut through the divisive, silencing impacts of armed violence. It is an oblique response to rhetorical aggressions from a state that still refuses to take responsibility for the crimes it has perpetrated.

173

I came to the Embroidering for Peace Initiative as a member of the Monterrey embroidering collective, comprised of mothers of the disappeared and other activists. We gathered weekly at the Lucila Sabella Kiosk in Monterrey (an industrial hub in northeastern Mexico), attended national protests together, showed solidarity with other groups, and later became an organization, Forces United in Search for Our Disappeared (FUNDENL). We followed the embroidery collective Fuentes Rojas's (Red Fountains) instruction to sew killings in red thread onto white handkerchiefs, and the mothers embroidered enforced disappearances in green to express the hope of seeing their loved ones return to their homes alive. Sewing stories of loss in the cloth challenged me to revise the intellectual frameworks I was trained to cherish. The research for this piece comes from online and offline participant observation and in-depth interviews from 2012 to 2015 with the Embroidering for Peace collective in my native Monterrey, Nuevo León, and with embroiderers from other collectives. I consulted electronic newspaper databases to contextualize events that sparked the embroiderers' early efforts. This inquiry is part of a larger project exploring touch through textile art as a site of political resistance.

The Embroidering for Peace Initiative's installations and embroidery in public spaces responded directly to the consequences of President Felipe Calderon's demonstration of power on December 11, 2006. That day, Calderon gave a congratulatory speech to the army and the newly created Federal Police in Ahuehuetes, Mexico State. Seven thousand troops were already positioned through Operativo Conjunto Michoacan (Michoacan Joint Operation), and more would go "wherever it would be necessary"[1] to eliminate the alleged social threat posed by drug trafficking. Military operations later intensified at the United States-Mexico border, where several historical epicenters of contraband and drug trafficking are located.

Operativo Conjunto Chihuahua (Chihuahua Joint Operation) focused on policing the border of Ciudad Juárez and El Paso, Texas. The scholar and journalist Dawn Marie Paley (2020) argued that "the border became an axis of the drug war in Mexico" (p.144), as part of her thesis that military operations essentially secure extractivist enterprises by displacing families in key territories. Ciudad Juárez, a former neoliberal haven for manufacturing industries, was known as the murder capital of the world by 2010, according to the Woodrow Wilson Center (Petersen, 2010). Federal and local governments stigmatized victims of shootouts. "Collateral damage" was the term used to justify the rising death toll, especially mass killings. Governmental agencies insisted that the increase in brutal violence was a sign of the success of their strategy to end drug trafficking. In a report on rhetorical devices used by Mexican authorities, Article 19's office in Mexico stated that during Calderon's presidency, "The discourse has been of combat, struggle, battle, collateral damage and war" (Rábago & Vergara, 2011, para. 1). Relatives of the victims eventually spoke out against this affront.

The Villas de Salvarcar massacre of 2010 in Ciudad Juárez was one of the effects of Operativo Conjunto Chihuahua. Calderon announced the sixteen young men murdered in the attack were criminals when the news broke. "President, I cannot welcome you here," cried Luz María Davila, one of the mothers of the dead young men, as Calderon waved to stop an aide who seemed to go to whisk Davila away. "We are living the consequences of a war we did not ask for" (Wilkinson, 2010, para. 7). Wilkinson commented in the *Los Angeles Times* on Davila's statement: "It was a highly unusual rebuke from a humble woman in a country that retains paternalistic tendencies and demands a certain reverence for presidential figures" (para. 8). Davila paved the way for more public opposition to official narratives of the drug war.

The renowned Mexican poet Javier Sicilia also spoke out against the logics of the drug war after his son was murdered in 2011. His public statement refuted reports that Juan Francisco Sicilia was member of a drug cartel, and he made a call to occupy the streets and prove the rationale of the war wrong by amplifying the voices of relatives of the victims. Sicilia's press conference—and later communications—reached a wide audience of Mexicans and garnered the support of high-profile public figures like Hollywood actor Edward James Olmos, Mexican actor and director Diego Luna, and human rights defenders like Raul Vera. With this support, Sicilia led two caravans to demand the end of the drug war: one inside Mexico and the other to the United States. The Embroidering for Peace initiative began in Mexico City with the Fuentes Rojas collective response to Sicilia's incitation. Added to the impact of the poet's discourse, visualization of handkerchiefs in the streets and in social media gradually expanded the initiative in Mexico City to a transnational network of activists. The action was simple, but it rode on the momentum of the caravans. Its spread proved that it spoke to people.

Embroidering for Peace responded to Sicilia's and Davila's cries by showing stories of the victims silenced in official narratives. Short accounts of where, when, and how someone was murdered were stitched onto white handkerchiefs. Finished pieces hung from clothing lines in public parks and squares such as Calle Madero or Parque de los Coyotes in Mexico City. Text written in the embroideries came from lists obtained from a district attorney's database, direct reports by the person's relatives, and the Barcelona-managed website Menos Días Aquí (menosdiasaqui.blogspot.com), where volunteers registered deaths reported by media outlets up until 2016. Thread colors express different messages: red represents the dead; green is the color of hope to embroider the disappeared; and purple is used to stitch feminicides (murders of women). Drawings or vignettes sometimes adorned the words. The motto of the activity, coined by Ernesto Aroche from the Puebla collective, became, "We are a voice of threads and needles that won't quit; this little place in the world has not succumbed, so we embroider for peace."

In this chapter, I weave fragments of media analysis, interviews, and personal interactions with embroiderers. My objective is to analyze the affective responses that guided the activists at a time when they had little information or idea of how to act. Leticia Hidalgo, the mother of Roy Rivera Hidalgo (disappeared in Monterrey in 2011), reiterated in a recent interview that state and social institutions failed to disclose information about the losses and impacts of their offensive against organized crime. This chapter is a snapshot of what the network of embroiderers became and the potential of the communities it created. I focus on its origins to capture how the initiative became a complex space of political articulation and contestation of the state's monopoly over information and memory.

Vulnerability and Memory Work in Mexico

Judith Butler's (2004) notion of "precarious life" proves useful to unravel Luz María Davila's defense of her right to mourn while she contests official state narratives. Precarity becomes very present in grief, where one feels "the thrall in which our relations with others hold us, in ways we cannot always recount or explain ... in ways that challenge the very notion of ourselves as autonomous and in control" (Butler, 2004, p. 23). In this case, the official state narrative discourages public outrage about Davila's sons' deaths. When held by a community in solidarity, mourning should healthily transmute the loss. On this topic, Butler signaled that "perhaps mourning has to do with agreeing to do a transformation (perhaps one should say *submitting* to a transformation) the full result of which one cannot know in advance [emphasis original]" (p. 21). Drawing on Butler's prompt about mourning, it would be reasonable to expect that the work of mourning involves a fair amount of unpredictability, a lack of control that is not supposed to be heroically mastered. I interpret Davila's and Sicilia's defense of their children's memories as a way to claim their right to have a space and a community to sit with the feeling of precarity that is so central to the experience of mourning.

Luz María Davila and Javier Sicilia were not alone in their bereavement, as the death toll suggests. Per the International Crisis Group (2013), the death toll after 2006 ascended to seventy thousand by 2013 (para. 4). According to news outlets *Animal Politico* and *Semanario Zeta*, the number in 2012 was closer to 150,000. Homicide victims included those killed in shootouts and extrajudicial executions, as well as innocent bystanders. Enforced disappearances were not even mentioned or reported officially until in 2012, when the Ministry of the Interior leaked to the *Washington Post* a list of more than twenty-six thousand people "missing" on President Calderon's last day in office.

Fuentes Rojas began the embroidering initiative in 2011 as a way to collectively share and hold space for the precarity of this loss. Their group's name was derived from their first public action, where they dyed several of Mexico City's water fountains red in solidarity with Javier Sicilia. Disruptive actions like theirs shook feelings of impotence and were crucial to raise awareness about the weight of the deaths, treated as "ungrievable" (Butler, 2004) by dominant narratives.

When authorities enforce stigmas and ungrievability, they interfere with the emotional tasks and memory work needed to transform loss. In thinking through bereavement, according to Leader (2009), "The sequential work of moving through memories and hopes tied to the loved person allows, so to say, a gradual process of fractioning the agony and nostalgia" (p. 171). Mourning implies additional stress through intensive examination of memories and sensations, for there is something that remains unknowable (Blanchot, 1989; Butler, 2004). Publicly defaming the dead and stereotyping them complicates the unknowability germane to grieving because it performs a denial of the spatial and communal conditions of possibility to mourn. Stigma implicitly instructs the larger community to deny the grieving person a space to host their process.

There is a wealth of insights coming from human rights reports in Latin America that chronicle the relationship between public stigmatization, trauma, and the inability to mourn. Carlos Beristain, a medical expert, stated in a lecture at the Mexican National Human Rights Commission about dealing with the aftermath of the infamous disappearance of the forty-three students from the Ayotzinapa Teaching College in May of 2015 that "the stigmatized victim is different than the one who is socially recognized." To better understand his statement, an earlier article addressing the victims of terrorism in the Basque Country expounds on why recognition is essential to mourning: "Many victims feel as injury that the perpetrators have not acknowledged the damage, and that there has not been a rejection of the violence [they exercised]" (Beristain, 2006, para. 9). Recognition therefore constitutes an immediate reparative gesture given that "the admission of the facts by the perpetrators as well as the actions that will aid to assume this truth as part of the moral conscience of the Basque and Spanish societies" contributes to the improvement of those who suffered in the conflict (para. 16). To admit blame publicly, as Beristain held, aids the sustenance of a communal space where the loss can be accompanied by others.

News outlets work to elide public and governmental responsibility in the rising death toll, complicating grieving processes. Journalist Michelle Garcia (2010) observed that deeper questions about militarization in Mexico are harder to ask when news pieces fixate on sensational aspects of the violence. She wrote about how such pieces "focus on body counts and decapitations and ignore a number of relevant questions that would have framed the story much differently. For instance, did Calderon launch an internal war to legitimize his presidency?" (p. 17). Citizen-led media outlets should pose deeper questions that could help to dismantle the logics of militarization. For example, an article published in *Borderland Beat* doubted government reports contending that those killed in shootouts could be simply called "collateral damage": "It is hard to believe that while the media have access to witnesses and personnel involved, they could not know that innocent people were killed and that the official statement was not credible. The reason we question this is because not long after several incidents we started to receive e-mails from people who were reporting that innocent people had been killed in some shootouts, contrary to military reports. The majority of reporting of these events has come from social media such as Facebook, Twitter, and blogs" (Buggs, 2015, para. 7). Citizen-led journalism—through blogs, Twitter, and Facebook—rose to prominence given the biases of news media outlets during this time. Even more sensational blogs like *El Blog del Narco* (elblogdelnarco.com) became popular outlets.

Embroidering for Peace: Finding a Grammar to Resist Erasure by the State

Embroidering as memory work establishes a counternarrative to totaling deaths and losses as "collateral damage." It directly follows Javier Sicilia's provocation to claim the streets and show that victims are not merely numbers. Before Sicilia's reckoning, Rossana Reguillo's (2011) work on the narco machine chronicled how citizen-led efforts to carefully create an inventory of the losses of the drug war paved the way for what embroidery eventually encompassed as a medium of expression: "We count the dead, but the gesture is useless because we cannot reclaim their humanity, nor stitch the tears the machine leaves in its wake. Violence is unidirectional, there is no reciprocal violence by virtue of it being inflicted by the phantasmagorical condition of the machine" (para. 9). Reguillo's conception of militarized violence aptly indicates the type of wound it inflicts. Militarized violence is designed to instill a haunting that continuously terrorizes the victims' loved ones and their community. Hence, the response to the language of this wound must be a gesture that adequately identifies the unidirectionality and impersonal quality of the machine. Embroidering words, dates, and numbers became a practice that made the phantasmagorical quality of death, violence, and loss manageable.

A first look at the Embroidering for Peace Initiative shows embroiderers directly countered the sensationalist coverage of violence by taking time to deal with each individual death. Even though not all of the deaths and disappearances found their way to embroidery, each one of them is rendered symbolically embroiderable. It enables each loss to achieve representation and to be humanized (Butler, 2004, p. 141). The complete name of Fuentes Rojas's project in 2011, fittingly, was Embroidering for Peace and Memory: One Victim, One Handkerchief. The call to action in February 2012 established that the objective of embroidering was to "posit a symbolic approximation to each individual tragedy that is known to us only as a spectacle through the media. The embroideries will be shown in public squares throughout the country! You can suggest other ways of making them noticeable" (Gargallo, 2014, p. 59).

The Oaxacan artist Monica Ituribarria's (2009) personal artistic project *1/40,000 Ante el Dolor de los Demás* (Regarding the pain of others) inspired Fuentes Rojas's decision to embroider. Ituribarria printed newspaper and magazine news pieces onto white handkerchiefs and then traced the text with thread.

Her project drew from Susan Sontag's (2003) writing on the spectacularity of war photography and challenged the inertia of mainstream media through embroidering. As Ituribarria stated in an artist statement, "I choose reflecting upon violent deaths and the indifference of those who listen to or read the chronicle of a death as if it was a war movie; [I reflect upon] humanity's indifference, only thinking that this sort of thing happens in the movies and as a spectacle."

Ituribarria was not involved in how her project was taken up by Embroidering for Peace and the momentum it established, as she acknowledged during an interview in 2014. Nevertheless, the form she chose allowed makers and spectators to pay attention to details of the story portrayed and resist the grip of sensationalist press. Ituribarria's conceptualization remains part of the history of the Embroidering for Peace Initiative, as Katia Olalde (2018) contended. Embroiderer Teresa Sordo, who founded the embroidering group in Guadalajara, recounted to me in November of 2013 how she has been attentive to the flow of activity at each embroidering meeting:

> The embroidery began as a protest, but each Sunday comes with something new: each person who arrives, and the chance to come together with the women who constitute the collective, and how we have come together to work, to understand, and to reflect what we did after each Sunday; we sit [there] to look, to understand what is going on. I have changed greatly and feel satisfaction when I see that there is a different way to pose the question. It is a denouncement, but it is also an invitation to change things, to reflect, to believe in a different way to communicate and finally to work for peace.

Sordo's testimony animates how communal embroidering exercises different ways of critiquing difficult events and dealing with painful experiences and how it mobilizes individuals and collectives politically.

As a practice and tradition, embroidery achieves several goals because of its symbolic and evocative nature. Elia Andrade Olea from Fuentes Rojas stressed that on the one hand, "It is an encounter with an other, and it is to repair, symbolically, the social fabric" (Montero, 2012, para. 9). The capacity to repair comes from the traditional character of embroidering and the pleasant associations that accompany its performance. The art therapist and semiologist Victor Fuenmayor (2011) described the pleasure in the practice of popular arts such as embroidering as a remembrance of a deeper procedural memory that is latent: "The real popular traditions, those we think of as our own, live inside us and are inscribed in our body. They are part of actions that we understand or part of knowledge of the procedures to create" (p. 5). As a metaphor for mending, sewing is one of the "diverse bodily practices" that humans engage in that are "complex expressive manifestations, including somatic, physical, cognitive, emotional, and spiritual dimensions, use of spaces, rhythmic synchronies that can be felt and followed by a community" (p. 10). This remembrance of something seemingly innate, as Fuenmayor stressed, is tied with pleasure, even if it is done to memorialize something painful.

Meetings to hang embroideries and place more handkerchiefs in public spaces transformed pleasant feelings and memories of sewing into increased awareness, information shared in conversation, and hope that something can be done against the machinery of the state. Several embroiderers reported feeling helpless when a certain piece of news touched them deeply. Mariana López from Puebla, whose mother Gabriela González List also embroidered there, contrasted this emotion with the sensation of possibility that embroidery gave her. In an interview toward the end of 2012, she put it as "knowing that despite the feelings of impotence, there is something you can actually do with your hands". While in the Plaza de la Democracia in Puebla, Mariana also had the opportunity to teach others to how to embroider.

Most embroiderers for peace in Mexico performed and exhibited their art in public; squares, parks, and populated pedestrian streets were filled with embroideries hanging from clothing lines. As the news pieces indicate, public spaces in some of these cities were considered unsafe. Gargallo (2014) rightly argued in her book about Embroidering for Peace that "in a country where the most uttered phrase is 'you can no longer leave the house,' embroidering in public space is revolutionary" (p. 51). A few groups chose to perform in private, especially in places where they endured harassment by police, such as Torreón, or spaces with cold weather, like Montreal and Paris. Some gathered periodically— weekly or monthly—to do this for years, including Fuentes Rojas in Mexico City, Embroidering for Peace in Mexico from Barcelona, Embroidering for Peace– Guadalajara, and Embroidering for Peace–Argentina. Others met once a week until the embroideries were exhibited on Avenida Juárez, one of the main streets in Mexico City, when Calderon left office on December 1, 2012.

Touch as Political Resistance and as Seed of Transnational Connection

I emphasize touch as a medium for memorialization because relating to a fearful community through talking about sensations became a crucial way to grow as a network of embroiderers. As makers, we shared stories of how it felt to prick the cloth with the needle. Through continuous sharing of sensations, the objective of the initiative became clear: an experience of feeling was at the center of our brand of memory work. These exchanges were more meaningful when pictures of made pieces showed up in social media and connected people via the shared practice of embroidering to protest militarized violence in Mexico. Small differences in materials, stitches, and environments tacitly showed each of the smaller groups that they were accompanied in their processes by more people, especially women, who shared emotions about violent events in the country.

To understand the force and continuity of the embroidering practice as a network, I look at it as a space of situated knowledge production. There are agreements about thread color and size of the cloth stick, but every hand that sews experiences something different. When embroiderers discuss these events, their conversations allow them to notice the unique labors differently located participants put into this political exercise. Alexander and Mohanty (2010) identified these often-ignored convergences in *Cartographies of Knowledge and Power*, where they signaled that "knowledge is produced by activist and community-based political work" (p. 27). Knowledge is not only produced but enriched because "some knowledges can only emerge within these contexts and locations" (p. 27). Therefore, though all sites adopted some form of embroidery, their interactions as sites of knowledge production in and of themselves also contributed to what is already known about embroidery as a form of praxis.

Embroidery is a practice of creating texture, which is felt with the tip of one's fingers. As a technique, embroidery mirrors mourning in that it requires focus, patience, and endurance. The practice of sewing in public spaces and displaying the products on social media provided material and virtual spaces for political assembly and the performance of loss. According to Manning's *Politics of Touch* (2006), touching enables a person who is wounded by violence to explore a way of expression, such as embroidery, and through its practice—characterized by perseverance—"invent, event-fully, what a body can do" (p. 59). Manning's description of a reinventing activity fits well with what embroiderers were implicitly finding through meditation, action, grassroots accounts of the war, and reaching out to others: there is an alternative to conforming to the government's lack of accountability.

Testimony from embroiderers like Marcela Valero in Monterrey also give insight into why embroidery endured as a way of protest. Valero embroidered weekly at Plaza Zaragoza in the center of Monterrey in 2012, after FUNDENL tried various other ways of raising awareness about enforced disappearances. In her own words in an interview in 2015, "I think [its appeal] has to do with several things, on the one hand, the ease of moving the materials and embroideries. On the other hand, I believe that the graphic expression of the embroidery is stronger compared to that of the shoes [previously also used to protest]. The letters in red, green, etc. capture the attention of the one who reads them the white background from where they stand out. The handkerchief is also more nostalgic."

De Alwis (this volume) talks about a similar context of enforced disappearances in Sri Lanka during the late 1980s and early 1990s. Because disappearance is the type of violence that "seeks to obliterate the body," objects might succeed in affectively conveying absence and the hope of finding the disappeared because they embody what is missed from them with poetic precision. She writes: "Particularly poignant was how this mother continued to articulate her relationship to this piece of clothing through her materialized labor of care-taking, of doing laundry. Such a labor also invoked her care-taking of her son—of washing him, of washing his clothes; both tasks which could no longer be performed because of his (physical) absence as well as his absent presence (his scent)." By literally touching the narration, whether the person is embroidering the words or touching them on a handkerchief that is already embroidered, the witness began to relate to that part of the war story sidelined by media outlets. That fragment of the story tended to be details about the ordinary lives of the disappeared that capture them as people—that humanize them. Textures, meant to be touched, center such details.

In the context of Embroidering for Peace, for embroiderer Diana Martínez from Monterrey (interviewed in 2015), touch is "presence; it makes someone tangible, to be there, to feel him or her." Thus, touch as an experience contrasts with the spectacular nature of mainstream information that aims to erase the person. Manning (2006) saw this disposition of care and concern in touch and wrote, "To touch is to tender, to be tender, to reach out tenderly" (p. 377). In most of the fragments of testimonies to which I refer, there is an implied desire to show care or to tend for the vulnerable ones—those who have been hurt by the war. Teresa Carmona Lobo, an embroiderer from Cancun whose son Joaquin García Jurado was murdered brutally in August of 2010 in Mexico City stated in an interview in 2015, "It is a very emotional sense [touch]; it allows me to caress and when a thread gets tangled; it is like an exercise of searching for meaning, of developing patience; it is an apt way to resolve difficulties; it allows me to undo the knot, stitch onto the fabric again, and build a loving and caressed memory." Carmona Lobo was part of the first cohort of activists and citizens who accompanied Javier Sicilia to both caravans in 2011. She slowly filled a white handkerchief with colorful stitching to honor her son.

Touch as a political resource is not new. It emerges from the persistent need to think differently about politics, outside of frameworks that ignore affectivity as a complex political means (Mouffe, 2007 p. 1) and that privilege speech and verbal language as means of truth-telling. Mouffe explored play and affect when discussing Wittgensteinian language games to advance her concept of agonistic pluralism. She stated that democratic action requires something other than the perfecting of verbal argumentation required in political activity. It demands "a manifold of practices and pragmatic moves aiming to persuade people to broaden the range of their commitments to others, to build a more inclusive community" (p. 4). Mouffe called to attention the limits and dangers of narrowing the notion of who is human and worthy through the tools aimed to craft democratic culture. Stigmas that dull the impact of some deaths, as mentioned before, are constructed and enforced through such discursivity. Touch interrupts the emphasis on discursivity and its vices that exclude nonhegemonic ideas, notions, and experiences of the human, instead inviting people to conceive of and explore political alternatives.

Manning (2006) leads us to look at what is engendered when we inform our political stances through touch, permitting us "to evoke a pluralism that radically departs from Aristotelian thought and celebrates a demystification of the naturalizations that allow ends to become means" (p. 286). Carmona's "caressed memory" is thus a means of resistance. When she spoke about "undoing the knot" in the embroidery, she reflected her personal stance but also represented the dead end that many families seem to encounter when they seek justice. The need to shift the discussion to a victim-centered approach is central for the mothers of the victims and shared by those who participate in the embroidering network, as depicted in Martinez's testimony. Manning referred to these capacities of touch as a political glue, as "resistance, this surge to touch others, wound against wound, that potentially creates a community of resistance, a complex, disorderly, incommensurable community of those who cannot keep themselves from reaching out toward the world" (p. 343).

Touch can facilitate different ways of relating to the often unshareable experiences of pain and grief. María Herrera, the mother of four young men who were disappeared in Guerrero and Michoacán between 2008 and 2010, expressed at the Universidad Autonoma Metropolitana Xochimilco in 2014 that "if there was a pain meter, our pain [mothers of the disappeared] would be off the scales." Respectful of the intensity of such distress, rather than trying to crack it open, "Touch induces a repetition, a response that is unique, since it is a search for the *unknowable*" (Manning, 2006, p.37). Mourning, as Butler stated, implies closeness to unknowability. Herrera does not know where her children are but refuses to deal with their absences as deaths. Touching is mindful of the inscrutability of pain like Herrera's and accepts its existence.

Distance, Frustration, and Connection outside of Mexico

Abroad, embroidering groups functioned to link Mexican migrants to a larger community of resistance trying to understand experiences of loss in the context of violence in their home country. Nina Hasegana, a Mexican migrant who has lived in Tokyo for more than half her life, holds that, "Embroidering connects us with the embroiderers from here [Tokyo], and it is an act of presence [with the wider community of activists]. First and foremost, we are all embroiderers for peace. We are a community." Nina belongs to the International Network for Peace in Mexico, and, as an activist, she translated videos into Japanese and was also in charge of updating social media. The group was composed of Mexicans, Colombians, Spaniards, and Japanese nationals who gathered regularly at the Cafe Lavanderia, owned by Colombians. They embroidered Japanese designs with Spanish texts. Hasegana emphasized in our conversation that the quietude of the act of embroidering was more appealing to the people in Tokyo than traditional public demonstrations.

Solidarity also came from non-Mexican nationals who exercise their right to be in solidarity with Mexico. A good example of transnational solidarity happened in Durham, United Kingdom, where Jamie-Leigh Ruse coordinated an embroidering group in 2013. On the community-articulating quality of textile protest she remarked, "One of the objectives was to raise awareness of what was happening in Mexico amongst Mexicans in the university, and amongst other foreign and home students." Her doctoral dissertation studied how a community of Mexican migrants in Barcelona got involved with activism that questioned the "war on drugs." Ruse also observed, "I think the main impact was the sense of community it gave to the group, and the awareness it raised amongst those who participated in it. I think it gave everyone a sense of contributing to something meaningful, but in a way which, at least verbally, is un-articulable." A Catalonian embroiderer from Barcelona, who asked to remain anonymous, described the reactions of the passers-by: "The reaction is positive. Besides how much we like the embroidery as a technique, I believe we have to appreciate it is well received to a great degree. It is something objectively beautiful, and, in any case, for a few highly conscientious persons, it can be considered too 'soft.'" It serves as a pedagogical tool to raise awareness but also, "It has happened that passers-by from Mexico stopped [to see the embroideries], either they live here temporarily or are only on vacation in the city. They ended up staying to embroider their own relatives." In this involvement, there is a political gesture that generates a positive sensation in those who grieve, even when they are far from home. Embroiderers touch the cloth but also are touched by the memories and the company of others.

Embroidering as Collective Flow

Even when the stitched stories do not identify the person by name, which happens often, no death or loss is deemed unworthy of being embroidered because each presence means something collectively. Regina Méndez, a member of Fuentes Rojas from Mexico City, clarified this decision: "The initial discussion of the group was whether we had to embroider, or not embroider, the names and the stories of military officials, police, and murdered criminals. We decided that their names must not be forgotten for us; they are essential in the search of a collectivity, in the reconstruction of public space. Each death speaks about one of us, because the people that inhabit public space constitute the 'we'" (Gargallo, 2014, pp. 55–56).

Embroidering couches experiences of wonder, tenderness, and political engagement, yet the same attributes that make it attractive are ironically the reasons why it is not viewed as serious enough. Lorde (1984) explored the patriarchal suspicion of experiences pleasure in seemingly mundane housework and feminine expressions of affect and enriched a narrow-minded notion of political and coalitional work by validating the excluded ways of knowing embodied in experiences of domestic labor and feminine emotion. She stressed that this immersion into wonderment is necessary and politically relevant: "As women we need to examine the ways in which our world can be truly different. I am speaking here of the necessity of reassessing the quality of all the aspects of our lives and our work and how we move toward and through them" (p. 55). The embroiderers' dedication to a domestic activity tacitly embraces Lorde's decision to hold the power of the erotic as a gift to be discovered and used. Sewing as a repetitive activity mimics the meditative quality of scrutinizing the political landscape that Lorde implies in the above passage, including assessing how those who protest can also exacerbate the conditions they intend to change.

In a 2013 interview, I asked Leticia Hidalgo how she thought one ought to face the machinery of the state she has intimately experienced while searching for her son Roy Rivera Hidalgo since 2011. Hidalgo mentioned that embroidery is the "sublime" weapon that can truly interpellate the monstrous apparatus of a state. In this case, a necessary consideration is that the state is in cahoots with the alleged criminals it is supposed to pursue. The persistence of embroidering as a memorialization practice opened numerous possibilities for the participants in Monterrey. After nine months of embroidering, conversing, and participating as a group in other political activities, Hidalgo and the other participants of Embroidering for Peace in Monterrey consolidated the aforementioned organization that searches for the disappeared, FUNDENL. Hidalgo stated several times that the embroidering initiative "created FUNDENL." Formalizing the constitution of the group gave her and others a more powerful presence with political interlocutors. Similarly, Guadalajara's Families United for our Disappeared in Jalisco started convening thanks to Embroidering for Peace in Guadalajara. Guadalajara's passionate group of embroiderers oriented their efforts after 2012 to supporting the mothers and relatives of the disappeared.

Conclusion: Undoing the Grammar of Violence

In this chapter, I set out to describe the emergence of the Embroidering for Peace Initiative as a response to militarized violence, an oppressive news cycle, and stigmatization of the victims of the "war on drugs." Instead of merely disputing what government and media report, activists sewing the stories of each victim in the cloth sought to embody what these outlets made too abstract: deaths and absence. As a process, embroidering is too slow to memorialize each of the losses, yet it remains powerful enough to engage participants in different, more transformative trains of thought and action.

Unfortunately, the term "collateral damages" is still used to report murders, enforced disappearances, and feminicides, and forced displacement and militarization as a response to organized crime has increased throughout Mexico. Yet the COVID-19 pandemic in 2020 witnessed the expansion of textile art used to protest repressive exercises of power in many parts of Latin America, including Mexico, and around the world. I do not take for granted why collectives and individuals stick with practices such as embroidering; their capacity to shape narratives via globalized social media is resilient. Thus, I recover testimony that speaks to the power of embroidery to create an experience of presence of those absented by political violence but also of the people who constitute the community of embroiderers. Embroidery's persuasiveness through this performance of presence can unsettle the stigmatization of the dead and the disappeared in Mexico and in other parts of the world. In short, the Embroidering for Peace Initiative memorializes violence and maps out territories of peace. Its capacity to hold violence while simultaneously making space to dream alternative futures makes it an effective means of protecting the work of mourning from the voices and actors that seek to undermine it.

Note

1   This is from a speech given by President Felipe Calderon Hinojosa on December 13, 2006, on the transference of national defense and the navy. The full speech used to be archived at calderon.presidencia.gob.mx. However, as of July 2024 this webpage has been taken down, likely for political reasons related to Calderon's sentencing hearing. References to the speech and its framing of the drug war can be found at https://www.youtube.com/watch?v=984NIjrQ9dw and https://www.resdal.org/caeef-resdal/assets/mexico---anuncio-sobre-la-operaci%C3%B3n-conjunta-michoac%C3%A1n.pdf

13

Epigraph 24584

● ●

In Which She Talks to the Dead and Sometimes the Dead Talk Back

CHARLOTTE HENAY

24584

An address a license plate a phone number   spotty   colloquy   at   the interstices
I asked some time ago if the number meant anything
before floundering speechless   a poet
finding voodoo apps bearing her name
she   blogbookperson
the home for an altar I almost committed our futures to
creating consciousness from collaboration

I must have taken them home forgetting
when my suffering became of service
freed from obligation I chose sister lover mother   I am not her
        child
recklesswildnotsafe binding water and electrical
channels bent to unbridled will
etched into my desk I hold gateways to cyberspace   roads and pathways
inadvertent scrollwork
attest to the knot slowly tightening over a fortnight
reaching at once into ghost story and deathwork
                       I been here waiting
she missed me breathing her in used to lonely
bereft of limbs and heavy silences calls me irresponsible
where she saw combination locks I saw fortune in the making

24584

The pattern clearly coordinates in an Algerian desert or maybe   The
                                          Democratic Republic
                                          of the Congo

archives in court cases a type MO star in the constellation Orion
meteor showers letting go of finding safety in liminal worlds
refuting binaries when I follow her direction I search out contacts
find lwas   ritual descriptions   invocations and crossroads
she favours gatekeepers then dances on coals
to trick stealthily | slipping | through   minute openings
making them into armies undisciplined she is bound
                           24584

to call her through flood and thunder
is foolish I hear there is no
prescription | recipe   single purposed learning
the practice takes a reverence for words
and magic transcendental nausea connects us and I am not

We gat so much god we ain't gat room for nuttin else

afraid

Because they lived there in the triangle of their   lives
doesn't mean they owned those stories you are   what your daddy is
transactions in a matrifocal society we eat that shit up

Despite it constantly spitting you out in the place where houses bear names yet most people don't know dey grammies'   I rise with her name on my tongue to the gaulin on the road home
Mail order death extinguishes any trade in hope the plantocrat in a seeming concession to pigmentocracy opens the door to fat shaming corrupt   darker skinned savages with the audacity to supplant their predecessors' rotten stewardship sewage overflows in the road what have we become
None of this seems odd to me not only that she would speak it and they all nod   come here for five   found wanting there's nothing to see
would you get the cake please I would like to serve it now
here

Move along

We gat so much god we ain't gat room for nuttin else

They serve Chinese food at Mandy's Healthy Kitchen and Bakery on Palmdale Avenue at Bradley
in the place of pencil cactus for shrinking warts
child cries for his daddynotfromhere can't find ease in this bed
              this house this now
pink mohair and thwarted plans to heal
speaking of a preponderance of feminist postcolonial bullshit Mumbo Jumbo
pushingeveryoneelseout

                              takingupallthespace

                              nottheartthattheymake

muddo emblazoned across my centre because your mouth was foul and it is almost dirty and easy yet still incomplete I've come to understand that these idead these talks they are for the moments of inbetween time space and place the ones that were so vibrant and all-consuming explosive love bound the very few breaths times fingertip brushes where you were fiercely my mother more than someone else's daughter far away sister bound these talks they are for revelatory instances of why the breaths were so very few what brought us to these oceans apart again again again is the only reason I am learning to bend time so that I can tell this all to you
without stone dirt sand as translator

We gat so much god we ain't gat room for nuttin else

It's a strange thing to know you are truly in   between. To feel it in your bones as irreversible. I'm trying a mantra today. Repeat the mantras you need.

My body aches. My handsfrom clenching at night. I'm always holding on. Slowly acclimating to what I now understand as being and becoming data, see the north as more comfortable and even less my own. Relinquish everything even my body, only responsibilities. I don't know where to begin that isn't also an ending. Call hardness my own. The effort required for things to run as I understand smoothly is exponential, I both welcome tomorrow and ward against it, lost touch with what my mother would say buried it in old photographs sent the wind packing afraid she won't recognize me as her granddaughter speculation all there is to be is run ya mout amidst this sea of yesterdays and nothingness wonder how many words ink how much.

Feel always as though you are running even in the dark even standing still even when not sure from what or whom this is not what you want to do leave it sit quietly for a while let go the words of others drop the books observe more sleep don't need to write it down smell the blood go deeper get lost in your own heartbeat wonder about nothing sit be so still.

Take time to want nothing.

they learned blackness the church and witness well enough for indentureship
so I sent them seeking contracts   now this one back again thought I told you to take that
fool child home?
Pinned between my assumptions and having perhaps participated in my own debasement
Grammie why are you so shtuuuupid?

night unfurls to the soundtrack of ground spiders escaping flooded lairs they wait for the
unsuspecting shout exhilaration in leaps and bounds covering seven times their body length
uphill after that one she always found trouble or it found her beacon of disbelief and confusion
traded ancestral memory for jaysus' story somebody else's son and the sweet sour smell on
his breath in the morning of all them girls she sold herself didn't need me to pose as mistress
broker strode mincingly beneath pleated cotton traded mother for accomplice smelled that
on him too long kept silences family heirlooms divide us rift upon rift upon rift who dances
with boogiemen and lives to rejoice she withers slowly watches while her own body betrays
her crumbling in time with that same spider soda poppa catch up from in between the louvers
she kept in rubbing alcohol as a curiosity shaken and examined by countless fingers bald
amputee in its old age caught in her own weaving that one floats in septic stasis spirit joined
she and the spider both caught by the same hand

The Contract

I've been listening

I've been thinking

about this seemingly privileged chaos under

tone

ofsurvivalofabuseofaddictionoftoday relatively
comfortable   compared to continued existence
uprootedness commodification bodyfamilyidentitysexyoualitygendher

paid for it   don't make it yours
thisisyourmealticket   if you begin to pay attention
what you have buried is reborn
eight chirren husband dead and

We gat so much god we ain't gat room for nuttin else

gone

under my tongue sandpaper tickles hope

1. By the 1880s, a comprehensive network of selection, transport and delivery of domestic workers to Canada had evolved. The role of Canadian immigration agents in this scheme was to advertise domestic employment and/or offer reduced fares to suitable applicants. Since prospective emigrants often lacked the funds to pay their own way (even at the reduced rate), the fare for passage was sometimes advanced to the Canadian immigration agent by her future employer or, more commonly, by one of the various organizations and businesses engaging in the import/export of domestic servants. The women would subsequently be contractually bound to a specified term of service ranging from six months to a year and would also be required to repay the cost of the assisted passage from wages. So began indentured servitude in Canada.

We gat so much god we ain't gat room for nuttin else

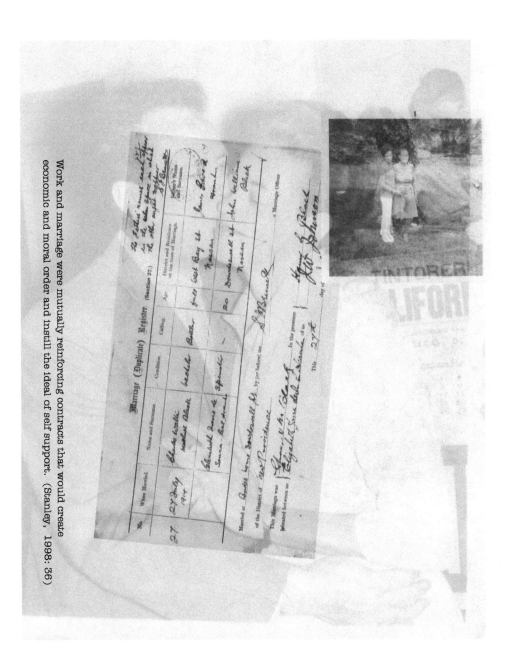

Work and marriage were mutually reinforcing contracts that would create economic and moral order and instill the ideal of self support. (Stanley, 1998: 36)

We gat so much god we ain't gat room for nuttin else

1. Caribbean women did tend to stay in the occupation longer than white domestic servants, though this had less to do with racist assumptions about how amenable Black women were to domestic service than with barriers to exit. Calliste suggests that these were related to discrimination in employment, a lack of recognition of education and skills attained abroad, the stigmatization of domestic work, and a lack of networks within the Canadian Caribbean community. The situation began to change by the late 1950s so that less than a quarter of Caribbean domestic workers stayed in the occupation for more than three years. [See Note 36 below]
2. Note 36: Ibid. at 145.

How much of your mother's retelling was tainted by her own irreconcilable exile, have you ever wondered? Big face and an emaciated body huge hands holding my face and crying, silent. You say you love me, listen to her, watch over her for you. Strongest presence calling twins to resist she sees, now, the power in taking us in. Shells weathered and broken mark her rest the hair on my body pays attention when I visit. I know you haven't given up telling tales, redrawing lines of blame and responsibility. But some stories aren't meant to be told not even in whispers what ifs and thens once uttered they converge into irrevocable quantum possibilities and I have to look away. Reprieve not sought from bottled guilt or half formed regret I ache from wounds leaking gin and need. As your heart malfunctions blossoms form flour frying pan freedoms sick up and you look so sad. They say wait, wait, waiting reverberates through my ancestry endless replay rests in mitochondria or maybe it's the lining of my gut and I can't tell the difference

That's your mother in the next breath she says don't let all that information go to waste there are three types of real magic we are conjuring not creating making silence sing working mirrors for glimpses into afterlives othermothers so random it can seem select through centuries I have abided with you

I come from heavy bottom women who stand up and pound fufu in the hot sun.

I come from Big Face fighter people-
On my mother side;
Carlota seed that slice that man head clean off with big machete.

I born from people who dig graves with their fingernails to put down dead babies...

Fly blown nose I hate this nose yours is much prettier small perfect you are just perfect except except for things have been different since you came he doesn't love me the same anymore it's your fault you've bewitched him that wasn't part of the deal girl Perfectly manicured hands in the middle of the morning when decent folks are climbing out of bed night shifts breed night habits You mussee gat dem genes from her she was a beauty hungry too always looking

I born from people that hang black bottles from the branches of the casuarina tree -Listening for 'sperrit

I born a gaulin woman...*

You start that writing yet oh yes I've started or rather it's started writing me

We gat so much god we ain't gat room for nuttin else

I did ask. I asked if she knew that while they drank frolicked and posed in paradise my father made a glove of my body I did not ask about my mother in her service I didn't want to know a wealthy white woman's perspective on servitude she was never given much to introspection or responsibility this is why my mother raised you kept photos of you and the man your mother never loved

We gat so much god we ain't gat room for nuttin else 198

I awoke to noise and the taste of my sister's pain licking my lips come come now don't be foolish I've waited long for you says the voice in the dark. People have choices, they can know better. At which point they can do better. Don't worry too much, open the archive.

ephemeral return to a land I never left

We gat so much god we ain't gat room for nuttin else

They may see their own dimensions but their eyes were clouds their voices beyond refutation have transcended the immediately relational to encompass diasporic PTSD their stories in my belly a constant nausea their deities forgotten mine have been taken I wander aimlessly errant finding listening and worse

this errantry is gender determined it is not safe to peregrinate so much these days for the violence might consume you your ethereal quest doesn't make you immune simpler moments where I cannot speak to anyone for hours and then days and then endless spans of time gently touching grandmothers the space for creation cinched in a furrow between my fingers seemingly minute though infinitely large the politics are in the refusal to be political is it not sacred enough to escape dissertation and doesn't it require care though unlooked for nonetheless it must be praised

These children are transients linger only for a while in the infinite tasks of many lives give me grace to make this one my own filled with kindness help me be full of benevolences to nurture I ask you for gentleness for the presence to recognize what I want and need grant me sleep patience the sacred and the sorrow

In ceremony
In ceremony and
In ceremony and dreams
In ceremony and dreams I
In ceremony and dreams I accept.
In ceremony and dreams, what am I accepting?

You should make some scholarly commitments   to which I reply I have already made too many   I sing at bedtime for love make sure there is toast in the freezer refrain from breaking dishes in a fit of rage not choke on the quality of despair while telling strangers to piss off I don't need your methodological framework to hold this paradox discipline middle no-thing   it hums inside me at superhuman pitch

We gat so much god we ain't gat room for nuttin else

ADDRESS
IMMIGRATION INSPECTOR-IN-CHARGE

901 Bleury St.,
Montreal 1, P.Q.

IN YOUR REPLY REFER TO
No. ED 1-6272
IMMIGRATION BRANCH

RD:VH

DEPARTMENT
OF
MINES AND RESOURCES

Montreal, January 20, 1950.

Dear Miss,

Regarding your request for permanent admission to Canada, I wish to advise that the authority has now been granted, provided you meet with our prevailing health regulations.

Would you be so kind to call at our office at your earliest convenience, in order that we may complete your case.

Thanking you in advance, I remain,

Yours very truly,

J. M. Langlais,

Miss Naomi L. Black,
746-A de L'Epee Street,
Montreal, P.Q.

---

1. Two factors contributed to the decision to admit Caribbean domestic workers as landed immigrants rather than on a temporary basis: First, the government retained the power to deport a woman during the first year if she proved "undesirable" by, say, becoming pregnant or severing her contract with her employer. Second, the prevailing belief was that Caribbean domestic workers, unlike their white cohorts, would remain in domestic service long after the one year compulsory period expired, presumably due to a natural affinity of Black women for domestic service. [See Note 31 below]
2. Note 31: Calliste, supra, note 13 at 143.
3. Because the Caribbean governments involved in the Scheme were anxious to make a good name for their citizens abroad, their selection process gave priority to educational attainment and ambition over domestic skills. Many candidates were actually nurses, teachers or civil servants in search of better job opportunities in Canada. [See Note 32 below] This "brain drain" of educated women was depicted in a mordant Trinidadian newspaper cartoon featuring a Caribbean girl saying: "I'll be a Civil Servant when I grow up and get a chance to go to Canada as a Domestic Servant!" [See Note 33 below]
4. Note 32: Ibid. at 143-44.
5. Note 33: Ibid. at 144.
6. Employers expressed general satisfaction with Caribbean domestic workers, finding them to be "more educated, `fond of children,' obliging and less demanding than other domestics." [See Note 34 below] Caribbean domestic workers were also cheap --- one commentator found that employers paid them up to $150 less per month than their white counterparts. [See Note 35 below]
7. Note 34: Ibid.
8. Note 35: Ibid. at 149. The Scheme brought 2,940 women to Canada as domestics between 1955 and 1966 (ibid. at 145).

We gat so much god we ain't gat room for nuttin else

My anger entombed along with her carried me over oceans and universes driven by the
syncretic sought safety in places where everyone else was righter whiter
immured by offspring and recall fresh from the turning of my entire body to meet
the teacher's eyes neck muscles
stiff from the combined force
of her will and her pulling twisting
plaits perfectly tight
bones hunger before they find cold earth come out   tree frogs call your name
I need you to show me story

There's nowhere to run
Cock crows in the middle of the afternoon
I hunker down against the storm comin'
and sit with my mother's bones

We gat so much god we ain't gat room for nuttin else

Artist's Statement

> Talking to the dead is a perceived ongoing exchange between living and deceased members of (these) communities.... Talking to the dead strengthens a sense of unity among members of these communities and gives individuals a way to communicate with deceased relatives.... Talking to the dead is a long-standing yet under-explored spiritual practice.... Talking to the dead facilitates their relationships to the past and is relevant to the ways they navigate and live out their faith.
>
> Embracing what Sheila Smith McCoy calls "limbo time," the fused contested space that Black diasporic cultures negotiate between linear and cyclical time ... taking one through a "figurative journey" that crosses the boundaries of time. (Maignault-Bryant, 2014, pp. xvi-xvii)

I wonder if the ancestors scatter when their abodes are razed. Do they stay, waiting, or find other places? How do they grieve? Is it given to us to carry what our ancestors felt and help them to grieve the losses?

Memorying enacts relationality—beyond recall, observation, and memorialization. It is both theory and method for Afro-Indigenous futurities and moves differentially through less than artificial notions of time, space, and place. It makes relative Blackness and Indigeneity in a reclamation of ancestors, voices, and silences in celebration and exceeding recentering. This is an embodied and explicitly self-conscious process—in part—of grieving, the absence of which has gotten us stuck in repeating cycles of trauma. It encompasses ancestral veneration, visionary thinking, and sitting with the bones. It is not remembering, though I am a rememberer. Memorying is not palliative; it exceeds the temporal. It is a casting, a retaking. In entering into conversation with the dead, there is an intention related to the future possibilities that reclamation of this methodology may serve. There are also questions: how does talking with the dead offer us access to modes of understanding beyond what we typically apprehend? How we language grief and memory has the power to enclose our imaginations and futurities. My work offers sitting with the bones as a way of being, with spirit, that resists despair and holds worlds together. In storying at the interstices of our collective memories, I write what Hartman (2008) identified as a history "within and against" (p. 12) the archive (see also Turner et al., this volume). I have found support for this endeavor in Michelle Wright's epiphenomenal time as undergirding for refusing separation of the secular and the profane (Kolia, 2016) in how we remember. Through a fusion of poetics, critical autoethnography, metaphor, images, and archival documents, the purpose is to engage a practice of ethnographic refusal (Simpson, 2007). Metaphor, allusion, and allegory are put to work for futurities, to mash it up. This mash-up encompasses narrative, witness and testimony, critical autoethnography, quantum science, and poetry as interpretive retelling in the imagining of something different. This creative process takes shape in between; Clark (2009) described diaspora as modality, going beyond transnationalism's referencing of ties and interactions across nation-state borders. Diaspora here reclaims the conditions that transnationalism seeks to qualify with embedded colonial continuities in its epistemic underpinnings, thematic concerns, and practices. It claims the liminal as a space of poesies, a making, uncovering silences inherent in portraying the subjectivity of Black womxn, Indigenous womxn, and womxn of color in an invitation to undo and remake in relationship.

I am inextricably tied to womxn across the continent in a weaving that is of both death and magic eternal one dreams my dreams holds me when I tarry left foot anchored in the veil entertains my mother hand in hand with nightblooms they too walk both sides I have surfaced from the same saltwaters that hold their dead I am marked by deathwork.

Responding to the call to use imagination, empathy, and dreaming to unshackle our relations in the futures we dream (Morrill et al., 2016), I ask how unearthing silences in Afrodescended womxn's stories and lives as archive could contribute to a radical poetic moment, engendering narratives for resisting hegemonic constructs (Sousanis, 2015). This work takes shape as a form in which document and art are indistinguishable because they serve the same purpose of rupturing existing boundaries of knowing. It is of indeterminate outcome, springing from a series of dreams, visions, and conversations with the dead—my dead—as catalyst for the work. The silences within are more than absence: they are refusal, letting go, a ceremony of survival. They are personal and collective, a weaving and a witnessing. They are those leaving their bodies, dreaming another life. They are archived in dreams, story, and soul visions. They form a decolonial library in the face of the denial and medicalization of death-related issues and the removal of death-related rituals from community (Littlewood, 1992).

This is a polyphony of matrilineal voices, words, and stories that have made themselves known in a multitude of ways. How do we think about Afro-Indigenous futurities at the interstices of public history and collective memorying—of which grief is an integral part—and poetics? The work itself is a practice of reciprocity, an amalgam of stories, lives, and dreams. Its design is experiential, its fracture meant to draw the reader through how it felt to take these stories in, to move through them and hear the voices of the dead. This piece conveys the fragmentation and confusion that are constants in the living of Black lives and the reflecting upon them in and through the archive. Story trickles in, and we contend with the unending violence modernity continues to exact on our material lives and on our imaginations. This is not a place for pretension; it is deliberately disruptive. The purpose was not to make it easy to read. These stories are scripted within and as alternative genealogies of Black diasporic feminisms and in part as a critique of transnationalism. They demonstrate, through citational practice, how existing works might produce praxes of talking to the dead. When we remember together, recognizing that multiverse is simultaneous and parallel, words are portal and anchor. As such, there is no definite break between the concepts that live in this work: memory/archive/futurities.

In developing a protocol for talking with the dead, poetry feeds the bones, and then, the stories. There is a story of nation-making in the margins (Beard, 2009), of inherited silences and secrets about family members. The silences are not a counterpoint to voice; rather, they embody it, in what Marriott (2017) called a provocation "to the point of a singular lack of transparency or a refusal to engage or cater to expectations" (p. 1). The prevailing expectation is that the writing will lay Black life bare, will explain itself, will offer its subjectivity up for consumption and display. Black transformative poetics refuse this. Form itself becomes questionable; the writing lives as "rhythmic experiment," as performance.

Behind my eyes I see global dialogues opening in the cavity of aching bellies
vomiting boundaries never knew they were ceremonies stand beside me
not behind me. In exploding categories I embrace the possibility of choosing that
    which is necessary to keep moving.
Go now, don't wait

Part 5

On Worlding

14

Dreams to Remember

● ●

A Conversation on *Unsilencing the Archive: An Afronautic Approach*

CAMILLE TURNER, MILA MENDEZ, AND HEATHER EVANS

Unsilencing the Archive: An Afronautic Approach was a virtual lab developed and facilitated by Toronto-based artist and scholar Camille Turner as part of the three-day workshop that gathered contributors to this edited volume in June 2021. It emerged from and builds on Turner's broader body of art and scholarship that combines Afrofuturism and historical research to explore issues of race, space, home, and belonging by listening for what and who is silenced in Canada's archive of transatlantic slavery in order to remember and care for the dead. The lab explored and put into practice Afronautics, a methodological frame that Turner developed that approaches colonial archives from the vantage point of a liberated future. At the beginning of the lab, Turner explained the four methodological principles of Afronautics: Blackness is central; time is nonlinear; silence speaks and yields information and direction; and imagination is a tool for building worlds. Participants were then divided into breakout groups to apply Turner's Afronautic approach to select colonial archival evidence that took the form of posters, newspaper and magazine clippings, and advertisements from eighteenth-century colonial Canada. Each group was assigned one document, and the task was to use the standpoint of a liberated future to recenter the silenced, buried, and absented Blackness in that archival evidence. The lab concluded with group presentations and debriefings. Some weeks after the workshop, Turner sat down with Mila Mendez and Heather Evans, both of whom participated in the workshop, to reflect on the lab and theorize the implications of Afronautics for how we understand memory and its practices. What follows is an edited version of their conversation. Readers unfamiliar with Turner's body of work are encouraged to visit www.camilleturner.com to view past iterations of the Afronautic Research Lab, a traveling reading room where participants were invited to consider evidence of Canada's coloniality and participation in the transatlantic slave trade.

*   *   *

TURNER I would love to hear your thoughts, Mila, about the lab and what happened there and what you observed. I think that the idea of centering Blackness was really, really difficult for people. And it's hard for me, too! I'm writing a didactic right now about people who were enslaved by the Bâby family for an artwork entitled *House of Bâby* that I just made with my collaborator Camal Pirbhai. How do I decenter whiteness in this piece? How do I center Blackness? The archive has nothing about the enslaved people besides their names and their racial identities. They were Black and Indigenous; some of them were mixed. But we don't know anything else about them. So how do you even write about them? That's, of course, the bigger question participants had to contend with in the lab.

MENDEZ When I think methodologically about centering Blackness, I recognize this work has a crucial felt element, a kind of "ah-ha!" that reverberates through the body. I feel it when I read the work of other theorists who are genuinely refusing the scripts of whiteness. We know whiteness centers Blackness in its own way, but not the way that you're asking for.

TURNER That's so true. It's as if this lens is so opaque that it's difficult to even see that's the lens we're looking through.

MENDEZ In the lab, I remember you trying to bring that lens into focus for participants. At one point, someone was zooming out of the document, tying it to other reference points, and you asked, "What happens when we zoom back into the document?" What happens when someone is present with the document they have and let it be enough—to say that Blackness is here in a significant enough way that you don't need to look anywhere else?

Yet, there's a resistance to being told that this might be a new process for you, that antiracist feminist or transnational feminist methodologies don't inherently teach you how to do this, and that it might take a while. Centering Blackness in the

Dreams to Remember • 211

Twenty Dollars Reward.

RAN Away, on Thursday evening, the 18th inst. a Negro Man Servant, the property of the Subscriber, named BELFAST; but who commonly goes by the name of BILL.——— At the time of his elopement he was in the service of William Forsyth, Esq; and had meditated an attempt to get on board a ship that night which lay in the harbour, bound to Newfoundland; but was frustrated: It is probable, however, he may still endeavour to escape that way, therefore, the masters of all coasters going along shore, or other vessels bound to sea, are hereby forewarn—

Crowdfunding for African Freedom Society

My name is [African name]. I liberated myself on Thursday evening by running toward freedom. I took my liberation by boarding a ship which lay in the harbour bound for Africa. Be on the lookout for William Forsyth, a brutal white man, known for torture, rape, and murder. The fugitive may be hiding in his barn on his property. I am liberating myself to join freedom fighters on the Gold Coast, to prevent the enslavement of more Africans. In lieu of a reward, please send donations to the African Freedom Society, PO Box 357.

FIGURE 14.1 Left: From *Nova Scotia Gazette and Weekly Chronicle*, March 15, 1794. Right: Afronautic lab group's response to this archival evidence from the June 2021 workshop.

Afronautic way is a practice and an affect. It is embodied work, and because of that, it can take time to learn.

TURNER It's funny because the seeds of the lab grew from my teaching. Each year I would bring my students into the archives, and so I was trying to look at different approaches. And this is the way that helped me to go into the archives as a descendant of ancestors who were enslaved. But it's one thing to put forward a methodology, but ... it's sort of like beta testing it, I suppose. It's not complete. I know that I'm doing something in my work, but how am I doing it? What is it? I know when something is successful because it does those things [that Mila mentioned]. But what is actually happening? I loved the very first piece by lab participants that was presented [see Figure 14.1]. I just thought it was brilliant.

EVANS It was also such a good piece [the archival document in figure 14.1] for the lab because it offered a subject, a certain subjectivity through which to enter the exercise. But as we saw, not all groups were able to apply the framework so effectively.

TURNER That's the thing, what are the right questions to ask? How do you present the frame so it's usable, so people understand what to do?

EVANS Permission is coming to mind for me. Some of us were confronted with internal blocks in relation to the task of centering Blackness. It in some ways illuminated how identity formulated through certain understandings of racialization prohibits imagination, or really anything outside of the episteme of access and recovery. I found myself asking, what permission do I have, as a non-Black person, to imagine Blackness in this space?

TURNER So, the imagination can really get stunted in this whole process.

212 • Camille Turner et al.

MENDEZ This brings to mind Saidiya Hartman's method of writing, which she describes in *Venus in Two Acts* (2008): critical fabulation. Hartman has taught us that by reconsidering and re-presenting historical events from the vantage point of the silenced, the dispossessed, and the unthought, we can imagine those events differently. It's critical history where imagination is central, and hers is grounded in the reality and the materiality of that which is absented by the dominant narrative. As you say, Heather, it shows us imagination is conditioned.

EVANS Mila and I were talking about critical fabulation after the workshop. You're doing something akin to this, but we can't quite articulate what's different about your approach. There's definitely something different happening, though. How do you see your methodology in relation to critical fabulation?

TURNER I've been thinking about Hartman's *Wayward Lives* (2019) and what she's doing because she's been my guide for walking through the archives and geographies of slavery, right? But I feel like I create from a liberated future; I'm looking at the past *from* that future, and I think that's what's different.

EVANS It's interesting to reflect on this anchoring in the future in relationship to the lab. I don't think that everyone got that, at least in terms of *how* to do it. The first group that presented certainly seemed anchored in that kind of liberated moment. But whoever is doing that has to be already there; they need to already have that anchor point. If you don't, it's an untethered imagination that can go in lots of directions. What future are you thinking from, and therefore what lens are you looking at these histories from? If you're remembering from the present, it's a limited vantage point. So, on a practical level, how do you get people to remember from the future?

TURNER Maybe there needs to be some sort of dreaming. I have a new piece that I'm conceptualizing, and it's all about dreaming. The dream is so important, being able to dream. And to be able to understand that in what you're projecting, saying, thinking, feeling, and putting into the world, you're creating something. So, that's where it needs to start.

MENDEZ I'm really curious now about exploring what the future orientation means because I remember that coming up in the workshop, but I don't remember it being primary.

TURNER It wasn't because I didn't know how important that was. This is what Honor [Ford-Smith; see Ford-Smith & Stephen, this volume] is trying to get me to talk about. I talk about nonlinear time or at least nonsequential time. Other people are doing that, but not in the same way that I am. Look at John Akomfra's *Vertigo Sea*, for instance, which imagines the sea as an archive from which crimes of the past are retrieved. He crosses temporalities by presenting disasters at sea through time, but he's not looking back from the future while he's doing this. He's looking back from the present. Toni Morrison (2007) talks about collaborating across time. She's writing into slave narratives what people couldn't say back then. She's doing the work of filling in blank spaces that had to be left blank in the past because it wasn't safe to do otherwise. She's definitely not rooting her understanding of the past in the future. Afronautic time is a different kind of time.

MENDEZ Exactly. I'm imagining the differences between the kind of approach to nonlinearity you're offering and some of the others that are about crossing temporalities. The visual metaphor is different, right? There's a difference between being anchored in the future and then time traveling versus blurred time spaces.

EVANS Or even, what would it mean to take out "future" and say the remembering is "anchored in the *dream*"?

TURNER Oh, I love that.

EVANS Because I think when we say "future," we get stuck in the linearity and lose the creative spaciousness of dreaming that you've been talking about.

TURNER Yes, and it's not always the future. Like you say, it's anchored in the dream.

MENDEZ So, it's a practice of critical dreaming? I love that, too. I find that one challenge with working from or around the future is that it forecloses any acknowledgement that these liberated events are already happening, even if in infinitely small moments. In your lab, for example. Even if it's just two seconds. But in that embodied moment, the two-second dream or the two-second vision, you *are* inhabiting it. It is not future, but it is *a* future accessed in the present dream.

When I think about folks who are working towards a liberated future for all, the articulations that resonate the most for me are not necessarily the clearest, but the affects are strongest. Because there are so many concurrent experiments taking place in the name of liberation, it's hard to know which plan is *the* plan. So, in the absence of these certain details, you don't necessarily know what the future looks like, but you know that none of the things that currently make you comfortable will make you comfortable in that place. Comfort will be a totally different thing, and relations and abundance will be wholly different, too. By these metrics, what you can do is *feel* how vastly different it will be from anything that you could name or understand now, and you can let that feeling be a guide.

EVANS You're saying that you can access it, you can experience it in those moments, you just can't . . .

214 • Camille Turner et al.

MENDEZ You probably can't articulate it, and you can't sustain it, and articulation might not be what is helpful to sustain it anyway.

EVANS Because sustaining it would require a collective. No one can do it alone. But there's a possibility that if everyone were experiencing those seconds more often, that we could sustain it longer.

TURNER Yes, because if I think about what's going on in the Afronautic lab, those things are happening, but it's hard to articulate. It's on us all to cocreate the future; it is a collective dreaming. If we could all bring ourselves together to sustain that dream, we would be living it. So, what does an invitation to step into that dream-space look like?

MENDEZ Perhaps it is giving people the right phrase or invitation to access that place and to trust that when people do access it, however brief, that it is significant. What permission do you need to keep chasing that feeling over and over again, until not chasing it cues you that something is off? Being able to answer that question seems like the thing you'd want people to carry forward. Similarly, how do you know when you're in the liberated future? How do you know when you're centering Blackness?

EVANS In so many ways, this volume is about what brings people to that collective dreaming, what are the tools and practices of remembrance that we need, and don't need, to get there. I'm thinking back, Camille, to our conversations years ago about your turn away from Memory Studies early on in your graduate work—what it didn't have to offer, why it wasn't helpful. You couldn't step into the space of Afronautics in the way you are now with the terms of that literature. What you seem to gesture towards in your work is the need for an ontological shift in our relationships to memory.

TURNER That's right. What I'm offering is a different way to look at memory, a way to look at the past, and in particular, painful pasts. I read this piece by Shoshana Felman (Felman & Laub, 1992) where she wrote about what happened when she showed her students these Holocaust testimonies and basically the students were shattered. They descended into talking about it obsessively and feeling very alone; there was trauma involved in witnessing. And so, she looked at that trauma. I referenced her work [in my doctoral dissertation] to talk about my own fears about going into the archive. What if this happens to me? How do I bring myself back? What are the stakes for me as a descendant going into this archive and confronting the traumatizing experiences of my ancestors?

Remember before we had talked about my film *Sarah* (2021),[1] which asks you to think about the purpose of remembering. Can we actually go into the future without memory? Is that what we're trying to do? Somehow it was necessary for the

Afronaut to know about the past even though they were living in a liberated future. You can't just sever the past and go on like you're a new entity. Somehow, we need it. And I don't know what that need is except that a necessary part of being human is having a past, and that past gives you a ground underneath your feet. *Sarah*, for me, was putting Afronautics into practice. It was conjuring this liberated future and looking at the past through that future. It's what enables me to survive going into the archive, doing that work, and facing the violence of the past. It's doing the work of methodology, but it's a conceptual frame as well. And I'm extracting it from what I'm doing. It was just, what did I do? How can this be useful? How can it be rolled out as a methodology?

EVANS And out of that methodology, as a means of teaching it and making available these tools, you've created these public labs that combine remembrance and the speculative in ways that foundationally unsettle normative understandings of what practices of memory can be and can do.

TURNER I think I mentioned to you before Lubaina Himid (2011). It was so brilliant what she did in her lecture. And to me, it's thinking Afronautically, in a way. She basically (re)envisioned Paris and London as if they were places where Black people's histories were remembered as an important part of the history of the place. I wasn't looking [at the video that was playing] when she was talking and didn't realize it was speculative until I looked at it. But in a way, it was more powerful just listening because it felt like there actually was a memorial on the Champs-Élysées that references Bob Marley! I was thinking, "Wow, I never noticed these things before." [Laughter] It was a brilliant performative lecture.

EVANS I love that it stays in the speculative.

TURNER Yes, and the speculative space does something. It brings us to the place of possibility. And when you think in those ways, it becomes an impetus for doing, or at least for being differently.

EVANS I think for so many of us at the workshop, the lab opened the possibility that imagination could go into our work. It asked us to take a step back and realize we're not going to get to where we want to go from where we are. It required us to question the terms upon which we are collectively invoking this past, but also invited us to access the past differently, to expand what we think of as being able to convey a past and as being able to haunt. Camille, in a previous conversation you were talking about your experience of haunting and how that really was the impetus for this work. Haunting has in so many ways become the entry point for those who are thinking critically about remembrance of violent or unjust pasts. Avery Gordon (2008) is ubiquitous at this point.

TURNER That's so true. And I'm also using Viviane Saleh-Hanna (2015), which I think is really important because she specifically references colonization and slavery as being intertwined and notes the way that this history permeates everything. She calls her theory Black feminist hauntology. She's talking about who is the center point of all of this. She's looking at Black women as a way to think about these histories and how they intersect. If you think about Black women at the center of the haunting, then you start seeing different things. I think about myself as a Black woman walking on this seemingly innocent white land of Newfoundland. I think about what I am bringing to this space with me and how can we read this space through my body. When I look at myself as a part of this story, I think about what that makes visible.

EVANS Mila, I think your understanding of the differences between Gordon (2008) and Christina Sharpe's (2016) understandings of haunting in relation to "wake work" in the afterlife of slavery are relevant to this, insomuch as you, Camille, are in some ways invoking and carrying forward haunting rather than trying to resolve it or address it.

MENDEZ Yeah, even though Gordon does not look for or write resolutions broadly in *Ghostly Matters* (2008), I read the attention to ghost stories as wanting a world eventually unhaunted. We're invited to attune to hauntings so that we can respond.

TURNER There's something to be done.

MENDEZ Yeah, something to be done.

EVANS But that's not the ontology, or hauntology, that you're working from, Camille. You're like, let's bring this out, let's haunt, let's have this with us, and that *is* the carrying of the past.

TURNER Absolutely. It's about recognizing it, about how we recognize the ghosts. Although I think what Gordon (2008) does is recognizing space itself as haunted. So, you know, thinking about the rocks and the waves as witness and what the land itself can tell us. And I found that very useful.

MENDEZ Right. And with Sharpe's *In the Wake: On Blackness and Being* (2016), I get the impression that the goal is not to put the ghosts to rest. This isn't about retraumatizing, but it's also not about *not* being with pain. It's not about a world in which those ghosts don't have to exist. It's about a paradox. Within the wake, which is impossible to briefly define but might be understood as the space in which Blackness is constituted or written, lived, mourned, imagined, and more in the afterlife of slavery, is violence, *and* within and in excess of the wake is also resolute life and care. This offers a way of being in the archives. This raises a question about

Afronautic research. What is its relationship to the pain? What is its relationship to the trauma?

TURNER It's still a question for me, but I know it was necessary. This is what kind of comes up in that piece *Sarah* (2021): what is that relationship to pain? Why was it important for the Afronaut to come back? And to know? Why couldn't they have just gone off and enjoyed living in this nice liberation? And that's important. There's something that we need to know in order to be, I think.

EVANS Part of what I'm wondering is how much in *Sarah* (2021) the liberated future is a future freed from certain terms of relations to violence that are set in this world.

TURNER That's a very good question. And how does the Afronaut's relationship to the past compare with, say, the researcher's relationship to the past?

MENDEZ Yes, exactly. I'm curious, too, in the methodology of Afronautics, in the four principles or steps that you outlined, about where pain is. Somewhere in there is also an invitation to encounter that violence differently, so that depending on who the researcher is, they're not retraumatizing themselves and/or, depending on positionality, set up to have a particular relation to that violence, whether it's a fragility or an apology or a defensiveness.

TURNER I love all the questions that this brings up, and I feel like I don't even want to close any possibilities because it could be so many things. All I know is that I created this as a way to survive the violence of the archives.

MENDEZ And so, for you, too, it was about how to relate to the pain.

TURNER Yes, and it's still not easy to do. But it's the whole idea that we've been talking about—the dreaming. Dreaming is so important, especially for remembrance, but it is difficult to sustain that dream. You're conjuring this liberated future, and you're anchoring yourself to that future, and yet you're encountering this past, and it is coming at you. When I did my dissertation research in Newfoundland, I basically went into the hold of a ship, and I'm on the Middle Passage, traveling through the records. And I was looking through these records, and they are telling me what's going on. And these are the records generated by the captains of the ships, you know? It's devastating. So, I had to invent a way to be able to do this work. And *Sarah* (2021) is what came out. I did not think through *Sarah* in any kind of chronological way. It's just that shit was going down. The lockdown, the lynching of George Floyd, this crazy moment of feeling exhausted, of wanting to close my eyes until it was over. All of the social media—the explosion of anti-Blackness that is always there but it was just more and more inundating—and you're locked in your apartment. All of this going on, and *Sarah* just kind of manifested itself. It really wrote itself. It was a way to think through, how do you survive? This character, this Afronaut, this idea of deliverance . . . everything just kind of fed into each other in my imagination. But that's the thing about worlding, you know, when you think about imagination as a tool for making worlds.

EVANS I still find the word "imagination" so interesting as it pertains to remembrance. In the colonial episteme, imagination has this weight of untruth, of not being grounded in truth, the binary opposite of memory. And yet the way you're talking about imagination invokes other worldviews.

TURNER I think about Toni Morrison (2007) because I found her methodology very useful for mine, and she talks about how facts can exist without human intelligence and its imaginative dimensions, but truth cannot. That's why she's trying to find a truth of the lived experience beyond those facts.

EVANS And this speaks to what's possible in terms of forms of remembrance.

TURNER Yes. It's about worlding, about evoking a speculative world, and of bringing into the mind, body, and existence the possibility. And that starts *from* the dream, not the other way around. And I love that.

Note

1   *Sarah* (2021) is a film by Camille Turner, one of the three artistic projects that constituted her dissertation. It is a documentary-style video that explores the experience of a Black researcher feeling the weight of anti-Blackness in the present while trying to do the work of unsilencing anti-Blackness in the past. The story takes place in the researcher's apartment where she sits at her computer researching the story of the *Sarah*, a slave ship constructed in Newfoundland, while she is bombarded by present-day media reports of Black people targeted by state violence. The story is narrated by an Afronaut—an African space/time traveler—from the future whose ancestors left earth in the twenty-first century when the planet had become unbearable for Black people. Now living in peace among the stars, their historians silenced the past to give them a fresh start. But silence is not seamless, and the past haunts their dreams. The Afronaut travels back in time to twenty-first century earth to find out why their ancestors had left. Through watching what the researcher recovers and what she is experiencing in the present, the Afronaut learns the truth.

Acknowledgments

As detailed in the preface, this project originated in Malathi de Alwis and Alison Crosby's collaborative work on the inhabitance of loss in Sri Lanka and Guatemala. Our attention to the transnational dimensions of memorialization practices extended and deepened when Heather Evans joined the team, bringing their work on the "comfort women" movement. We are grateful to the Toronto-based memory reading group, as well as M. Brinton Lykes and Ramsey Liem, for earlier conversations that helped shape the project's framework. As members of the editorial committee, de Alwis, Honor Ford-Smith, Shahrzad Mojab, and Carmela Murdocca were instrumental in this volume coming into being, shaping its conceptual parameters, participating in grant writing, giving input into the call for participants, and selecting contributors. This volume would not have been possible without their time, enthusiasm, grace, and generosity. We held a (much delayed, due to the pandemic) three-day virtual workshop for contributors in June 2021. Tremendous thanks and appreciation to Camille Turner, Ford-Smith, and Juanita Stephen for organizing and running two of the central sessions in the workshop, details of which are discussed in this volume. We are indebted to Emily Coussons and Mila Mendez for all their hard work in ensuring that the workshop ran smoothly and that we could all breathe together. Although we lamented being unable to gather in-person, many thanks to participants for so enthusiastically embracing the virtual format and making it such a generative dialogical space. We received permission to reprint de Alwis's chapter, Tracing Absent Presence, originally published in *States of Trauma: Gender and Violence in South Asia* (Zubaan, 2009, pp. 238–253). We are very grateful to Zubaan Books, Urvashi Butalia, Piya Chatterjee, Manali Desai, and Parama Roy for their enthusiastic and positive response to our request. Our deep appreciation to Pradeep Jeganathan for his support of this project during a time of such intense grief, as well as to the Friends of Mala WhatsApp group for providing an ongoing space of mutual care as we mourn the loss of our very dear friend. The digital archive that is being developed to accompany and enrich this volume owes much to Emily Coussons, Hasini Haputhanthri, and Marian Iñiguez Perez for their logistical, conceptual, and curatorial efforts; to Patrick Evans for his generous technical expertise; and to the archive contributors who have entrusted us with their materials. Many thanks to all of them and the Centre for Feminist Research at York University for housing and administering this project. It was supported financially by the Social Sciences and Humanities Research Council of Canada, as well as the Faculty of Liberal Arts and Professional Studies, the Office of the Vice-President Research and Innovation, and the York Research Chair in Reparative and Racial Justice at York University. We acknowledge and appreciate this support. Many thanks to our editor at Rutgers University Press, Margaret Solic, as well as Kimberly Guinta, for their enthusiastic support for and guidance of this project, and to the anonymous reviewers for their helpful feedback. We are beyond grateful to our loved ones for holding us throughout this project and for their never-ending patience with the vast amounts of time and energy it has required. And lastly, our deep appreciation to each other; this has truly been a collaborative undertaking, deepened by the loss of our coeditor and friend, Mala. "No drama" is truly a motto to live by.

References

Abdo, N. (2014). *Captive revolution: Palestinian women's anti-colonial struggle within the Israeli prison system*. Pluto.

Abiral, B. (2016). Silencing sexual violence and vulnerability: Women's narratives of incarceration during the 1980–1983 military junta in Turkey. In A. G. Altinay & A. Petö (Eds.), *Gendered wars, gendered memories: Feminist conversations on war, genocide and political violence* (pp. 93–106). Routledge.

Abrahamian, E. (1989). *The Iranian Mojahedin*. Yale University Press.

Afraz, M., & Afraz, R. (2015). *With the Omani revolutionaries: The Dhofar war diary*. Andeeseh va Peykar.

Agamben, G. (1999). *Remnants of Auschwitz: The witness and the archive* (D. Heller-Roazen, Trans.). Zone Books.

Ahmed, S. (2000). *Strange encounters: Embodied others in post-coloniality*. Routledge.

Ahmed, S. (2004). *The cultural politics of emotion*. Edinburgh University Press.

Ahmed, S. (2006). *Queer phenomenology: Orientations, objects, others*. Duke University Press.

Ahmed, S., & Stacey, J. (2001). Testimonial cultures: An introduction. *Cultural Values*, *5*(1), 1–6. https://doi.org/10.1080/14797580109367217

Aijazi, O. (2018). *Fictions of social repair: Chronicity in six scenes* [Unpublished doctoral dissertation]. University of British Columbia.

Aikau, H. K., Arvin, M., Goeman, M., & Morgensen, S. (2015). Indigenous feminisms roundtable. *Frontiers: A Journal of Women Studies*, *36*(3), 84–106.

Akkaya, A. H. (2016). *The Kurdistan Workers' Party (PKK): National liberation, insurgency and radical democracy beyond borders* [Unpublished doctoral dissertation]. Ghent University.

Alexander, M. J. (2005). *Pedagogies of crossing: Meditations on feminism, sexual politics, memory and the sacred*. Duke University Press.

Alexander, M. J., & Mohanty, C. T. (2010). Cartographies of knowledge and power: Transnational feminism as radical feminist praxis. In A. L. Swarr & R. Nagar (Eds.), *Critical transnational feminist praxis* (pp. 23–45). SUNY Press.

Allam, N. (2018). *Women and the Egyptian revolution: Engagement and activism during the 2011 Arab uprisings*. Cambridge University Press.

Altınay, A. G., José Contreras, M., Hirsch, M., Howard, J., Karaca, B., & Solomon, A. (Eds.) (2019). *Women mobilizing memory*. Columbia University Press.

Alvarez, S. (2014). Enacting a translocal feminist politics of translation. In S. E. Alvarez, C. de Lima Costa, V. Feliu, R. J. Hester, N. Klahn, M. Thayer, & C. C. Bueno (Eds.), *Translocalities/translocalidades: Feminist politics of translation in the Latin/a Americas* (pp. 1–18). Duke University Press.

Amadou Diallo Foundation (n.d). *About us*. Retrieved July 8, 2024, from https://www .amadoudiallofoundation.org/about.html

Anderson, K., & Jack, D. C. (2015). Learning to listen: Interview techniques and analyses. In R. Perks & A. Thomson (Eds.), *The oral history reader* (3rd ed., pp. 179–192). Routledge.

Arboleda Quiñónez, S. (2011). *Le han florecido nuevas estrellas al cielo: Suficiencias íntimas y clandestinización del pensamiento afrocolombiano* [Unpublished doctoral dissertation]. Universidad Andina Simón Bolivar.

Argenti-Pillen, A. (2003). *Masking terror: How women contain violence in Southern Sri Lanka*. University of Pennsylvania Press.

Arias, A. (Ed.). (2001). *The Rigoberta Menchú controversy*. University of Minnesota Press.

Arvin, M., Tuck, E., & Morrill, A. (2013). Decolonizing feminism: Challenging connections between settler colonialism and heteropatriarchy. *Feminist Formations, 25*(1), 8–34. https://doi.org/10.1353/ff.2013.0006

Ashika, M. (2019). Memory as encounter: The Saturday Night mothers in Turkey. In A. G. Altınay, M. José Contreras, M. Hirsch, J. Howard, B. Karaca, & A. Solomon (Eds.), *Women mobilizing memory* (pp. 133–151). Columbia University Press.

Asociación Campesina Integral del Atrato. (2002). *Medio atrato: Territorio de vida*. Red de Solidaridad Social.

Ayala, A. G. (2011). *Rituales mortuorios y afroatrateños en el alto y medio Atrato*. Mundo Libre.

Aydin, A., & Emerence, C. (2015). *Zones of rebellion: Kurdish insurgents and the Turkish State*. Cornell University Press.

Badilla, M., & Aguilera, C. (2021). The 2019–2020 Chilean anti-neoliberal uprising: A catalyst for decolonial monumentalization. *Memory Studies, 14*(6), 1226–1240. https://doi.org/10.1177/17506980211054305

Badran, M. (2013). Theorizing oral history as autobiography: A look at the narrative of women revolutionary in Egypt. *Journal of Women's History, 25*(2), 161–170. https:// doi.org/10.1353/jowh.2013.0018

Baldwin, J. (1962, December 1). A letter to my nephew. *The Progressive*. https://progressive .org/magazine/letter-nephew/

Balfour, G. (2013). Do law reforms matter? Exploring the victimization–criminalization continuum in the sentencing of Aboriginal women in Canada. *International Review of Victimology, 19*(1), 85–102. https://doi.org/10.1177/0269758012447213

Bambara, T. C. (1980). *The salt eaters*. Vintage Books.

Barad, K. (2007). *Meeting the universe halfway: Quantum physics and the entanglement of matter and meaning*. Duke University Press.

Barthes, R. (1981). *Camera lucida: Reflections on photography* (R. Howard, Trans.). Farrar, Straus and Giroux.

Bazargan, P. (n.d.). *My memory of women's participation in a section of the armed movement of the two decades of 1960s and 1970s*. Retrieved July 8, 2024, from www .peykarandeesh.org.

Beard, L. J. (2009). *Acts of narrative resistance: Women's autobiographical writing in the Americas*. University of Virginia Press.

Beetham, S. (2016). From spry cans to minivans: Contesting the legacy of confederate soldier monuments in the era of "Black Lives Matter." *Public Art Dialogue, 6*(1), 9–33. http://dx.doi.org/10.1080/21502552.2016.1149386

Bello, M. N., Martín, E., Millan, C., Pulido, B., & Rojas, R. (2005). *Bojayá, memoria y río. Violencia política, dano y reparación.* Universidad Nacional de Colombia.

Benjamin, W. (1972). A short history of photography. *Screen, 13*(1), 5–26. https://doi.org /10.1093/screen/13.1.5

Beristain, C. (2006, February, 19) *Memoria y reconciliación: debates y desafíos en el caso vasco.* Grupo Antimilitarista Tortuga. http://www.grupotortuga.com/Carlos -Martin-Beristain-Memoria-y#sthash.FgqzXrVY.dpuf

Beverley, J. (2004). *Testimonio: On the politics of truth.* University of Minnesota Press.

Bevins, V. (2020). *The Jakarta Method: Washington's anticommunist crusade and the mass murder program that shaped our world.* Public Affairs.

Bhanji, N. N. (2018). Trans necrointimacies: Affect, race, and the chalky geopolitics of trans memorialization [Unpublished doctoral dissertation]. York University. http://hdl.handle.net/10315/35797

Biennial Foundation. (2015). *Jogja Biennale Equator #3. Hacking conflict: Indonesia meets Nigeria.* https://www.biennialfoundation.org/2015/06/the-jogja-biennale -team-challenged-us-to-create-a-theme-beyond-just-the-similarities-between -indonesia-and-nigeria-we-needed-to-create-a-theme-that-went-beyond-just -similarities-a-theme-that-could-a/

Bilbija, K., & Payne, L. A. (Eds.). (2011). *Accounting for violence: Marketing memory in Latin America.* Duke University Press.

Blackwell, M., & Naber, N. (2002). Intersectionality in the era of globalization: The implications of the UN World Conference against Racism for transnational feminist practices–A conference report. *Meridians, 2*(2), 237–248.

Blanchot, M. (1989). *The space of literature.* University of Nebraska Press.

Bold, C., Knowles, R., & Leach, B. (2002). Feminist memorializing and cultural countermemory: The case of Marianne's Park. *Signs: Journal of Women in Culture and Society, 28*(1), 125–148. https://doi.org/10.1086/340905

Botman, S. (1988). The experience of women in the Egyptian communist movement, 1939–1954. *Women's Studies International Forum, 11*(2), 117–126.

Boylorn, R. (2015). Stories from Sweetwater: Black women and narratives of resilience. *Departures in Critical Qualitative Research, 4*(1), 89–96. https://doi.org/10.1525/dcqr .2015.4.1.89

Boym, S. (2002). *The future of nostalgia.* Basic Books.

Boym, S. (2011). Nostalgia and its discontents. In J. K. Olick, V. Vinitzky-Seroussi, & D. Levy (Eds.), *The collective memory reader* (pp. 452–457). Oxford University Press.

Braithwaite, K. (1977). *Mother poem.* Oxford University Press.

Branche, J. (2015). *The poetics and politics of diaspora: Transatlantic musings* (Vol. 7). Routledge.

Brand, D. (2017). An Ars poetica from the blue clerk. *The Black Scholar, 47*(1), 58–77, https://doi.org/10.1080/00064246.2017.1264860

Brand, D. (2020, July 4). On narrative, reckoning, and the calculus of living and dying. *Toronto Star.* https://www.thestar.com/entertainment/books/2020/07/04/dionne -brand-on-narrative-reckoning-and-the-calculus-of-living-and-dying.html

Briggs, L., & Spencer, R. (2019). Introduction to the issue radical transnationalism: Reimagining solidarities, violences, empires. *Meridians: Feminism, race, transnation-alism, 18*(2), 253–260. https://doi.org/10.1215/15366936-7775619

Brown, W. (2001). *Politics out of history.* Princeton University Press.

Budiardjo, C. (1996). *Surviving Indonesia's gulag: A western woman tells her story*. Cassell.

Bueno-Hansen, P. (2015). *Feminist and human rights struggles in Peru: Decolonizing transitional justice*. University of Illinois Press.

Buggs. (2010, March 29). *The Mexican Drug War's collateral damage*. Borderland Beat. http://www.borderlandbeat.com/2010/03/mexican-drug-wars-collateral-damage.html

Burns, I. (2021, May 12). Ontario court decision on bias against black Canadians called "a game changer." *The Lawyer's Daily*. https://www.thelawyersdaily.ca/articles/6431/ontario-court-decision-on-bias-against-black-canadians-called-a-game-changer

Burt, J-M. (2016, February 11). *Human remains presented as evidence in Sepur Zarco trial*. International Justice Monitor: Guatemala Trials. https://www.ijmonitor.org/2016/02/human-remains-presented-as-evidence-in-sepur-zarco-trial/

Butler, J. (1993). *Bodies that matter: On the discursive limits of "sex."* Routledge.

Butler, J. (2004). *Precarious life: The powers of mourning and violence*. Verso.

Butler, J. (2015, March). *Vulnerability and resistance revisited*. [Conference paper]. Programa Universitario de Estudios de Género, Mexico City, Mexico.

Cabi, M. (2022). *The formation of modern Kurdish society in Iran: Modernity, modernization and social change 1921–1979*. I. B. Tauris.

Cabnal, L. (2019). El relato de las violencias desde mi territorio. In X. Leyva Solano & R. Icaza (Eds.), *En tiempos de muerte: Cuerpos, rebeldías, resistencias* (pp. 113–126). Consejo Latinoamericano de Ciencias Sociales; Cooperativa Editorial Retos.

Çaglayan, H. (2019). *Women in the Kurdish movement: Mothers, comrades, goddesses*. Palgrave Macmillan.

Campbell, C. (2010). *Running the dusk*. Peepal Tree Press.

Campt, T. (2017). *Listening to images*. Duke University Press.

Cansiz, S. (2018). *Sara: My whole life was a struggle* (J. Biehl, Trans.). Pluto. (Original work published 2015)

Cansiz, S. (2019). *Sara: Prison memoir of a Kurdish revolutionary* (J. Biehl, Trans.). Pluto.

Caruth, C. (1995). Introduction. In C. Caruth (Ed.), *Trauma: Explorations in memory* (pp. 3–12). Hopkins University Press.

Cavarero, A. (2005). *For more than one voice: Toward a philosophy of vocal expression*. Stanford University Press.

Cavarero, A., Thomaidis, K., & Pinna, I. (2018). Towards a hopeful plurality of democracy: An interview on vocal ontology with Adriana Cavarero. *Journal of Interdisciplinary Voice Studies, 3*(1), 81–93. https://doi.org/10.1386/jivs.3.1.81_1

Centro para la Acción Legal en Derechos Humanos, & Pérez Sián, M. J. (2014). *Las voces de las mujeres persisten en la memoria colectiva de sus pueblos: Continuum de violencias y resistencias en la vida, cuerpo y territorio de las mujeres*.

Chakraborty, C. (2012). Air India Flight 182: A Canadian tragedy? *Topia: Canadian Journal of Cultural Studies, 27*, 173–76. https://doi.org/10.3138/topia.27.173

Chakraborty, C. (2015). Official apology, creative remembrances, and management of the Air India tragedy. *Studies in Canadian Literature, 40*(1), 111–130.

Chakraborty, C. (2016). Remembering Air India flight 182 in an age of terror. In A. De (Ed.), *South Asian racialization and belonging after 9/11: Masks of threat* (pp. 1–20). Lexington.

Chakraborty, C., Dean, A., & Failler, A. (Eds.). (2017). *Remembering Air India: The art of public mourning*. University of Alberta Press.

Chandraprema, C. A. (1991). *Sri Lanka: The years of terror. The J.V.P. insurrection 1987–1989*. Lakehouse Bookshop.

Chatterjee, P., Desai, M., & Roy, P. (Eds). (2009). *States of trauma: Gender and violence in South Asia*. Zubaan.

Cheng, A. (2001). *The melancholy of race*. Oxford University Press.

Chevrie, M., & Le Roux, H. (2007). Site and speech: An interview with Claude Lanzmann about Shoah. In S. Liebman (Ed.), *Claude Lanzmann's Shoah: Key essays* (pp. 37–50). Oxford University Press.

Chirix García, E. D. (2019). Cuerpos, sexualidad y pensamiento maya. In X. Leyva Solano & R. Icaza (Eds.), *En tiempos de muerte: Cuerpos, rebeldías, resistencias* (pp. 139–160). Consejo Latinoamericano de Ciencias Sociales; Cooperativa Editorial Retos.

Choudry, A., & Vally, S. (Eds.). (2020). *The university and social justice: Struggles across the globe*. Pluto.

Christian, B. (1987). The race for theory. *Feminist Studies, 14*(1), 67–79.

Clark, V. (2009). Developing diaspora literacy and Marasa consciousness. *Theatre Survey, 50*(1), 9–18. https://doi.org/10.1017/S0040557409000039

Clarke, K. (2009). *Fictions of justice: The international criminal court and the challenges of legal pluralism in sub-Saharan Africa*. Cambridge University Press.

CNN. (2016, July 26). *Mothers of the movement: Entire DNC convention* [Video]. YouTube. https://www.youtube.com/watch?v=WvMaSzRuKjg

Cohen, D. W. (1994). *The combing of history*. University of Chicago Press.

Cole, J. (2001). *Forget colonialism? Sacrifice and the art of memory in Madagascar*. University of California Press.

Collins, P. H. (1986). Learning from the outsider within: The sociological significance of Black feminist thought. *Social Problems, 33*(6), S14–S32. https://doi.org/10.1525/sp.1986.33.6.03a00020

Comisión para el Esclarecimiento Histórico. (1999). *Guatemala: Memoria del silencio Tz'inil Na'tab'al*. Oficina de Servicios para Proyectos de las Naciones Unidas. http://www.centrodememoriahistorica.gov.co/descargas/guatemala-memoria-silencio/guatemala-memoria-del-silencio.pdf

Connerton, P. (1989). *How societies remember*. Cambridge University Press.

Connerton, P. (2006). Cultural memory. In C. Tilley, W. Keane, S. Küchler, M. Rowlands, & P. Spyer (Eds.), *Handbook of memorial culture* (pp. 315–324). Sage. https://dx.doi.org/10.4135/9781848607972.n21

Connerton, P. (2011). *The spirit of mourning: History, memory and the body*. Cambridge University Press.

Cook, T., & Schwartz, J. (2002). Archives, records, and power: From (postmodern) theory to (archival) performance. *Archival Science, 2*(3), 171–85. https://doi.org/10.1007/BF02435620

Cooper, B. C. (2015). Love no limit: Towards a black feminist future (in theory). *The Black Scholar, 45*(4), 7–21. https://doi.org/10.1080/00064246.2015.1080912

Corcoran, K. (2011, February 9). *Felipe Calderon, Mexico President, vows to fight drug cartels*. HuffPost. http://www.huffingtonpost.com/2011/09/02/felipe-calderon-drug-cartels_n_946967.html

Cordoba, J. O. (2009). *Resistencia festiva: Fiesta de San Antonio de Padua en Tangui (Chocó) en el contexto del conflicto armado (1996–2008)*. Uniandes.

Coronado, E. (2017, November 11). *Sepur Zarco: La historia de los abusos sexuales contados en un comic*. Plaza Pública. https://www.plazapublica.com.gt/content/sepur-zarco-la-historia-de-los-abusos-sexuales-contados-en-un-comic

Crenshaw, K. (1991). Mapping the margins: Intersectionality, identity politics, and violence against women of color. *Stanford Law Review, 43*(6), 1241–1279.

Crosby, A. (2023). Lost in translation? Agency and incommensurability in the transnational travelling of discourses of sexualized harm. *Genealogy, 7*(3), 69, 1–16. https://doi.org/10.3390/genealogy7030069

226 • References

Crosby, A., & Lykes, M. B. (2011). Mayan women survivors speak: The gendered relations of truth-telling in postwar Guatemala. *International Journal of Transitional Justice, 5*(3), 456–476. https://doi.org/10.1093/ijtj/ijr017

Crosby, A., & Lykes, M. B. (2019). *Beyond repair? Mayan women's protagonism in the aftermath of genocidal harm*. Rutgers University Press.

Coulthard, G. (2014). *Red skin, white masks: Rejecting the colonial politics of recognition*. University of Minnesota Press.

Das, V. (2000). The act of witnessing: Violence, poisonous knowledge, and subjectivity. In V. Das, A. Kleinman, M. Ramphele, & P. Reynolds (Eds.), *Violence and subjectivity* (pp. 205–225). University of California Press.

Das, V. (2007). *Life and words: Violence and the descent into the ordinary*. University of California Press.

de Alwis, M. (1998). Motherhood as a space of protest: Women's political participation in contemporary Sri Lanka. In A. Basu & P. Jeffrey (Eds.), *Appropriating gender: Women's activism and the politicization of religion in South Asia* (pp. 185–201). Routledge.

de Alwis, M. (1998). *Maternalist politics in Sri Lanka: A historical anthropology of its conditions of possibility* [Unpublished doctoral dissertation]. University of Chicago.

de Alwis, M. (1999). Millennial musings on maternalism. *Asian Women, 9*, 151–170.

de Alwis, M. (2000). The "language of the organs": The political purchase of tears in Sri Lanka. In W. Hesford & W. Kozol (Eds.), *Haunting violations: Feminist criticisms and the crisis of the "real"* (pp. 195–216). University of Illinois Press.

de Alwis, M. (2004). Feminism. In J. Vincent & D. Nugent (Eds.), *A companion to the anthropology of politics* (pp. 121–134). Blackwell.

de Alwis, M. (2009). Disappearance and displacement in Sri Lanka. *Journal of Refugee Studies, 22*(3), 378–391. https://doi.org/10.1093/jrs/fep024

Dean, A. (2012). The importance of remembering in relation: Juxtaposing the Air India and Komagata Maru disasters. *Topia: Journal of Canadian Cultural Studies, 27*, 197–214. https://doi.org/10.3138/topia.27.197

Dean, A. (2013). Public mourning and the culture of redress: Mayerthorpe, Air India, and murdered or missing Aboriginal women. In P. Wakeham & J. Henderson (Eds.), *Reconciling Canada: Critical perspectives on the culture of redress* (pp. 181–198). University of Toronto Press.

Dean, A. (2015). *Remembering Vancouver's disappeared women: Settler colonialism and the difficulty of inheritance*. Toronto University Press.

Dean, J. (2008). Enjoying neoliberalism. *Cultural Politics, 4*(1), 47–72. https://doi.org /10.2752/175174308X266398

de la Torre, G. (2003). *"Alabaos"* del Centro Cultural MAMA Universidad de Quibdó Chocó [CD Audio Recording]. In *Historia del Pueblo afrocolombiano: perspectiva pastoral* [Brochure]. Centro de Pastoral Afrocolombiana.

de Lima, C. (2014). Lost (and found?) in translation/feminisms in hemispheric dialogue. In S. E. Alvarez, C. de Lima Costa, V. Feliu, R. J. Hester, N. Klahn, M. Thayer, & C. C. Bueno (Eds.), *Translocalities/translocalidades: Feminist politics of translation in the Latin/a Americas* (pp. 19–36). Duke University Press.

Derrida, J. (1974). *Of grammatology* (G. C. Spivak, Trans.). Johns Hopkins University Press. (Original work published 1967).

Derrida, J. (1978). *Spurs/Éperons* (B. Harlow, Trans.). University of Chicago Press.

Derrida, J. (1994). *Specters of Marx: the state of the debt, the work of mourning, and the new international*. Routledge.

Dialita. (2016). *Dunia milik kita* [Our own world]. Cakrawala Record.

Dipa, A. (2019, May 17). Dialita 1965 survivors choir to accept Gwangju human rights award. *The Jakarta Post*. https://www.thejakartapost.com/news/2019/05/17/dialita-1965-survivors-choir-to-accept-gwangju-human-rights-award.html

Doctor, F. (2015). *All inclusive*. Dundurn.

Doss, E. (2010). *Memorial mania: Public feeling in America*. University of Chicago Press.

Douglass, A. (2003). The Menchú effect: Strategic lies and approximate truths in texts of witness. In A. Douglass & T. Vogler (Eds.), *Witness and memory: The discourse of trauma* (pp. 55–88). Routledge.

Drabold, W. (2016). Read what the mothers of the movement said at the Democratic convention. *Time*. https://time.com/4424704/dnc-mothers-movement-transcript-speechvideo/

Eagleton, T. (2009, November 16). Waking the dead. *The New Statesman*, 4975(138), 44–45.

Ebrahimi, M. (2019). *Women, art, and literature in the Iranian diaspora*. Syracuse University Press.

El Tiempo Editorial (2016, September 27). 'Miembros de las FARC, bienvenidos a la democracia.' https://www.eltiempo.com/politica/proceso-de-paz/firma-del-acuerdo-final-de-paz-con-las-farc-en-cartagena-34636

Eng, D. L., & Han, S. (2019). *Racial melancholia, racial dissociation: On the social and psychic lives of Asian Americans*. Duke University Press.

Erll, A. (2008). Cultural memory studies: An introduction. In A. Erll & A. Nunning (Eds.), *Cultural memory studies* (pp. 1–18). De Gruyter.

Erll, A. (2011). Travelling memory. *Parallax*, 17(4), 4–18.

Ermine, W. (2007). The ethical space of engagement. *Indigenous Law Journal*, 6(1), 193–203.

Ernst, W., & Parikka, J. (2012). *Digital memory and the archive*. University of Minnesota Press.

Escobar, A. (2015). Territorios de diferencia: la ontología política de los "derechos al territorio." *Cuadernos de Antropología Social* (41), 25–38.

Eslava, L., Fakhri, M., & Nesiah, V. (2017). *Bandung, global history, and international law: critical pasts and pending futures*. Cambridge University Press.

Espinosa, Y., Gómez, D., & Ochoa, K. (Eds.). (2014). Introducción. In *Tejiendo de otro modo: Feminismo, epistemología y apuestas decoloniales en Abya Yala* (pp. 13–43). Editorial Universidad del Cauca.

Erengezgin, Ç. (2021). *Coloniality and solidarity: An intersectional study of the relationship between the Turkish feminist movement and the Kurdish women's movement since the 1980s* [Unpublished doctoral dissertation]. University of British Columbia.

Failler, A. (2009). Remembering the Air India disaster: Memorial and countermemorial. *Review of Education, Pedagogy, and Cultural Studies*, 31(2), 150–176. https:doi.org/10.1080/10714410902827168

Failler, A. (2010). "Remember me nought": The 1985 Air India bombings and cultural Nachträglichkeit. *Public: Art/Culture/Ideas*, 42, 101–124.

Failler, A. (2012). "War-on-terror" frames of remembrance: The 1985 Air India bombings after 9/11. *Topia: Canadian Journal of Cultural Studies*, 27, 253–270. https://doi.org/10.3138/topia.27.253

Faist, T. (2010). Diaspora and transnationalism: What kind of dance partners? In R. Bauböck & T. Faist (Eds.), *Diaspora and transnationalism: Concepts, theories and methods* (pp. 9–34). Amsterdam University Press.

Falcón, S. M., & Nash, J. C. (2015). Shifting analytics and linking theories: A conversation about the "meaning-making" of intersectionality and transnational feminism. *Women's Studies International Forum*, 50, 1–10.

Farid, H. (2005). Indonesia's original sin: mass killings and capitalist expansion, 1965–66. *Inter-Asia Cultural Studies, 6*(1), 3–16. https://doi.org/10.1080/1462394042000326879

Felman, S., & Laub, D. (1992). *Testimony: Crises of witnessing in literature, psychoanalysis, and history.* Taylor & Francis.

Fernando, P. (n.d.) A fisherman mourned by his wife. In Y. Gooneratne (Ed.), *Poems from India, Sri Lanka and Malaysia.* Heinemann.

Ferreira Da Silva, D. (2014). Toward a black feminist poethics: The question of blackness toward the end of the world. *The Black Scholar, 44*(2), 81–97. https://doi.org/10.1080/00064246.2014.11413690

Final report of the Commission of Inquiry into involuntary removal or disappearance of persons in the Western, Southern and Sabaragamuwa Provinces. (1997). Government Publications Bureau.

Finch, A. (2020). Cécile Fatiman and Petra Carabalí, late eighteenth-century Haiti and mid-nineteenth-century Cuba. In E. Ball, T. Seijas, & T. Snyder (Eds.), *As if she were free: A collective biography of women and emancipation in the Americas* (pp. 293–311). Cambridge University Press.

Ford-Smith, H. (2011). Local and transnational dialogues on memory and violence in Jamaica and Toronto: Staging *Letters from the Dead* among the living. *Canadian Theatre Review, 148*(148), 10–17. https://doi.org/10.3138/ctr.148.10

Ford-Smith, H. (2014). Gone but not forgotten: Memorial murals, vigils, and the politics of popular commemoration in Jamaica. In *At the limits of justice: Women of colour on terror* (p. 263–288). University of Toronto Press. https://doi.org/10.3138/j.ctt9qh983.19

Franco, J. (1985). Killing priests, nuns, women, children. In B. Marshall (Ed.), *On Signs* (pp. 414–420). Johns Hopkins University Press.

Frank, S., & Ristic, M. (2020). Urban fallism: Monuments, iconoclasm and activism. *City, 24*(3–4), 552–564. https://doi.org/10.1080/13604813.2020.1784578

Freeman, E. (2005). Time binds, or, erotohistoriography. *Social Text, 23*(3–4), 57–68. https://doi.org/10.1215/01642472-23-3-4_84-85-57

Freire, P. (2000). *Pedagogy of the oppressed* (30th anniversary ed.). Continuum.

Friedmann, S. (2006). Cantadoras que se alaban de poetas: Reivindicaciones colectivas en la construcción de cultura. *Palimpsesto, 1,* 142–147.

Friscolanti, M. (2017, March 17). *Ontario's "poetic" judge is back with another ruling.* Macleans.ca. https://www.macleans.ca/news/canada/ontarios-poetic-judge-is-back-with-another-ruling/

Fuenmayor, V. (2011). El signo de la tradición en el cuerpo. In T. Hernández (Ed.), *60 años de Tradiciones Populares Venezolanas: de la fiesta de la tradición a la tradición global-izada* (pp. 101–128). Fundación Cultural Chacao.

Fulchiron, A., Paz, O. A., & López, A. (2009). *Tejidos que lleva el alma: Memoria de las mujeres mayas sobrevivientes de violación sexual durante el conflicto armado.* ECAP, UNAMG, & F&G Editores.

Fulton, S., & Martin, T. (2017). *Rest in power: The enduring life of Trayvon Martin.* Spiegel & Grau.

Galappatti, A. (2004). Psychological suffering, "trauma," and PTSD: Implications for women in Sri Lanka's conflict zones. In W. Giles, M. de Alwis, E. Klein, N. Silva, & M. Korac (Eds.), *Feminists under fire: Exchanges across war zones* (pp. 115–129). Between the Lines.

Garcia, M. (2009). Myths of Mexico: The U.S. simplistic depiction of the drug war. *Columbia Journalism Review, 48*(4), 16–18.

Gargallo, F. (2014). *Bordados de paz, memoria y justicia: un proceso de visibilización.* Grafisma Editores.

Gelles, P. H. (1998). Testimonio, ethnography and processes of authorship. *Anthropology News*, *39*(3), 16–17. https://doi.org/10.1111/an.1998.39.3.16.1

Ghaddar, J. J., & Caswell, M. (2019). "To go beyond": Towards a decolonial archival praxis. *Archival Science*, *19*(2), 71–85. https://doi.org/10.1007/s10502-019-09311-1

Ghamari-Tabrizi, B. (2004). Contentious public religion: Two conceptions of Islam in revolutionary Iran: Ali Shariati and Abdolkarim Soroush. *International Sociology*, *19* (4), 504. https://doi.org/10.1177/0268580904047371

Ghobadi, G. (2015). *Shaqāyiq-hā bar Sanglākh: Zindigī wa Zamānah-yi yik Zan-i Kurd* [Poppies on rocks: The life and times of a Kurdish woman]. Self-published.

Ghobadi, G. (Ed.) (2020). *Gulzār-i Shaqāyiq-hā: Nāguftah-hā-yi Zanān-i Mubāriz Kurdestān 'Īrān* [Field of poppies: The untold stories of Iranian Kurdish women in struggle]. Noghteh.

Ghoshal, R. A. (2013). Transforming collective memory: Mnemonic opportunity structures and the outcomes of racial violence memory movements. *Theory and Society*, *42*(4), 329–350. https://doi.org/10.1007/s11186-013-9197-9

Giles, W., & Hyndman, J. (2004). *Sites of violence: Gender and conflict zones*. University of California Press.

Giles, W., de Alwis, M., Klein, E., & Silva, N. (Eds). *Feminists under fire: Exchanges across war zones*. Between the Lines.

Gómez-Barris, M. (2009). *Where memory dwells: Culture and state violence in Chile*. University of California Press.

Goodison, L. (1992). *Selected poems*. The University of Michigan Press.

Good Morning America. (2020, July 13). *Their painful bond: Black mothers speak out together on their unimaginable loss* [Video]. YouTube. https://www.youtube.com/watch?v=vuBLCqZ2s5w

Gopinath, G. (2005). *Impossible desires: Queer diasporas and South Asian public cultures*. Duke University Press.

Gordon, A. (2008). *Ghostly matters: Haunting and the sociological imagination*. University of Minnesota Press.

Gossett, C. (2013). Silhouettes of defiance: The memorialization of historical sites of queer and transgender resistance in the age of neoliberal inclusivity. In Stryker, S. & Aizura, A.Z. (Eds.), *The transgender studies reader 2* (pp. 565–579). Routledge.

Gossett C., & McManemin, J. (2020). *Monumental collapse: Toppled statues and reimagining archives*. Art Papers. https://www.artpapers.org/monumental-collapse/

Grassian, D. (2013). *Iranian and diasporic literature in the 21st century: A critical study*. McFarland.

Grewal, I. (2005). *Transnational America: Feminisms, diasporas, neoliberalisms*. Duke University Press.

Grewal, I. (2017). *Saving the security state: Exceptional citizens in twenty-first century America*. Duke University Press.

Grewal, I., & Kaplan, C. (1994). Introduction: Transnational feminist practices and questions of postmodernity. In I. Grewal & C. Kaplan (Eds.), *Scattered hegemonies: Postmodernity and transnational feminist practices* (pp. 1–36). University of Minnesota Press.

Grewal, I. & Kaplan, C. (1994). *Scattered hegemonies: Postmodernity and transnational feminist practices*. University of Minnesota Press.

Grewal, I., & Kaplan, C. (2000). Postcolonial studies and transnational feminist practices. *Jouvert: A Journal of Postcolonial Studies*, *5*(1). https://legacy.chass.ncsu.edu/jouvert/v5i1/grewal.htm

Grupo de Memoria Histórica de la Comisión Nacional de Reparación y Reconciliación. (2010). *Bojayá: La guerra sin límites.* http://www.centrodememoriahistorica.gov.co/descargas/informes2010/informe_bojaya.pdf

Gutiérrez, D. (2016). *Ejercicios del cuidado. A propósito de la piel de la memoria* [Unpublished doctoral dissertation]. Universidad Nacional Autónoma de México.

Haaken, J. (2002). Cultural amnesia: Memory, trauma, and war. *Signs: Journal of Women in Culture and Society, 28*(1), 455–457. https://doi.org/10.1086/340870

Halbwachs, M. (2011). The collective memory. In J. K. Olick, V. Vinitzky-Seroussi, & D. Levy, (Eds.), *The collective memory reader* (pp. 139–149). Oxford University Press.

Halbwachs, M., & Coser, L. A. (1992). *On collective memory.* University of Chicago Press. https://doi.org/10.7208/chicago/9780226774497.001.0001

Hall, K. Q. (2016). A transnational Black feminist framework: Rooting feminist scholarship, framing contemporary Black activism. *Meridians: Feminism, race, transnationalism, 15*(1), 86–104. https://doi.org/10.2979/meridians.15.1.06

Haritaworn, J., Kuntsman, A., & Posocco, S. (Eds.). (2014). *Queer necropolitics.* Routledge.

Harper, S. (2010). Statement by the Prime Minister of Canada at the Commemoration Ceremony for the 25th anniversary of the Air India Flight 182 atrocity. In C. Chakraborty, A. Dean, & A. Failler (Eds.), *Remembering Air India: The art of public mourning* (pp. 153–158). University of Alberta Press.

Hartman, S. (1997). *Scenes of subjection: Terror, slavery, and self-making in nineteenth-century America.* Oxford University Press.

Hartman, S. (2007). *Lose your mother: A journey along the Atlantic slave route.* Farrar, Straus and Giroux.

Hartman, S. (2008). Venus in two acts. *Small Axe, 12*(2), pp. 1–14. https://doi.org/10.1215/-12-2-1

Hartman, S. (2019). *Wayward lives, beautiful experiments: Intimate histories of social upheaval.* W.W. Norton.

Hasanpour, S. (2012). *Dechmewe Sablax* [Going back to Sablaq]. Apec Förlag.

Hatfield, J. E. (2019). The queer kairotic: Digital transgender suicide memories and ecological rhetorical agency. *Rhetoric Society Quarterly, 49*(1), 25–48. https://doi.org/10.1080/02773945.2018.1549334

Hayner, P. B. (2002). *Unspeakable truths: Facing the challenge of truth commissions.* Routledge.

Henderson, M. G. (2005). Speaking in tongues: Dialogics, dialectics, and the black woman writer's literary tradition. *The Scholar & Feminist XXX: Past Controversies, Present Challenges, Future Feminisms, 3*(3) & *4*(1), 1–21. http://sfonline.barnard.edu/sfxxx/documents/henderson.pdf

Henry, N. (2009). Witness to rape: The limits and potential of international war crimes trials for victims of wartime sexual violence. *International Journal of Transitional Justice, 3*(1), 114–134. https://doi.org/10.1093/ijtj/ijn036

Heryanto, A. (1999). Where communism never dies: Violence, trauma and narration in the last cold war capitalist authoritarian state. *International Journal of Cultural Studies, 2*(2), 147–177. https://doi.org/10.1177/136787799900200201

Heryanto, A. (2006). *State terrorism and political identity in Indonesia: Fatally belonging.* Routledge.

Himid, L. (2011). *What are monuments for? Possible landmarks on the urban map: London and Paris* [Video]. Vimeo. https://vimeo.com/22938970

Hirsch, M. (2019). Introduction: Practicing feminism, practicing memory. In A. G. Altinay, M. J. Contreras, M. Hirsch, J. Howard, B. Karaca, & A. Solomon (Eds.), *Women mobilizing memory* (pp.1–23). Columbia University Press.

Hirsch, M., & Smith, V. (2002). Feminism and cultural memory: An introduction. *Signs: Journal of Women in Culture and Society, 28*(1), 1–19. https://doi.org/10.1086/340890

Holland, S. H. (2000). *Raising the dead: Readings of death and (Black) subjectivity.* Duke University Press.

Honna, J. (2000). Military ideology in response to democratic pressure during the late Suharto era: political and institutional contexts. In B. R. O'G. Anderson (Ed.), *Violence and the state in Suharto's Indonesia* (pp. 54–89). Cornell University Press.

Hoskins, A. (2011). Media, memory, metaphor: Remembering and the connective turn. *Parallax, 17*(4), 19–31. https://doi.org/10.1080/13534645.2011.60557

Hoskins, A. (Ed.) (2017). The restless past: An introduction to digital memory and media. In A. Hoskins (Ed.), *Digital memory studies: Media pasts in transition* (pp. 1–21). Routledge.

Hoskins, A. (2018). Memory of the multitude: The end of collective memory. In A. Hoskins (Ed.), *Digital memory studies: Media pasts in transition* (pp. 85–109). Routledge.

Hoskins, A., & Halstead, H. (2021). The new grey of memory: Andrew Hoskins in conversation with Huw Halstead. *Memory Studies, 14*(3), 675–685. https://doi.org10.1177/17506980211010936

Hughes, L. (1994). Harlem [2]. In A. Rampersad & D. Roessel (Eds.), *The collected poems of Langston Hughes* (p. 426). Vintage Classics.

Huyssen, A. (2003). *Present pasts: Urban palimpsests and the politics of memory.* Stanford University Press.

Ibrahim, I. (2018, September 25). Ontario judge gives light sentence to Black offender citing systemic racism. *The Black Youth Project.* https://blackyouthproject.com/ontario-judge-gives-light-sentence-to-black-offender-citing-systemic-racism/

Impunity Watch & Alliance to Break the Silence and Impunity. (2017, July 18). *Changing the face of justice: Keys to the strategic litigation of the Sepur Zarco case.* https://www.impunitywatch.org/wp-content/uploads/2017/07/Changing_the_face_of_justice_final.pdf

International Crisis Group. (2013). *Peña Nieto's challenge: Criminal cartels and rule of law in Mexico.* http://www.crisisgroup.org/en/regions/latin-america-caribbean/mexico/048-pena-nietos-challenge-criminal-cartels-and-rule-of-law-in-mexico.aspx

Iran Tribunal. (2012). *On the abuse and mass killings of political prisoners in Iran, 1981–1988.* Iran Tribunal Press.

Ituribarria, M. (2009) *1/40,000: Ante el dolor de los demás.* Artist Statement. http://mo-itu.com/

Jacobs, J. (2010). *Memorializing the Holocaust: Gender, genocide and collective memory.* I. B. Tauris.

Jaleel, R. (2021). *The work of rape.* Duke University Press.

James, S. L. (2017). Remarks for a roundtable on transnational feminism. *Meridians, 18*(2), 471–479.

Jaramillo, P. (2014). *Etnicidad y victimización. Genealogías de la violencia y la indigenidad en el norte de Colombia.* Universidad de los Andes.

Jeganathan, P. (2004). *The work of melancholia: Aspects of nationalist thought in the island formerly called Ceylon* [Keynote address]. Institute of Postcolonial Studies Bi-Annual Conference, Munich, Germany.

Jelin, E. (2002). *Los trabajos de la memoria.* Madrid Siglo XXI de España Editores.

Jelin, E. (2003). *State repression and the labors of memory.* University of Minnesota Press.

Jeong-ho, M. (2004). Disappeared, but still alive in their minds. In S. Puvimanasinghe, (Ed.), *An exceptional collapse of the rule of law: Told through stories by families of the disappeared in Sri Lanka* (pp. 123–127). Asian Legal Resource Centre, Asian Human Rights Commission and Families of the Disappeared.

Kaba, M. (2021). *We do this 'til we free us: Abolitionist organizing and transforming justice.* Haymarket Books.

Kakabaveh, A., & Ohlson, J. (2021). *Amineh–"No Bigger than a Kalashnikov": A Peshmerga in Parliament* (S. Berger, Trans.). Buxus.

Kamangar, A. (2016). *Farāzhā-yi az Zindigī* [Moments of life]. Shamlo Kulturhus.

Kammen, D., & McGregor, K. (Eds.). (2012). *The contours of mass violence in Indonesia, 1965–68.* ASAA Southeast Asia Publication Series.

KBI Telegraf. (2017, January 4). *20 Judul Album Musik Indonesia Terbaik 2016.* https://telegraf.co.id/20-judul-album-musik-indonesia-terbaik-2016/

Kelley, R. D. G. (2002). *Freedom dreams: The black radical imagination.* Beacon.

Kolia, Z. (2016). The aporia of indigeneity: (Dis)enchanting identity and the modular nation form. *Interventions, International Journal of Postcolonial Studies, 18*(4), 605–626. http://doi.org/10.1080/1369801X.2015.1131181

LaCapra, D. (1999). Trauma, absence, loss. *Critical Inquiry, 25,* 696–727. https:doi.org /10.1086/448943

Lamble, S. (2008). Retelling racialized violence, remaking white innocence: The politics of interlocking oppressions in transgender day of remembrance. *Sexuality Research & Social Policy, 5*(1), 24–42. https://doi.org/10.1525/srsp.2008.5.1.24

Langer, L. (1997). The alarmed vision: Social suffering and Holocaust atrocity. In A. Kleinman, V. Das, & M. M. Lock (Eds.), *Social suffering* (pp. 47–68). University of California Press.

Lawrence, D. (2007). *And still I rise: A mother's search for justice.* Faber and Faber.

Leader, D. (2009). *The new Black: Mourning, melancholia, and depression.* Penguin Books.

Leal, C. (2018). *Landscapes of freedom: Building a postemancipation society in the rainforests of western Colombia.* The University of Arizona Press.

Leathem, H. M. V. (2020). *Monumental destruction.* Monument Lab. https://www .monumentlab.com/bulletin/monumental-destruction

Leebaw, B. (2011). *Judging state-sponsored violence, imagining political change.* Cambridge University Press.

Leonidas, V. (2009). *Al son que me toquen canto y bailo. Cartilla de iniciación musical.* Ministerio de Cultura.

Leung, M. (2015, March 9). "Transformative" decision: How a judge's decision is turning legal heads. *CTVNews.* https://www.ctvnews.ca/canada/transformative-decision -how-a-judge-s-decision-is-turning-legal-heads-1.2270358

Lifton, R. J. (1967). *Death in life: Survivors of Hiroshima.* The University of North Carolina Press.

Littlewood, J. (1992). The denial of death and rites of passage in contemporary societies. *The Sociological Review, 40,* 69–84. https://doi.org/10.1111/j.1467-954X .1992.tb03387.x

Locke, C. (2020). Digital memory and the problem of forgetting. In S. Radstone (Ed.), *Memory and methodology* (pp. 25–36). Routledge.

Lorde, A. (1984). The uses of the erotic: The erotic as power. In *Sister outsider: Essays and speeches* (pp. 53–59). Crossing.

Losonczy, A. M. (1991). El luto de sí mismo. Cuerpo, sombra y muerte entre los negros colombianos del Chocó. *América Negra, 1,* 43–65.

Love, H. (2007). *Feeling backward: Loss and the politics of queer history.* Harvard University Press.

Lowe, L. (1996). *Immigrant acts: On Asian American cultural politics*. Duke University Press.

Lowe, L. (2015). *The intimacies of four continents*. Duke University Press.

Lugones, M. (2014). Colonialidades y genero. In Y. Espinosa Miñoso, D. Gómez Correal, & K. Ochoa Muñoz (Eds.), *Tejiendo de otro modo: Feminismo, epistemología y apuestas decoloniales en Abya Yala* (pp. 57–74). Editorial Universidad del Cauca.

MacKinnon, C. (2006). Defining rape internationally: A comment on Akayesu. *Columbia Journal of Transnational Law, 44*(3), 940–958.

Maignault-Bryant, L. S. (2014). *Talking to the dead: Religion, music, and lived memory among Gullah/Geechee women*. Duke University Press.

Makaremi, C. (2011). *Aziz's notebook: At the heart of the Iranian revolution* (R. Georges, Trans.). Gallimard.

Makaremi, C. (2013). *Aziz's notebook. At the hearth of the Iranian Revolution* (R. Georges, Trans.) Yoda.

Makaremi, C. (Director). (2019). *Hitch: An Iranian story* [Film]. Alter Ego Production.

Manning, E. (2006). *Politics of touch*. University of Minnesota Press.

Maya Restrepo, L.A. (1996). "África: legados espirituales en la Nueva Granada, siglo XVII." *Historia Crítica* (12): 29–42.

Maracle, L. (1996). *I am woman: A native perspective on sociology and feminism* (2nd ed.). Raincoast.

Marjara, E. (Director). (1998). *Desperately seeking Helen* [Film; DVD]. National Film Board of Canada.

Marriott, D. (2017). Introduction: Black experimental poetics. *The Black Scholar, 47*(1), 1–2. http://doi.org/10.1080/00064246.2017.1264826

Matin-Asgari, A. (2002). *Iranian student opposition to the Shah*. Mazda.

Mavor, C. (1995). *Pleasures taken: Performances of sexuality and loss in Victorian photographs*. Duke University Press.

Mavor, C. (1997). Collecting loss. *Cultural Studies, 11*(1), 111–137. https://doi.org/10.1080/09502389700490071

The May 18 Memorial Foundation. (2019, June). *The completion of the 2019 Gwangju Prize for Human Rights Awards Ceremony*. 518. http://518.org/Mayzine/201906/subpage/sub0201.php?ckattempt=1

The May 18 Memorial Foundation. (2020, April). *Dialita Choir (Indonesia): Socio cultural movement for peace*. 518. http://www.518.org/Mayzine/202004/subpage/sub0502.php

Mawani, R. (2012). Law's archive. *Annual Review of Law and Social Science, 8*(1), 337–365. https://doi.org/10.1146/annurev-lawsocsci-102811-173900

McAllister, C. (2013). Testimonial truths and revolutionary mysteries. In C. McAllister & D. M. Nelson (Eds.), *War by other means: Aftermath in post-genocide Guatemala* (pp. 93–115). Duke University Press.

McGregor, K. (2012). The Cold War, Indonesian women and the global anti-imperialist movement, 1946–65. In J. E. P. Mooney & F. Lanza (Eds.), *De-centering Cold War history local and global change* (pp. 31–51). Routledge.

McGregor, K., & Setiawan, K. (2019). Shifting from international to "Indonesian" justice measures: Two decades of addressing past human rights violations. *Journal of Contemporary Asia, 49*(5), 837–861. https://doi.org/10.1080/00472336.2019.1584636

McLean, L. (2020). A question that has no end: The politics of life and death in the search for disappeared migrants in Mexico. *Citizenship Studies, 24*(8), 994–1009. https://doi.org/10.1080/13621025.2020.1769027

McSpadden, L. (2016). *Tell the truth and shame the devil: The life, legacy, and love of my son Michael Brown*. Simon and Schuster.

Megill, A. (2011). History, memory, identity. In J. K. Olick, V. Vinitzky-Seroussi, & D. Levy (Eds.), *The collective memory reader* (pp. 193–197). Oxford University Press.

Meijer, I. C., & Prins, B. (1998). How bodies come to matter: An interview with Judith Butler. *Signs: Journal of Women in Culture and Society, 23*(2), 275–286. https://doi.org/10.1086/495251

Menchú, R. (1984). *I, Rigoberta Menchú: An Indian woman in Guatemala* (E. Burgos-Debray, Ed.; A. Wright, Trans.). Verso.

Metz, C. (1990). Photography and fetish. In C. Squires (Ed.), *The critical image: Essays on contemporary photography*. Bay.

Meza, C. A. (2010). *Tradiciones elaboradas y modernizaciones vividas por pueblos afrochocoanos en la vía al mar*. Instituto Colombiano de Antropología e Historia.

Millán, C. (2009). *Ya no llega el Limbo porque la gente bailando está: Prácticas de memoria en Bojayá-Chocó* [Unpublished master's thesis]. Universidad Nacional de Colombia.

Million, D. (2009). Felt theory: An Indigenous feminist approach to affect and history. *Wicazo Sa Review, 24*(2), 53–76. https://doi.org/10.1353/wic.0.0043

Million, D. (2013). *Therapeutic nations: Healing in an age of Indigenous human rights*. The University of Arizona Press.

Milton, C. E. (Ed.). (2014). *Art from a fractured past: Memory and truth-telling in post-Shining Path Peru*. Duke University Press.

Minow, M. (1998). *Between vengeance and forgiveness: Facing history after genocide and mass violence*. Beacon.

Mnjama, N. (2008). The Orentlicher principles on the preservation and access to archives bearing witness to human rights violations. *Information Development, 24*(3), 213–25. https://doi.org/10.1177/0266666908094837

Moghadam, V. M. (2005). *Globalizing women: Transnational feminist networks*. John Hopkins University Press.

Moghissi, H. (1994). *Populism and feminism*. St. Martin's.

Mohajer, N. (2020). *Voices of a massacre: Untold stories of life and death in Iran, 1988*. Oneworld Publications.

Mohajer, N. (Ed.). (2020). *Voices of a massacre: Untold stories of life and death in Iran, 1988*. Simon and Schuster.

Mohanty, C. T. (2003). *Feminism without borders: Decolonizing theory, practicing solidarity*. Duke University Press.

Mohanty, C. T. (2013). Transnational feminist crossings: On neoliberalism and radical critique. *Signs, 38*(4), 967–991. https://doi.org/10.1086/669576

Mojab, S. (2007). Introduction: Years of solitude, years of defiance: Women political prisoners in Iran. In A. Agah, S. Mehr, & S. Parsi (Eds.), *We lived to tell: Political prison memoirs of Iranian women* (pp. 1–18). McGilligan.

Mojab, S. (2015). Introduction: Marxism and feminism. In S. Mojab (Ed.), *Marxism and feminism* (pp. 1–29). Zed.

Mojab, S. (2019). Forward: Forget-me-not. In *Lives lost: In search of a new tomorrow* (viii-xv). Prison Poetry Project. Trace.

Mojab, S. (2022). Women and revolution in the Middle East. In S. Joseph & Z. Zaatari (Eds.), *Handbook of Middle East women* (pp. 197–211). Routledge.

Mojab, S. (2024). The *past* and the *absences* are *present* in Kurdish women's memoirs. In S. Mojab (Ed.). *Kurdish women through history, culture, and resistance* (pp. 222–243). Mazda Publishers.

Montero, M. P. (2012, December 5). *Bordando por la paz: la herida en el pañuelo*. Sin Embargo. https://www.sinembargo.mx/05-12-2012/449678

Mookherjee, N. (2015). *The spectral wound: Sexual violence, public memories, and the Bangladesh war of 1971*. Duke University Press.

Moon, J. (2004). Disappeared, but still alive in their minds. In *An exceptional collapse of the rule of law: Told through stories by families of the disappeared in Sri Lanka*. Asian Legal Resource Centre, Asian Human Rights Commission and Families of the Disappeared

Morrill, A., Tuck, E., & Super Futures Haunt Qollective. (2016). Before dispossession, or surviving it. *Liminalities, 12*(1), 1–20. http://liminalities.net/12-1/

Morrison, T. (1995). Site of memory. In W. Zinsser (Ed.), *Inventing the truth: The art and craft of memoir* (pp. 83–102). Houghton Mifflin.

Morrison, T. (2010). *Beloved*. Vintage Classics.

Motha, S. (2015). As if law, history, ontology. *UC Irvine Law Review, 5*(2), 327–348.

Mouffe, C. (2007). *En torno a lo político* (S. Laclau, Trans.). Fondo de Cultura Económica. (Original work published by Verso in 1993)

Mullings, B. (2009). Neoliberalization, social reproduction and the limits to labour in Jamaica. *Singapore Journal of Tropical Geography, 30*(2), 174–188. https://doi.org/10.1111/j.1467-9493.2009.00363.x

Murdocca, C. (2013). *To right historical wrongs: Race, gender, and sentencing in Canada*. UBC.

Murrell, N. S. (2010). *Afro-Caribbean religions*. Temple University Press

Nagar, R., & Swarr, A. L. (2010). Theorizing transnational feminist praxis. In A. Lock Swarr & R. Nagar (Eds.), *Critical transnational feminist praxis* (pp. 1–20). SUNY Press.

Naghibi, N. (2016). *Women write Iran: Nostalgia and human rights from the diaspora*. University of Minnesota Press.

Nammi, D., & Attwood, K. (2020). *Girl with a gun: Love, loss and the fight for freedom in Iran*. Unbound.

Nash, J. C. (2021). Beyond antagonism: Rethinking intersectionality, transnationalism, and the women's studies academic job market. In A. Tambe & M. Thayer (Eds.), *Transnational feminist itineraries: Situating theory and activist practice* (pp. 37–51). Duke University Press.

Nash, J. C., & Pinto, S. (2020). Strange intimacies: Reading black maternal memoirs. *Public Culture, 32*(3), 491–512. https://doi.org/10.1215/08992363-8358686

National Inquiry into Missing and Murdered Indigenous Women and Girls. (2019). *Reclaiming power and place: The final report of the national inquiry into missing and murdered Indigenous women and girls, Volume 1a and 1b*. Privy Council. https://www.mmiwg-ffada.ca/final-report/

Nemequene Tundama. (2016, April 13). *You cannot decolonize colonialism* [Video]. YouTube. https://youtu.be/hXJS8d2T1IE

Nice, G., Sabi, H., Sakhi, S., & Ghiasi, R. (2019). The Iran Tribunal: An international people's tribunal for the promotion of truth and justice. In R. M. Paulose (Ed.), *People's tribunals, human rights and the law* (pp. 99–111). Routledge.

Nobel Women's Initiative. (2016, February 24). *Nobel laureates call Sepur Zarco trial "victory for sexual violence survivors worldwide."* https://nobelwomensinitiative.org/nobel-laureates-call-sepur-zarco-trial-victory-for-sexual-violence-survivors-worldwide/?ref=18

Notosusanto, N., & Saleh, I. (1968). *The coup attempt of the "September 30 Movement" in Indonesia*. Pembimbing Masa.

Ochoa, A. M. (2014). *Aurality. Listening and knowledge in nineteenth-century Colombia*. Duke University Press.

Oficina de Derechos Humanos del Arzobispo de Guatemala. (1998). *Nunca más: Impactos de la violencia, informe del proyecto interdiocesano de recuperación de la memoria*. Litografía e Imprenta LIL, SA.

Oglesby, E. (2007). Educating citizens in postwar Guatemala: Historical memory, genocide, and the culture of peace. *Radical History Review, 97*, 77–98. https://doi.org/10.1215/01636545-2006-013

Olalde, K. (2019). *Bordando por la paz: bordado y acción colectiva contra la violencia en México*. Red Mexicana de Movimientos Sociales.

Olick, J. K., Vinitzky-Seroussi, V., & Levy, D. (Eds.). (2011). Introduction. In *The collective memory reader* (pp. 9–62). Oxford University Press.

Orjuela Villanueva, C. (2020). ¿Qué hacemos con tanto muerto junto? Tratar la muerte violenta y masiva en el Medio Atrato. *Revista Colombiana de Antropología, 56*(2), 51–78.

Paley, D. M. (2020) *Capitalismo antidrogas: una guerra contra el pueblo*. Libertad Bajo Palabra.

Perera, S. (2001). Spirit possessions and avenging ghosts: Stories of supernatural activity as narratives of terror and mechanisms of coping and remembering. In V. Das, A. Kleinman, M. M. Lock, M. Ramphele, & P. Reynolds (Eds.), *Remaking a world: Violence, social suffering and recovery* (pp. 157–200). University of California Press.

Petersen, B. (2010, August 12). Juarez, México—Murder capital of the world. *CBS News* https://www.cbsnews.com/news/juarez-mexico-murder-capital-of-the-world/

Pethes, N. (2019). *Cultural memory studies: An introduction*. Cambridge Scholars.

Philip, N. (2011). *Zong!* Wesleyan University Press.

Powell, K. J. (2016). Making #BlackLivesMatter: Michael Brown, Eric Garner, and the specters of Black life—of Blackness. *Cultural Studies, Critical Methodologies, 16*(3), 253–260. https://doi.org/10.1177/1532708616634770

Prescod-Weinstein, C. (2016, December 19). *The physics of melanin: Science and the chaotic social construct of race*. bitchmedia. https://www.bitchmedia.org/article/physics-melanin/science-and-chaotic-social-construct-race

Prime Minister of Canada. (2007). *Prime minister unveils memorial dedicated to the victims of Air India Flight 182*. http://pm.gc.ca/eng/media.asp?id=1719

Puar, J. (2007). *Terrorist assemblages: Homonationalism in queer times*. Duke University Press.

Quiceno, N. (2016). *Vivir sabroso. Luchas y movimientos afroatrateños en Bojayá, Chocó, Colombia*. Universidad del Rosario.

Rábago, O., & Vergara, L. (2011, August 19). *La violencia en México y el discurso gubernamental*. Artículo 19. https://articulo19.org/la-violencia-en-mexico-y-el-discurso-gubernamental/

Radstone, S. (2000). Working with memory: An introduction. In S. Radstone. (Ed.), *Memory and methodology* (pp. 1–24). Routledge.

Radstone, S., & Hodgkin, K. (2003). Regimes of memory: An introduction. In K. Hodgkin & S. Radstone (Eds.), *Regimes of memory* (pp. 1–22). Routledge.

Razack, S. H. (1999). *Looking white people in the eye*. University of Toronto Press.

Razack, S. (2017). The impact of systemic racism on Canada's pre-bombing threat assessment and post-bombing response to the Air India bombings. In C. Chakraborty, A. Dean, & A. Failler (Eds.), *Remembering Air India: The art of public mourning* (pp. 85–117). University of Alberta Press.

Reading, A. (2014). Making memory work for feminist theory. In M. Evans, C. Hemmings, M. Henry, H. Johnstone, S. Madhok, A. Plomien, & S. Wearing (Eds.), *The SAGE Handbook of Feminist Theory* (pp. 196–214). Sage.

Reading, A. (2016). *Gender and memory in the globital age*. Palgrave Macmillan.

Reguillo, R. (2011). *La narcomáquina y el trabajo de la violencia: Apuntes para su decodificación*. Hemispheric Institute. https://hemisphericinstitute.org/es/emisferica-82/reguillo5.html

Riaño-Alcalá, P. (2012, Sept. 28–29). *Quitar espacio a la guerra: Mapping everyday responses to violence in contexts of armed violence* [Paper presentation]. Surviving Violence: Comparative Perspectives Workshop, Halifax, Nova Scotia, Canada.

Riaño-Alcalá, P. (2015). Emplaced witnessing: Commemorative practices among the Wayuu in the Upper Guajira. *Memory Studies, 8*(3), 282–297. https://doi.org/10.1177/1750698014563970

Riaño-Alcalá, P. (2023). i—iglesia. Iglesia San Pablo Apóstol (Bellavista Viejo), Medio Atrato, Chocó—Colombia. In D. Ruiz-Serna, D. & D. Ojeda (Eds.), *Belicopedia* (pp. 94–103). Universidad de los Andes.

Riaño-Alcalá, P., & Baines, E. (2011). The archive in the witness: Documentation in settings of chronic insecurity. *International Journal of Transitional Justice, 5*(3), 412–433. https://doi.org/10.1093/ijtj/ijr025

Riaño-Alcalá, P., & Chaparro Pacheco, R. (2020). Cantando el sufrimiento del río. Memoria, poética y acción política de las cantadoras del Medio Atrato chocoano. *Revista Colombiana de Antropología, 56*(2), 79–110. doi:10.22380/2539472X.793

Rivera-Cusicanqui, S. (2012). Ch'ixinakax utxiwa: A reflection on the practices and discourses of decolonization. *South Atlantic Quarterly, 111*(1), 95–109. https://doi.org/10.1215/00382876-1472612

Roberts, D. E. (1997). *Killing the Black body: race, reproduction, and the meaning of liberty*. Random House.

Robertson, G. (2010). *The massacre of political prisoners in Iran, 1988, Report of an inquiry*. The Abdorrahman Boroumand Foundation.

Robinson, G. (2017). "Down to the very roots": The Indonesian army's role in the mass killings of 1965–66. *Journal of Genocide Research, 19*(4), 465–486. https://doi.org/10.1080/14623528.2017.1393935

Robinson, G. B. (2018). *The killing season: A history of the Indonesian massacres, 1965–66*. Princeton University Press.

Rodríguez, D. (2006). (Non)scenes of captivity: The common sense of punishment and death. *Radical History Review, 2006*(96), 9–32. https://doi.org/10.1215/01636545-2006-002

Roosa, J. (2006). *Pretext for mass murder: The September 30th movement and Suharto's coup d'etat in Indonesia*. University of Wisconsin Press.

Roosa, J. (2020). *Buried histories: The anticommunist massacres of 1965–1966 in Indonesia*. University of Wisconsin Press.

Rothberg, M. (2009). *Multidirectional memory: Remembering the Holocaust in the Age of Decolonization*. Stanford University Press.

R. v. Gladue, 1 SCR 688 (1999). https://scc-csc.lexum.com/scc-csc/scc-csc/en/item/1695/index.do

R. v. Morris, ONSC 5186 (2018). http://canlii.ca/t/hv19g

R. v. Morris, ONCA 680 (2021). https://canlii.ca/t/jjhd9

Sakamoto, R. (2001). The women's international war crimes tribunal on Japan's military sexual slavery: A legal and feminist approach to the 'comfort women' issue. *New Zealand Journal of Asian Studies, 3*(1), 49–58. https://www.nzasia.org.nz/uploads/1/3/2/1/132180707/comfortwomen.pdf

Saleh-Hanna, V. (2015). Black feminist hauntology: Rememory the ghosts of abolition? *Penal Field, 12*. https://doi.org/10.4000/champpenal.9168

238 • References

Salih, A. (2018). *The stillborn: Notebooks of a woman from the student-movement generation in Egypt* (S. Selim, Trans.). Seagull Books.

Samarasinghe, G. (1999). Strategies of coping. In S. Perera (Ed.), *Stories of survivors: Socio-Political contexts of female headed households in post-terror Southern Sri Lanka*. Vikas.

Sarat, A., & Kearns, T. R. (Eds.). (1999). *History, memory, and the law*. University of Michigan Press.

Schirmer, J. (1989). Those who die for life cannot be called dead: Women and human rights protest in Latin America. *Feminist Review, 32*, 3–29. https://doi.org/10.2307/1395361

Schirmer, J. (1994). The claiming of space and the body politic within nation-security states: The plaza de Mayo Madres and the Greenham common women. In J. Boyarin (Ed.), *Re-mapping memory: The politics of timespace* (pp. 185–220). University of Minnesota Press.

Scott, D. (1982). Lemonsong. In *Dreadwalk* (pp. 16–19). New Beacon.

Scott, D. (2017). Toward a Caribbean theatre. *Caribbean Quarterly, 63*(2–3), 370–381. https://doi.org/10.1080/00086495.2017.1352285

Sedgwick, E. K. (2003). *Touching feeling: Affect, pedagogy, performativity*. Duke University Press.

Shamshiri, M. (2023). The gendered politics of dead bodies: Obituaries, revolutionaries, and martyrs between the Iranian, Palestinian, and Dhufar Revolutions. In C. R. Elling & S. Haugbolle (Eds.), *The fate of third worldism in the Middle East: Iran, Palestine and beyond* (pp. 99–120). One World.

Shange, N. (2010). *For colored girls who have considered suicide/when the rainbow is enuf*. Simon and Schuster.

Shapiro, A., & Pao, M. (2017, February 22). *After slavery, searching for loved ones in wanted ads*. NPR Code Switch. https://www.npr.org/sections/codeswitch/2017/02/22/516651689/afterslaverysearching-for-loved-ones-in-wanted-ads

Shariati, A. (2003). *Religion vs. religion* (L. Bakhtiar, Trans.). ABC International Group.

Sharma, P. (2021, February 9). *Anti-black racism reports in R v Morris*. TheCourt.Ca. http://www.thecourt.ca/systemic-oppression-in-sentencing-onca-to-rule-on-anti-black-racism-reports-in-r-v-morris/

Sharpe, C. (2016). *In the wake: on blackness and being*. Duke University Press.

Sharpe, J. (2003). "The rebels old Obeah woman": History as spirit possession. In *Ghosts of slavery: A literary archaeology of Black women's lives* (pp. 1–43). University of Minnesota Press.

Simpson, A. (2007). On ethnographic refusal: Indigeneity, "voice" and colonial citizenship. *Junctures, 9*, 67–80.

Simpson, B. R. (2008). *Economists with guns: Authoritarian development and U.S.-Indonesian relations, 1960–1968*. Stanford University Press.

Simpson, L. (2004). Anticolonial strategies for the recovery and maintenance of Indigenous knowledge. *American Indian Quarterly, 28*(3–4), 373–384. https://doi.org/10.1353/aiq.2004.0107

Soni, R., & Varadharajan, A. (2012). Between securocratic historiography and the diasporic imaginary: Framing the transnational violence of Air India Flight 182. *Topia: Journal of Canadian Cultural Studies, 27*, 177–195. https://doi.org/10.3138/topia.27.177

Sontag, S. (1973). *On photography*. Farrar, Straus and Giroux

Sontag, S. (2003). *Regarding the pain of others*. Penguin.

Sousanis, N. (2015). *Unflattening*. Harvard University Press.

Spivak, G. C. (1974). Translator's preface. In J. Derrida (Ed.), *Of grammatology* (pp. ix–lxxxvii). Johns Hopkins University Press.

Stengers, I. (2013). Introductory notes on an ecology of practices. *Cultural Studies Review, 11*(1), 183–196. https://doi.org/10.5130/csr.v11i1.3459

Stoler, A. L. (2009). *Along the archival grain: Epistemic anxieties and colonial common sense.* University of Princeton Press.

Stoll, D. (2008). *Rigoberta Menchú and the story of all poor Guatemalans.* Westview.

Sturken, M. (1997) *Tangled memories: The Vietnam war, the AIDS epidemic, and the politics of remembering.* University of California Press.

Swarr, A. L., & Nagar, R. (2010). Theorizing transnational feminist praxis. In A. L. Swarr & R. Nagar (Eds.), *Critical transnational feminist praxis* (pp. 1–20). SUNY Press.

Talebi, S. (2011). *Ghosts of revolution: Rekindled memories of imprisonment in Iran.* Stanford University Press.

Talebi, S. (2019). Ethnography of witnessing and ethnography as witnessing: Topographies of two court hearings. *Political and Legal Anthropology Review, 42*(2), 226–243. https://doi.org/10.1111/plar.12316

Tambe, A., & Thayer, M. (Eds.) (2021). *Transnational feminist itineraries: Situating theory and activist practice.* Duke University Press.

Taussig, M. (1992). *The nervous system.* Routledge.

Taussig, M. (2010). *Walter Benjamin's grave.* University of Chicago Press.

Taylor, D. (2003). *The archive and the repertoire: Cultural memory and performance in the Americas.* Duke University Press.

Taylor, D. (2019). Traumatic memes. In A. G. Altinay, M. J. Contreras, M. Hirsch, J. Howard, B. Karaca, & A. Solomon (Eds.), *Women mobilizing memory* (pp. 113–132). Columbia University Press.

Tecú Osorio, J. (2012). *Memoir of the Río Negro massacres: My parents' tragic story lives on in the memories of my children.* Editorial Maya Wuj.

Teitel, R. (2000). *Transitional justice.* Oxford University Press.

Thomson, S. (2013). *Whispering truth to power: Everyday resistance to reconciliation in postgenocide Rwanda.* University of Wisconsin Press.

Till, K. (2005). *The new Berlin: Memory, politics and place.* University of Minnesota Press.

Tobón, A. (2016). *Romances del Atrato: Cantos de la vida y de la muerte.* Instituto Caro y Cuervo.

Tobón, A., Ochoa, F., López Marín, S., & Serna Gallego, J. (2015). *El río que baja cantando. Estudio etnomusicológico sobre romances de tradición oral del Atrato medio.* Universidad de Antioquia.

Tomlins, C., & Comaroff, J. (2011). "Law as . . .": Theory and practice in legal history. *UC Irvine Law Review, 1*(3), 1039–1080.

Toppled Monuments Archive (2022). *Toppled monuments archive list.* https://www.toppledmonumentsarchive.org/new-page-1

Trotz, D. A. (2006). Rethinking Caribbean transnational connections: Conceptual itineraries. *Global Networks, 6*(1), 41–59. https: doi.org//10.1111/j.1471-0374.2006.00132.x

Trotz, D. A. (2014). "Lest we forget": Terror and the politics of commemoration in Guyana. In S. Perera & S. Razack (Eds.), *At the limits of justice: Women of colour on terror* (pp. 289–308). University of Toronto Press.

Tuck, E. (2009). Suspending damage: A letter to communities. *Harvard Educational Review, 79*(3), 409–428. https://doi.org/10.17763/haer.79.3.n0016675661t3n15

Tuhiwai-Smith, L. (2012). *Decolonizing methodologies: Research and Indigenous peoples.* Zed.

Turner, C. (Director). (2022). *Nave.* [Multimedia Installation]. Central Art Garage, Toronto, Canada. https://www.camilleturner.com/nave

Unión Nacional de Mujeres Guatemaltecas. (2017). *La luz que vuelve: Juicio Sepur Zarco.* Historieta nivel de educación media.

United Nations General Assembly (UNGA) Resolution 60/147, December 16, 2005, https://www.ohchr.org/sites/default/files/2021-08/N0549642.pdf

University of Saskatchewan. (2016, March 28). *Indigenous feminisms power panel* [Video]. Youtube. https://www.youtube.com/watch?v=-HnEvaVXoto

UofT Daniels. (2016, March 9). *"They paid their sentences with the removal of their feet" with Candace Hopkins* [Video]. YouTube. https://www.youtube.com/watch?v=3CYVNjUq8-I

Vafaei, N. (2018). *Jilvah-hā-yi Zindigī* [The effects of life]. Kitabi-Arzan.

Valencia, L. (2009). *Al son que me toquen canto y bailo.* Bogotá: Ministerio de Cultura.

van Bruinessen, M. (1994). Genocide in Kurdistan? The suppression of the Dersim rebellion in Turkey (1937–38) and the chemical war against the Iraqi Kurds (1988). In G. J. Andreopoulos (Ed.), *Conceptual and historical dimensions of genocide* (pp. 141–170). University of Pennsylvania Press.

van Voorhis, B. (2004). The pain has not disappeared. In *An exceptional collapse of the rule of law: Told through stories by families of the disappeared in Sri Lanka.* ALRC, AHRC & Families of the Disappeared.

Vasvari, L. O., & Wang, I. (2015). Introduction to life writing and the trauma of war. *CLCWeb: Comparative Literature and Culture, 17*(3), 2–8. https://docs.lib.purdue.edu/clcweb/vol17/iss3/

Velásquez Nimatuj, I. A. (2012). Peritaje cultural. In I. Mendia Azkue & G. Guzmán Orellana (Eds.), *Ni olvido, ni silencio: Tribunal de conciencia contra la violencia sexual hacia las mujeres durante el conflicto armado en Guatemala* (pp. 119–126). Universidad de País Vasco, Hegoa, and UNAMG.

Velásquez Nimatuj, I. A. (2013). *Peritaje cultural: Violaciones sexuales a mujeres q'eqchi' en el marco del conflict armado interno (1960–1996) de Guatemala, caso Sepur Zarco, municipio de El Estor, departamento de Izabal.* Unidad del Conflicto Armado, Fiscalía de Derechos Humanos, Ministerio Público de Guatemala. Juzgado Primero de Primera Instancia Penal, Narcoactividad y Delitos con el Ambiente por Procesos de Mayor Riesgo "B" del departamento de Guatemala, Causa No.C-01076-2012-00021 Oficial 1.B Expediente Ministerio Público: MP001-2011-118096, Guatemala.

Velásquez Nimatuj, I. A. (2019). Las abuelas de Sepur Zarco: Esclavitud sexual y Estado criminal en Guatemala. In X. Leyva Solano & R. Icaza (Eds.), *En tiempos de muerte: Cuerpos, rebeldías, resistencias* (pp. 89–107). Consejo Latinoamericano de Ciencias Sociales; Cooperativa Editorial Retos.

Vergara Figueroa, A. (2017). *Afrodescendant resistance to deracination in Colombia.* Palgrave Macmillan.

Vergara Figueroa, A., & Arboleda Hurtado, K. (2014). Feminismo Afrodiaspórico. Una agenda emergente del feminismo Negro en Colombia. *Universitas Humanística, 78*(78), 109–134.

Vice Staff. (2017, January 1). Our favorite local music of 2016. Vice. https://www.vice.com/en/article/pgp9v9/rilisan-musik-indonesia-terfavorit-2016-pilihan-vice

Viera, B. (2016, May 11). Michael Brown's mother Lezley McSpadden: "I feel like I can't enjoy anything." *Cosmopolitan.* https://www.cosmopolitan.com/entertainment/books/q-and-a/a58286/lezleymcspadden-tell-the-truth-and-shame-the-devil-interview/

Viswanathan, P. (2014). *The ever after of Ashwin Rao*. Random House Canada.

Viveros, M. (2018). Race, indigeneity, and gender: Lessons for global feminism. In J. W. Messerschmidt, P. Y. Martin, M. A. Messner, & R. Connel (Eds.), *Gender reckonings: New social theory and research* (pp. 90–110). New York University Press.

Wahyuningroem, S. L. (2013). Seducing for truth and justice: Civil society initiatives for the 1965 mass violence in Indonesia. *Journal of Current Southeast Asian Affairs, 32*(3), 115–142.

Walcott, D. (1992, Dec 7). *The Antilles: Fragments of epic memory*. Nobel Prize. https://www.nobelprize.org/prizes/literature/1992/walcott/lecture/

Walcott, R. (2021). *On property*. Biblioasis.

Whitlock, G. (2007). *Soft weapons: Autobiography in transit*. University of Chicago Press.

Wieringa, S. (2002). *Sexual politics in Indonesia*. Palgrave Macmillan.

Wilderson, F. B. (2010). *Red, white and black: Cinema and the structure of U.S. antagonisms*. Duke University Press.

Wilkinson, T. (2010, February 20). Juarez massacre may mark a turning for Mexico. *Los Angeles Times*. http://articles.latimes.com/2010/feb/19/world/la-fg-mexico-tipping-point20-2010feb20

Williams, R. K. (2016). Toward a theorization of black maternal grief as analytic. *Transforming Anthropology, 24*(1), 17–30. https://doi.org/10.1111/traa.12057

Wilson, S. (2008). *Research is ceremony: Indigenous research methods*. Fernwood.

Winter, J. (2006). Notes on the memory boom. In D. Bell (Ed.), *Memory, trauma and world politics* (pp. 54–73). Palgrave Macmillan.

Woodly, D. (2019). Black feminist visions and the politics of healing in the movement for Black lives. In A. G. Altınay, M. José Contreras, M. Hirsch, J. Howard, B. Karaca, & A. Solomon (Eds.), *Women mobilizing memory* (pp. 219–237). Columbia University Press.

Wright, M. (2015). *The physics of blackness: Beyond the middle passage epistemology*. University of Minnesota Press.

Wüstenberg, J. (2020). Introduction: Agency and practice in the making of transnational memory. In J. Wüstenberg & A. Sierp (Eds.), *Agency in transnational memory politics* (pp. 1–20). Berghan.

Wüstenberg, J., & Sierp, A. (Eds.). (2020). *Agency in transnational memory politics*. Berghan.

Wynter, S. (2003). Unsettling the coloniality of being/power/truth/freedom: Towards the human, after man, its overrepresentation–An argument. *The New Centennial Review, 3*(3), 257–337.

Xan Xi. (2021, June 8). I born a Gaulin woman. *New Limestone Review*. https://newlimestonereview.as.uky.edu/2021/06/08/first-place-xan-xi/

Yes No Wave Music. (2016, Oct 18). *Dialita—Konser peluncuran album "Dunia Milik Kita"* [Video]. YouTube. https://www.youtube.com/watch?v=21Dq3yGlSpg

Yogyakarta, Y. B. (2020). *Opening stage of Biennale Jogja XIII: Traveling across eras from survivors of 65 to Senyawa*. http://www.biennalejogja.org/2015/berita/opening-stage-of-biennale-jogja-xiii-traveling-across-eras-from-survivors-of-65-to-senyawa/?lang=en

Young, J. E. (1989). "After the Holocaust: National attitudes to Jews": The texture of memory: Holocaust memorials and meaning. *Holocaust and Genocide Studies, 4*(1), 63–76. https://doi.org/10.1093/hgs/4.1.63

Young, J. E. (1992). The counter-monument: Memory against itself in Germany today. *Critical Inquiry, 18*(2), 267–296. https://doi.org/10.1086/448632

Young, J. E. (2016). *The stages of memory: Reflections on memorial art, loss and the spaces between*. University of Massachusetts Press.

Yuliantri, R. D. A. (2012). LEKRA and ensembles: Tracing the Indonesian musical stage. In J. Lindsey & M. H. T. Liem (Eds.), *Heirs to world culture: Being Indonesian 1950–1965* (pp. 421–452). KITLV Press.

Yuval-Davis, N. (1997). *Gender and nation*. Sage.

Notes on Contributors

ALISON CROSBY is an associate professor in the School of Gender, Sexuality and Women's Studies at York University and the former director of the Centre for Feminist Research (2014–2019). Her research uses a transnational feminist lens and participatory methodologies to accompany protagonists' multifaceted struggles to redress and memorialize colonial racialized gendered violence in Guatemala, where she has worked for over thirty years. With M. Brinton Lykes she is the author of *Beyond Repair? Mayan Women's Protagonism in the Aftermath of Genocidal Harm* (Rutgers University Press, 2019), which received the 2021 Lemkin Book Award from the Institute for the Study of Genocide. The book was published in Guatemala as *Más Allá de la Reparación: Protagonismo de Mujeres Mayas en las Secuelas del Daño Genocida* by Cholsamaj in 2019.

MALATHI DE ALWIS (1963–2021) was a renowned Sri Lankan cultural anthropologist, feminist, and environmental activist. She published widely on social movements associated with "disappearances" as well as on nationalism, militarism, displacement, suffering, and memorialization. Her publication, *Archive of Memory*, curated and edited with Hasini Haputhanthri and simultaneously published in English, Sinhala, and Tamil, offers a people's object-related history of the past seventy years of independence in Sri Lanka. A section of this work toured the island as part of the It's About Time traveling history museum. De Alwis led "memory walks" around Colombo and collaborated on a "memory map" to document sites of violence across Sri Lanka; see http://historicaldialogue.lk/map/.

MARÍA DE LOS ÁNGELES AGUILAR is a Guatemalan Maya-K'iche' historian and a postdoctoral associate and lecturer at the Council on Latin American and Iberian Studies at Yale University. Her work focuses on policing and criminalization in Guatemala during the country's civil war (1960–96). In Guatemala, she has worked on collaborative research projects centered on historical memory, collecting testimony from Indigenous communities and genocide survivors.

AMBER DEAN is a professor of English and cultural studies at McMaster University. Her research focuses on public mourning, violence, and cultural memory. She is also interested in how creative forms of cultural production (fiction, art, photography, film, and performance) disrupt and reframe commonsense understandings of whose lives (and deaths) matter to wider publics. She is the author of *Remembering Vancouver's Disappeared Women: Settler Colonialism and the Difficulty of Inheritance*. With Chandrima Chakraborty and Angela Failler, she has also coedited *Remembering Air India: The Art of Public Mourning*.

KARINE DUHAMEL is Anishinaabe-Métis and a member of Red Rock Indian Band in northwestern Ontario. A historian by training, she has worked as a curator, an adjunct professor, and in the field of legal research. From 2018 to the end of its mandate in 2019, Duhamel was the director of research for the National Inquiry into Missing and Murdered Indigenous Women and Girls, drafting the final report and managing the Forensic Document Review Project and the Legacy Archive. She is now the director of the Indigenous Strategy for the Social Sciences and Humanities Research Council (Canada).

HEATHER EVANS is a doctoral candidate in the gender, feminist, and women's studies program at York University. Their research draws on transnational feminist theory, critical human trafficking studies, and memory studies to examine how militarized sexual harm and racialized, gendered resistance are constructed through the transnational memorialization practices of the "comfort women" movement. Their work is informed by thirteen years of experience as an activist, researcher, and educator with the "comfort women" movement in the South Korean and Canadian contexts, as well as nearly a decade of research on memorialization landscapes and critical interrogations of human trafficking and modern slavery discourses.

HONOR FORD-SMITH is a poet, theater worker, and scholar and an associate professor emerita at York University. Her most recent performance work is the ten-year performance cycle "Letters to the Dead" and "Vigil for Roxie," coauthored with Carol Lawes, Eugene Williams, and others. Her publications include *Lionheart Gal: Life Stories of Jamaican Women* (with Sistren), *3 Jamaican Plays: A Postcolonial Anthology 1977–1987*, and *My Mother's Last Dance*. As the founding artistic director of the Sistren Theatre Collective in Jamaica, an early Black and Caribbean feminist organization, she cowrote and directed Sistren's *Bellywoman Bangarang, Bandoolu Version, Domestics, Sweet Sugar Rage*, and more.

Notes on Contributors • 245

CHARLOTTE HENAY is a weaver and poet, multidisciplinary scholar, and spiritworker. She was an assistant professor in women's and gender studies at Brock University. Henay's deathwork sits with the bones as protocols for cultural reclamation and spiritual reparations, making Afro-Indigenous futurities in diaspora. Integral to this work are Black-Indigenous land relationships, where land—and the archive—are embodied. The substantive goal of this work is the design of alternate worlds in relational frameworks. Henay's work renders explicit in poetic form this process of talking with the dead and, through that, of confronting and ultimately transforming absences and silences in the archive. Her writing has been published in literary magazines and academic journals, and her multidisciplinary work has been exhibited at the Nasher Museum of Art, the National Art Gallery of the Bahamas, and at conferences and galleries in Toronto, Canada.

ERICA S. LAWSON is an associate professor in the Department of Gender, Sexuality, and Women's Studies at Western University, Canada. She teaches in the areas of feminist and critical race theories and gender and post-conflict recovery. Her research focuses on the politics of Black women's maternal activism for social change. Her most recent project is an initiative with women in Liberia who are working for peace and gender justice at Peace Hut sites, a study that documents how Liberian women utilize community councils in Peace Huts to advance gender equality and address domestic disputes through conflict resolution and mediation.

CHOWRA MAKAREMI is a writer, director, and anthropologist at the National Center for Scientific Research in Paris. She has conducted fieldwork and coordinated several research collectives on border control in Europe. She is working on post-revolution violence in Iran and leading the ERC research program Off-Site on this subject. She published *Aziz's Notebook at the Iranian Revolution* and wrote *Enghelab Street: A Revolution Through Books 1979–83* with Hannah Darabi. Makaremi also directed the documentary movie *Hitch: An Iranian Story*.

MILA MENDEZ is a queer, Black Chinese doctoral candidate in gender, feminist, and women's studies at York University. They are interested in the capaciousness of Black feminisms and ontological Blackness when brought to bear on archives of Black and Asian entanglements. In particular, their work explores Black and Chinese intimacies in settler colonial Canada that resist and challenge historical and contemporary narratives of racial antagonisms or solidarities, and that gesture instead to processes of co-constitution and intertwined pathways to liberation.

SHAHRZAD MOJAB, scholar, teacher, and activist, is internationally known for her work on the impact of war, displacement, and violence on women's learning and education and Marxist feminism and antiracism pedagogy. She is a professor emerita of adult education and community development and of women and gender studies at the University of Toronto. Her most recent books include *Kurdish Women Through History, Culture, and Resistance*; *Women of Kurdistan: A Historical and Bibliographical Study* (coauthored with Amir Hassanpour); *Youth as/in Crisis: Young People, Public Policy, and the Politics of Learning* (coedited with Sara Carpenter); *Revolutionary Learning: Marxism, Feminism and Knowledge* (coauthored with Sara Carpenter); *Marxism and Feminism*; *Educating from Marx: Race, Gender and Learning* (coedited with Sara Carpenter), and *Women, War, Violence, and Learning*.

CARMELA MURDOCCA is the York Research Chair in Reparative and Racial Justice and a professor in the Department of Sociology at York University. She is appointed to graduate programs in sociology, sociolegal studies, and social and political thought. Her research is concerned with the intersections of racial carceral violence and the social and legal politics of repair, redress, and reparations.

OLA OSMAN is a Gates-Cambridge Scholar and is currently pursuing a doctoral degree at the Cambridge University Centre for Gender Studies. Her work focuses primarily on mapping the continuities between racial slavery, its attendant anti-Black logics, and the Liberian civil war. She received a Master of Studies in women's studies from the University of Oxford and is a Clarendon Scholar.

AYU RATIH is a PhD candidate in the history/interdisciplinary studies program at the University of British Columbia in Vancouver. She co-coordinated an oral history project to document the stories of victims of anticommunist violence and established an archive, the Indonesian Institute of Social History. She served as the lead researcher at the National Commission for Violence against Women to investigate gender-based violence during the 1965–66 military operation. She is involved in the SSHRC-funded Transformative Memory International Network, which studies various ways of dealing with past atrocities among communities in Canada, Uganda, Colombia, and Indonesia.

PILAR RIAÑO-ALCALÁ is a professor at the Institute for Gender, Race, Sexuality and Social Justice Institute, University of British Columbia, and coprincipal investigator of the Transformative Memory International Network. Her scholarly work and research creation explore questions on the afterlives and worlds of mass violence and focus on themes of memory, traces and social repair, and methodological engagements with difficult knowledge and knowledge exchanges. She is the author of *Dwellers of Memory: Youth and Violence in Medellin, Colombia* and the editor of *Remembering and Narrating Conflict*. She is also completing the manuscript *In the Interstices of War and Peace: Memory and Social Repair in the Afterlives of Violence in Colombia*.

Notes on Contributors • 247

CORDELIA RIZZO is a scholar-activist, maker, and doctoral candidate in performance studies at Northwestern University, where she was awarded the Lilla A. Heston Award for Academic Excellence. Her research probes the language of touch through textile making to theorize what makes memory work possible in violent contexts. Her work straddles the intersection of performance studies, critical feminist methodologies, human rights activism, and critical phenomenology. Workshop facilitation and activism with feminist collectives and mothers of the disappeared in her native Monterrey inform her work.

JUANITA STEPHEN is an assistant professor of women's and gender studies and Black studies at the University of Windsor. Her current research is concerned with how care is taught and learned in self-organized and state-regulated care systems. Her scholarly, creative, and community practice are more broadly invested in exploring models of noncarceral care that attend to the safety, health, and wellbeing of Black children, families, and communities. Stephen holds a PhD from York University and is the cofounder of The Black Care Network.

CAMILLE TURNER is an explorer of race, space, home, and belonging. Born in Jamaica and currently based in Toronto, her work combines Afrofuturism and historical research. Her interventions, installations, and public engagements have been presented throughout Canada and internationally. Turner graduated from Ontario College of Art and Design and York University's environmental studies graduate program, through which she completed a PhD in 2022. She is currently a postdoctoral scholar at the University of Toronto where her research confronts the silences and fissures in colonial Canada's historiography.

IRMA ALICIA VELÁSQUEZ NIMATUJ was the 2019–2021 Edward Laroque Tinker Visiting Professor at the Center for Latin American Studies, Stanford University. She is an international spokeswoman for Indigenous communities in Central America and was the first Maya-K'iche' woman to earn a doctorate in social anthropology in Guatemala. She was instrumental in making racial discrimination illegal in Guatemala and was featured in *500 Years*, a documentary about Indigenous resistance movements, for her role as an activist and expert witness in war crime trials. The author of several books, she wrote a weekly column for the *El Periódico* newspaper in Guatemala.

Index

Abdo, N., 117n1

accountability, 17, 80

active forgetting, 140

activism: for Black Lives Matter, 2; against forced disappearance, 26n13; for indigenous people, 91; memory, 13–14; for Mexico, 183–184; race and, 7–8; revolutionary pasts and, 12–13; on social media, 74; UN advocacy spaces, 79; in United States, 148–149. *See also* maternal activism

Afghanistan, 113–114, 116, 148

Afraz, Mahbubeh, 106, 114–116

Afraz, Rafat, 106, 114–116

Africa, 101n12, 130–131, 138. *See also specific topics*

African communities, 150

African slavery, 32

African spiritual repertoires, 93

Afro-Colombian women, 89

Afrodiasporic movements, 91

Afrofuturism, 14–15, 203–205, 209–210

Afronautics, 14–15, 209–218, *211*, 218n1

agency, 82–83

Agency in Transnational Memory Politics (Wüstenberg and Sierp), 5–6

Aguilera, C., 2–3

Ahmed, Sara, 47–48, 95

Aijazi, Omer, 95

Aikau, H. K., 7–8

Air India Flight 182: artistic memorializations of, 55n2; Canada and, 43–44, 55n1;

docudramas about, 55n3; queer diasporic remembrance of, 43–46, 49–50, 54–55; as transnational tragedy, 46–48

Akan language, 153–154

Akomfra, John, 212–213

alabaos, 12, 88–90, 92–95, 98–99, 100n8

Alexander, Jacqui, 7

Alexander, M. J., 181

All Inclusive (Doctor), 44–45, 50–51, 53

Altinay, A. G., 6

Alvarez, S., 8–9

de Alwis, Malathi, xi–xiii, 86n1; legacy of, 11, 74–75, 113; scholarship from, 6, 181–182; Sri Lanka and, 83–84, 165–166

André, Brigitte, 66

André, Veronique, 66

And Still I Rise (Lawrence, D.), 163

Angola, 109

anthropology, 81

anti-Blackness, 217–218, 218n1

anti-Black racism: anti-Indigenous racism and, 40; in British empire, 46–48; in Canada, 55n2; in collective memory, 33; colonialism and, 35–36; gendered, 32; history of, 36–37; Middle Passage and, 162; by police, 29–30, 38; racial capitalism and, 172; racial gendered violence and, 40–41; racial governance and, 38; in sentencing, 30–31; subjectivity and, 42; systemic racism and, 29–30, 36; violence and, 1–2, 32, 34, 169–170

anti-Black violence, 1–2

250 • Index

anticolonial agenda, 8–9
anticolonial remembering, 59–65, 71
anticolonial writers, 62
anticommunist mass violence, 131, 133–135
anti-Indigenous racism, 40
apartheid, 5
Arango, Germán, 100n9
Archaeology of a Silence in Twelve Traces (film synopsis), *123*, 123–124
Archive of Memory project, xiii
Argentina, 21–22, 26n14, 84, 166–167, 180
Armed Revolutionary Forces of Colombia (FARC), 87–88, 92–93, 96–99, 100n1, 101n15
artistic memorializations, 44–45, 55n2
artist's statement, 203–205
Asia, 32, 130–131, 134–135, 138, 143n7, 150. *See also specific countries*
Asia Afrika Bersatu, 138
Asian Human Rights Commission, 19–20, 25n8, 25nn8–9
Assadi, Mina, 118n8
athurudahanvuna (forced disappearance), 18
Aziz's notebook (Makaremi), 105–106, 112–114, 116

bad death, 95–96
Badilla, M., 2–3
Baldwin, James, 157
Balfour, G., 30–31
Bandar-Abbas, Iran, 124, *125–128*, 126–129
Bandung Conference, 130
Barad, Karen, 10
Barrios Torres, Mayra Nineth, 78
Barthes, Roland, 22–23
Bazargan, Pouran, 114–115
Bear Clan wall mural, 66
Bella Spirit (painting), 65–66
Beloved (Morrison), 158
Benjamin, Walter, 23, 26n16, 41, 123–124, 153–154
Beristain, Carlos, 177
Bevins, V., 143n2
Biberman, Herbert J., 118n6
Black boys, 156–158
Black communities, 94, 96–99
Black feminism: Black feminist hauntology, 11, 216; Black feminist intellectuals, 7; diasporic Black mothers in, 8–9; Indigenous feminism and, 7–8, 12, 76; in

maternal activism, 162–165; in Mothers of the Movement, 13–14; praxis, 162, 164; scholarship from, 161; slavery in, 13–14
Black liberation, 161
Black Lives Matter, 2, 148–149, 163, 167–168
Black maternal activism, 164–165
Black motherhood, 148, 166–167, 171–172
Blackness, 38, 203–205, 209–218, *211*, 218n1
Black social consciousness, 162
Black subjectivity, 37
Black transnational feminism, 162–163
Black women, 96
Black womxn, 204
Bland, Sandra, 160
bodily practices, 141
Bojayá (Historical Memory Group), 89–90
Bojaya massacre, 91–99
Bollywood, 52
Botman, S., 117n1
Brand, D., 1–2, 16
Breaking the Silence and Impunity Alliance, 80
British empire, 46–48, 54–55
Brown, Michael, 160, 163, 170–171
Brown, W., 41
Buller, Marion, 67
Burgos-Debray, Elisabeth, 81
Bush, George W., 143n3
Butler, Judith, 23–24, 25n4, 45, 51–52, 143n3, 176, 183

Cabnal, Lorena, 77
Cabral, Amílcar, 62, 109
Calderon, Felipe, 173–178, 180, 186n1
Calliste, 196n1
Campt, T., 90, 96
Canada: Air India Flight 182 and, 43–44, 55n1; anti-Black racism in, 55n2; anticolonial remembering in, 59–60, 63–65, 71; Canadian Museum for Human Rights, 70–71; Canadian Museum of History, 70; Centre for Feminist Research in, 6; Colombia and, 91; colonialism in, 12, 15, 209–210; Court of Appeal, 39–40; decolonizing memorialization in, 60–63; exile in, 116; France and, 180; genocide in, 2; heterosexuality in, 44; India and, 46–48, 55; Indigenous feminism in, 8–9; Indigenous people in, 36, 39, 60–61; Jamaica and, 13, 148–150,

152, 153–154; Mexico and, 50; MMIWG in, 67, 69, 71; MMIWG2S+, 68; Namgis First Nation in, 67; NunatuKavut Nation in, 68–69; politics in, 47; prison in, 29–31, 34–35, 37–40; scholarship on, 194n1, 201n3; sentencing hearings in, 33; slavery in, 218n1; Social Sciences and Humanities Research Council of, 86n1; systemic racism in, 29–30; 2SLG-BTQQIA+ people, 59–62, 65–67, 70–71; University of Toronto, 9

canonical feminism, 91

Cansiz, Sakine, 105–112, 116–117

cantadoras, 12, 87–95, 97–99, 100n8

care, 13–14, 154

Caribbean diaspora, 148–150

Caribbean domestic workers Scheme, 201n1, 201n3, 201n6, 201n8

Carpenter, Sara, 117

Carr, Gwen, 160

Cartographies of knowledge and power (Mohanty and Alexander M. J.), 181

Castro, Fidel, 109

Caswell, M., 64

Catholic Church, 73–74, 92–93

Centre for Feminist Research, 6

Césaire, Aimé, 62

Chandraprema, C. A., 25n2

Chandrasiri, Hemantha, 21

Chaparro, Ricardo, 89–90

Chapman, Kindra, 168

Cheng, A., 164

Chevannes, Amber, 150–151

Chile, 3, 6

chronic mourning, 17–25

Circle Bear, Sarah Lee, 168

Circle of Mothers, 163

Civil War, United States, 165–166

Clark, V., 8, 204

Clinton, Chelsea, 168

Clinton, Hillary, 161, 167–169

Cold War, 132

collaborative performance, 13, 147–151, *152*, 153–159

collective memory, 3–4, 16, 33, 38–39

collective mourning, 13–14

Colombia, 8–9, 12, 87–99, 101n15, 183

colonialism: Afronautics and, 14–15; anti-Black racism and, 35–36; by British empire, 54–55; in Canada, 12, 15,

209–210; colonial extractivism, 82; colonial hauntings, 79; colonial violence, 34; decolonialism, 2–3, 8–9, 60–63, 77–78; imperial logic in, 11–12; for Indigenous people, 40–41, 68–69, 77; intersectionality after, 62–63; knowledge in, 61; patriarchy and, 105–106; slavery and, 32, 38–39, 41–42; by Spain, 92–93; systemic racism and, 37

Comaroff, J., 35

Commission of Inquiry into Involuntary Removal or Disappearance of Persons in the Western, Southern and Sabaragamuwa Provinces, 25n3

communism, 109, 114, 117, 117n1, 130–131, 133–136, 140–142

community activism, 91

Community Art Piece, 69

composition, 91–95

Connerton, Paul, 154, 156

contracts, domestic service, *195*

Cook, T., 64

Cooper, B. C., 163

Cooper-Jones, Wanda, 172n2

Cornell, Drusilla, 41

cosmovision, 75, 77–78, 82

counter-aesthetic, 2

counterdemonstrations, 3, 9–10

counter-memorial, 5, 10–11. *See also* countermemorializing; counter-monument

countermemorializing, 140–142

countermemory, 122–123, *123*, 162–163

counter-monument movements, 5

COVID-19, 1–2, 185–186

Cree people, 63–64

Cristo Mutilado, 92

Croatia, xii

Cruz Valencia, Jose de la, 100n9

Cuba, 96–97, 109–110, 148–149, 154

cultural memory, 4, 132, 164

Curnell, Joyce, 168

Cusicanqui, Sylvia Rivera, 99

Daniel, Smitri, xiii

Das, Veena, xiii, 84, 154

Davila, Luz María, 175–176

Davis, Jordan, 160, 168

Dean, Jodi, 149

decolonialism, 2–3, 8–9, 60–63, 77–78

252 • Index

defiance. *See* dissent
demonstrations, 2–3
denial, 119–120, 124, *125–128*, 126–129
depoliticization, 142
Derrida, Jacques, 11, 17–20, 25n1, 26n15, 33, 76
desire, 43, 45, 50–54
Desperately Seeking Helen (docudrama), 44–45, 50–54, 55n3
Dialita choir, 13, 131–133, 135–142, 143n3
Diallo, Amadou, 163
Diallo, Kiatou, 163
diaspora, 8–9, 14, 50, 91, 107, 148–149, 204. *See also* queer diaspora
digital media, 15–16
Disappearance Day, 25n9
discrimination, in employment, 196n1
dissent: by Aziz, 105–106, 112–114; by Cansiz, 105–112; in Oman, 114–116; revolution and, 116–117
Doctor, Faranza, 44–45, 50–51, 54
Doğan, Fidan, 108
domestic workers, Caribbean, 194n1, *196*, 196n1, 201n1, 201n3, 201n6, 201n8
Dream in Awakening, A (Assadi), 118n8
dreaming, 14–15, 217–218
Dunia Milik Kita, 137, 140, 142

Eagleton, Terry, 153–154
Eastern culture, 48
Embera people, 93
embodied knowledge, 96
embodied performance, 154
Embroidering for Peace Initiative, 13–14, 173–176, 178–186
Eng, D. L., 32
Ephemeral return to a land I never left, 199
Epigraph 24584, 187–189
epistemology, 9–10, 85–86
Ereiza, 92
Ermine, Willie, 63–64
erotohistoriography, 45
ethnocentric knowledge, 79
Europe, 4, 49–50, 79, 91, 116, 130–131. *See also specific countries*
evangelization, 93
Ever After of Ashwin Rao, The (Viswanathan), 46–48

Faist, T., 49
Falcón, S. M., 7–8

Fanon, Frantz, 62
Fauzia, Uchikowati, 136–138, 141
Felman, S., 80
feminism: canonical, 91; embodied performance in, 154; feminist politics, 173–176, 178–186; independence and, 24; Indigenous, 7–9, 12; international feminists, 75–76; Islamic, 117; in Latin America, 91; leadership in, xi–xii; in postmodernism, 8–9; South Asian feminists, 49; stigma against, 139; Western, 130–131. *See also specific feminist movements*
Finch, Aisha, 154
Floyd, George, 2, 161, 169, 217–218
forced disappearance: activism against, 26n13; denial of, 119–120; FUNDENL, 174, 181, 185; in Indonesia, 143n2; in Iran, 119–124, *123*, *125–128*, 126–129; in Mexico, 175–177, 182–183; in *muxuk chaq'rab* concept, 78; scholarship on, 17–25, 25n2, 25n9, 25nn2–3, 26n11
Forces United in Search for Our Disappeared (FUNDENL), 174, 181, 185
For Neelan (de Alwis), xi–xii
France, 180
Frank, S., 3
Freeman, Elizabeth, 45
French, Joan, 150
frictions, 96–99
Fucik, Julius, 109
Fuenmayor, Victor, 179–180
Fuentes Rojas, 174–176, 178–180, 184
Fulton, Sybrina, 160, 163, 169–171

Gandhi, Indira, 47–48
García, Chirix, 78–79
Garcia, Michelle, 177–178
Garcia, Rosario Tio, 86n1
García Jurado, Joaquin, 182
Gargallo, F., 180
Garner, Eric, 160
gender, 6–9, 32, 81, 96
genocide: in Canada, 2; mass graves, 84; post-genocide, 72–75, 82–86; in Rwanda, 76; UN on, 143n1; in Yugoslavia, 76
Germany, 5
Ghaddar, J. J., 64
Ghostly Matters (Gordon), 11, 216
ghosts, 11

girls. *See specific topics*
Gislason, Mylinda, 68
Gladue principle, 30, 36
globalization, 185–186
Global North, 7, 79
González, Gabriela, 180
Goodison, Lorna, 149
Good Morning America (TV show), 161, 169–171
Gopinath, G., 8, 44, 46, 49–53
Gordon, Avery, 11, 215–216
Gorky, Maxim, 109
Gossett, C., 2
governance, 64
government systems, 1–2
Grandmothers' and Elders' Advisory Circle, 67
Grewal, Inderpal, 7, 40
grief: Butler on, 23–24; chronic mourning, 17–25; collective memory and, 3–4; collective mourning, 13–14; desire and, 45, 51–52; grievability, 143n3; memory and, xi–xii, 15–16; performance and, 149; precarity and, 176; ungrievability, 177; unrepresentable element of, 153; unshareability of, 18. *See also* lingering grief; precarious life
Guatemala: Mujeres Transformando El Mundo in, 86n1; post-genocide, 72–75; post-genocide memory in, 85–86; Q'eqchi Maya people in, 12, 14, 72–75, 85–86; Sepur Zarco trial in, 72–75, 77–78, 80–85; sexual violence in, 72–75, 82–84; Sri Lanka and, xii, 6, 74–75; *testimonios in*, 79–82; transnational feminist research project in, 75–76; transnational public memory in, 75–79; UNAMG, 73–75, 80
Gwangju massacre. *See* Indonesia
Gwangju Prize for Human Rights, 137

Haiti, 148–149, 154
Halbwach, Maurice, xii, 4
Hall, K. Q., 163
Hamilton, Dontre, 160
Hamilton, Maria, 160
Han, S., 32
Haputhanthri, Hasini, xiii
Harper, Stephen, 47–48
Hartman, Saidiya, 161–162, 204, 212
Hasegana, Nina, 183

hegemonic memorialization practices, 132
Heiltsuk First Nation, 65–66
Herbert, Travis, 63
Herrera, María, 183
heteronormativity, 52
heterosexuality, 44
Hidalgo, Leticia, 176, 185
Hidalgo, Roy Rivera, 176, 185
Himid, Lubaina, 215
Hirsch, M., 60–61, 165
Historical Clarification Commission, 73
Historical Memory Group, 89–90
Hitch (documentary), 13, 119–124, *123*, *125–128*, 126–129
Ho Chi Minh, 109
Hodgkin, K., 10
hooks, bell, 163–164
Hopkins, Candace, 9–10, 14, 16n1
Hoskins, A., 16
House of Baby, 210
Hughes, Langston, 151
human rights: advocates, 127; Asian Human Rights Commission, 19–20, 25n8, 25nn8–9; Canadian Museum for Human Rights, 70–71; Gwangju Prize for Human Rights, 137; Mexican National Human Rights Commission, 177; in Truth and Reconciliation Commissions, 135–136; UN Human Rights Commission, 64–65; World Human Rights Day, 25n9
Huyssen, A., 4

identity, 51–54, 59–67, 70–71
imperial logic, 11–12
India, 46–48, 50, 52, 55. *See also* Air India Flight 182
Indigenous people: activism for, 91; anti-Indigenous racism, 40; in Canada, 36, 39, 60–61; in Chocó Department, 100n10; colonialism for, 40–41, 68–69, 77; communities, 78–79, 150; decolonial memory work by, 77–78; Embera people, 93; evangelization of, 93; Grandmothers' and Elders' Advisory Circle, 67; Heiltsuk First Nation, 65–66; Indigeneity, 203–205; Indigenous feminism, 7–9, 12, 60–63, 66–67, 76; Indigenous women, 59–60; Indigenous womxn, 204; land of, 73, 84; MMIWG, 67, 69, 71; MMIWG2S+, 68;

254 • Index

Indigenous people (cont)
  NunatuKavut Nation, 68–69; Q'eqchi
  Maya people, 12, 14, 72–75, 85–86;
  subjectivity of, 42; as survivors, 96–99;
  Two-Spirit people, 67–68; UNDRIP for,
  64–65; Urban Indigenous Advisory
  Committee, 67; violence against, 71
Indonesia: anticommunist mass violence in,
  131, 133–135; communism in, 130–131,
  134–136, 140–142; countermemorializing
  performance in, 140–142; Dialita choir
  in, 13; forced disappearance in, 143n2;
  mass violence in, 143n1; in Olympics,
  143n7; transnational cultural practices in,
  138–139; women survivors in, 130–133,
  135–138, 142
Inhabitance of Loss, The (de Alwis), xii
Inhabitance of Loss, The (research
  project), 6
Integral System for Truth, Justice and
  Reparation, 100n7
interdependence, 93
International Centre for Ethnic Studies, xiii
International Criminal Court, 76
international feminists, 75–76
internationalism, 133
International Network for Peace in
  Mexico, 183
interpellations, 96–99
intersectionality, 7–8, 38, 62–63
In the Wake (Sharpe), 216–217
Iran: forced disappearance in, 119–124, *123,
  125–128,* 126–129; Kurds in, 13, 107–112,
  116–117; MENA and, 112–114; politics in,
  105–107, 114–117, 119–122, 129n1
Iraq, 110, 143n3, 148
I Rigoberta Menchú (Menchú), 80–81
Islam, 107–114, 116–117, 118n7
Israel, 143n7
Ituribarria, Monica, 178–179

Jamaica, 13, 148–150, *152,* 153–154
Janatha Vimukthi Peramuna (JVP), 18, 20–21
Japan, 79, 183
Jarrico, Paul, 118n6
Jean, Allison, 170, 172n2
Jean, Botham, 170
Jeganathan, Pradeep, 24–25
Jewish Holocaust, 165
Joinet, Louis, 64–65

Joinet-Orentlicher Principles, 64–65
Jones, Allen, 165
Jones, Nancy, 165–166
Jones, Ralkina, 168
Jordan, Anique, 147–148

kanamal podathu (forced disappearance), 18
Kaplan, Caren, 7
Karimi, Fatemeh, 118n2
Kearns, T. R., 41
Keefer, P. C., 29
Kenney, Michelle, 168–169
Khoi, Esmail, 107
knowledge, 60–61, 79, 90–91, 96, 181
Komagata Maru (ship), 48
Kurds, 13, 106–112, 116–117, 118n2

La Capra, Dominick, 19, 23, 26n19
land, 73, 84–86
Lanzmann, Claude, xii
Latin America, 4–5, 80–81, 91, 185–186.
  See also specific countries
Laub, D., 80
law: as racial memory, 29–35, 41–42;
  reparative juridics, 35–41
Lawes, Carol, 150–151
Lawrence, D., 163
Lawrence, Stephen, 163
Leader, D., 177
Lebanon, 114–115
Legacy Archive, 60, 63–71
Lenin, Vladimir, 109
Leninism, 109, 114, 117
lesbians, 51–54
Letters from the Dead (play), 149–151
*Letter to my Nephew, A, "My Dungeon
  Shook"* (Baldwin), 157
Levinas, Emmanuel, 33
Levy, Horace, 150
liberalism, 12, 31–33, 38, 40–42, 51–52, 154
Liberation Tigers of Tamil Eelam (LTTE),
  18, 25n7
lingering grief, 106
Lobo, Teresa Carmona, 182–183
Londoño, Rodrigo, 87–88
López, Mariana, 180
Lorde, A., 184–185
Lose Your Mother (Hartman), 161–162
loss, xi–xiii, 12, 45, 50–54, 153
Lowe, L., 12, 31–34, 41–42, 164

Lucila Sabella Kiosk, 174
Luna, Diego, 175
Luz que Vuelve, La (government pamphlet), 72–73, 80, 85
Lykes, M. Brinton, 75, 82, 86n1

Macdonald, John A., 2
MacEwan University, 68
Makaremi, C., 105–106, 112–114, 116
Manning, E., 181–183
Maoism, 109, 117
Marjara, Eisha, 44–45, 50–54, 55n3
Marley, Bob, 215
Marriott, D., 205
Martin, Trayvon, 160, 163, 169–170
Martínez, Diana, 182–183
Marxism, 109, 114, 117
mass graves, 84, 119–122, 124, *125–128*, 126–129
material culture production, 63
maternal activism: Black, 164–165; Black feminism in, 162–165; Mothers of the Movement and, 160–162, 171–172; transnational, 166–167; in United States, 167–171
maternity, 22
Mavor, C., 26n18
Mawani, R., 33–35
Máxima, 94, 98–99
Maya people, 73–75, 77–79, 82, 85–86. *See also* Q'eqchi Maya people
Mazo, Jorge Luis, 92
McAllister, C., 81
McBath, Lucy, 160, 167–168
McCoy, Sheila Smith, 203
McGovern, Alexis, 168
McManemin, J., 2
McSpadden, Lezley, 160, 163, 170–171
Megill, A., 11
melancholia, 19
Memmi, Albert, 62
memoirs: political, 13, 105–106, 108–117, 118n5, 118nn2–3; of prison, 105–112, 116
memorialization. *See specific topics*
memorialization theory, 163–165
memory: activism, 13–14; Archive of Memory project, xiii; collective, 3–4, 16, 33, 38–39; countermemories, 122–123, *123*; cultural, 4, 132, 164; Derrida on, 33; in digital media, 15–16, 119–124, *123*, *125–128*,

126–129; dreaming and, 14–15, 217–218; governance and, 64; grief and, xi–xii, 15–16; Historical Memory Group, 89–90; idea of, 161–162; of kin, 22–23; land and, 85–86; lapse, 122–123; memorying, 8–9, 203–205; memory-making, 34, 41–42; memory studies, 214–215; of Middle Passage, 155; mourning and, 155–156; Nora on, 33; in oral history projects, 79–80; the past and, 19–20; from photographs, xiii, 20–21; place and, xii; poetics and, 91–95; politics, 5–6; post-genocide, 85–86; public, 12; remembering, 153; rememory, 166; REMHI project, 73–74, 79; revealing, 124, *125*; sound, 87–90, 99; in statues, 2–3; studies, 164–165; transnational public, 75–79; in Truth and Reconciliation Commissions, 135–136; in Western culture, 10–11; work, 12, 75, 77–78, 90, 176–178. *See also specific topics*
Menchú, Rigoberta, 80–81
Méndez, Regina, 184
Metz, Christian, 25n5
Mexico: activism for, 183–184; Calderon for, 173–178, 180, 186n1; Canada and, 50; Colombia and, 183; Embroidering for Peace Initiative in, 13–14; forced disappearance in, 175–177, 182–183; International Network for Peace in Mexico, 183; memory work in, 176–178; Mexican National Human Rights Commission, 177; Spain and, 183–184; United States and, 167, 178–186; War on Drugs in, 173–176
Middle East and North Africa (MENA): Iran and, 112–114; Kurds in, 106–112; scholarship on, 117n1, 118n3, 118n5; women in, 105–106, 114–117. *See also specific countries*
Middle Passage, 153, 155, 162
Million, D., 61
Missing and Murdered Indigenous Women and Two-Spirit+ (MMIWG2S+), 68
Mnjama, N., 64–65
Moghissi, H., 117n1
Mohanty, Chandra Talpade, 7, 181
Monument Lab, 3
monuments, 2–3, 5, 9, 25n9
Mookherjee, N., 76
Moorcroft, D. C., 29

Morris, Kevin, 29–32, 35–40
Morrison, Toni, 158, 166, 218
Morrissette, Suzanne, 16n1
Mother, The (Gorky), 109
motherhood: Asian Human Rights
 Commission and, 25n8; Black, 148,
 166–167, 171–172; with Black boys,
 156–158; Circle of Mothers, 163; maternity,
 22; Mothers' Front, 20–22, 25n9, 26n13;
 Mothers of Missing Migrants, 167; Plaza
 del Mayo Madres, 21–22, 84, 166–167;
 psychology of, 17, 19–20; Saturday Night
 Mothers, 167; violence and, 111–112.
 See also Mothers of the Movement
Motherly Love (Rumbolt), 68–69
Mothers of the Movement: maternal
 activism and, 160–162, 171–172; members
 of, 172n2; memorialization theory and,
 163–165; on television, 161, 169–171;
 transnational historical context for,
 165–166; in transnational maternal
 activism, 166–167; in United States,
 13–14, 161, 167–169
"Mother the Great Stones Got to Move"
 (Goodison), 149
Mouffe, C., 182
mourning, 87–88, 93–99, 151, *152*, 155–156
Mujeres Transformando El Mundo, 86n1
Muñoz Lascarro, Félix Antonia (Pastor
 Alape), 97–99
murdered and missing Indigenous women
 and girls (MMIWG), 67, 69, 71
Musqueam people, 91
muxuk chaq'rab concept, 78

Nagar, R., 8
Naimpally, Ravi, 155
Nakatsuru, Shaun, 29–30, 35–40
Namgis First Nation, 67
Naranjo Morse, Nora, 9–11
Nash, J. C., 7–8, 163
National Inquiry into Missing and
 Murdered Indigenous Women and Girls:
 Legacy Archive in, 60, 63–71; scholarship
 on, 12, 59–63, 71
National Union of Guatemalan Women
 (UNAMG), 73–75, 80
National Victims' and Land Restitution
 Law, 100n6
nation-building, 135

Nave (multimedia installation), 15
Negra, La, 97–99
Nietzsche, Friedrich, 123
Nigeria, 138
non-Western ontology, 9
Nora, Pierre, 33
Nova Scotia Gazette and Weekly Chronicle, 211
NunatuKavut Nation, 68–69

Olalde, Katia, 179
Olea, Elia Andrade, 179–180
Olick, V., 4, 116
Olmos, Edward James, 175
Oman, 13, 106, 114–117
Oñate, Don Juan de, 9, 11
Oneida, 88, 90–91, 94–95, 97–98
ontology, 9–10
Operation Blue Star, 47–48
oral history projects, 79–80
Orentlicher, Diane, 64–65
Orjuela, Camila, 100n9

Padi untuk India, 138
Pakistan, 113–114, 116
Palacios, Delis, 88, 100n9
Palacios, Leyner, 100n9
Palestine, 114–115
Paley, Dawn Marie, 174
Palmer, Tamika, 172n2
Patterson, Mikhayla, 68
Peace Management Initiative, 150
Pelkey, Samantha, 67
Pendleton, Hadiya, 160
Pendleton-Cowley, Cleopatra, 160
performance: collaborative, 13, 147–151, *152*,
 153–159; countermemorializing, 140–142;
 by Dialita choir, 131–132; embodied, 154;
 mourning and, 87–88; scholarship on,
 91–99
permanent loss, 19
phenomenology, 22
photographs: Benjamin on, 23, 26n16;
 Mavor on, 26n18; memory from, xiii,
 20–21; Plaza del Mayo Madres in, 21–22;
 representation in, 76; Sontag on, 26n10;
 symbolism in, 25n5
Pinto, S., 163
Plato, 123
Plaza del Mayo Madres, 21–22, 84, 166–167
poetics, 87–95

poetry, 149, 155–156. *See also specific poems*

police, 29–30, 38, 111

political agency, 99

political community of the sorrowing, xii, 6, 24

political memoirs, 13, 105–106, 108–117, 118n5, 118nn2–3

political present, 41

political prisoners, 13, 135–137

political stakes, 26n19

political violence, 4–5

politics: in Canada, 47; of care, 154; Cold War, 132; of collective memory, 16; at Democratic National Convention, 161, 167–169; depoliticization, 142; of diaspora, 107; feminist, 173–176, 178–186; geopolitics, 131, 134–135; in Iran, 105–107, 114–117, 119–122, 129n1; of knowledge, 60–61; of loss, 23; of memorialization, 160–165, 171–172; memory, 5–6; poetics and, 87–90; in post-genocide Guatemala, 72–75; of War on Drugs, 176–178

Politics of Touch (Manning), 181–183

post-genocide, 72–75, 82–86

postmodernism, 8–9

poststructuralism, 4

Pour-Mohammadi, Mostafa, 129n1

precarious life, Butler, 176

prison: in Canada, 29–31, 34–35, 37–40; collective memory and, 38–39; memoirs of, 105–112, 116; political prisoners, 13, 135–137; songs, 141–142

Protocols for Native American Archival Materials, 64–65

psychic numbing, 19

public memory, 12

Pueblo people, 9

Qambari, Ali-Mohammad, 121, 124

Q'eqchi Maya people, 12, 14, 72–75, 77–82, 85–86

queer diaspora: queer diasporic remembrance, 43–46, 49–50, 54–55; transnational feminism and, 46–48, 50–54

Quiceno, Natalia, 100n9

race: activism and, 7–8; gender and, 9; religion and, 46–48; sexuality and, 6; systemic racism, 29–30, 36–37; in United States, 169–170. *See also specific topics*

racial capitalism, 172

racial gendered violence, 40–41

racial governance, 31–32, 38

racialized Others, 44

racial memory: law as, 29–35, 41–42; in sentencing, 35–41

racial stereotypes, 48

racial violence, 148–149

Radstone, S., 10

Raissi, Ebrahim, 119–120, 129n1

Reclaiming Justice (conference), 6–7

Reclaiming Power and Place (National Inquiry), 62

reconciliation, 158–159

Recovery of Historical Memory (REMHI) project, 73–74, 79

Red River Métis, 66, 68

Reed-Veal, Geneva, 160, 168

Reguillo, Rossana, 178

religion, 46–48, 73–74, 107–112. *See also specific topics*

remembering, 153

remembrance, 60–63

rememory, 166

repair, 158–159

reparative juridics, 35–41

Report from the Gallows (Fucik), 109

responsibility, 80

Rest in Power (Fulton and Martin), 163

Restrepo, Adriana Maya, 101n12

Rhodes, Cecil, 3

Rice, Samaria, 169

Rice, Tamir, 169

Richard, Irene, 66

Richard, Lorraine, 66

Ríos Montt, José Efraín, 74

Ristic, M., 3

Rodríguez, D., 35

Rohani, Hassan, 119–120

Rolling Stone magazine, 137

Roosa, J., 143n1

Rose, Antwon, II, 168–169, 172n1

Rumbolt, Dee-Jay Monika, 68–69

Ruse, Jamie-Leigh, 183–184

R v. Morris, 29–32, 35–40

Rwanda, 76

Ryerson, Egerton, 2

Saa-ust Centre, 67

Sacred feminine, 66–67

St. Onge, Jean, 67
Saleh-Hanna, Viviane, 11, 216
Salt of the Earth (film), 110, 118n6
Sankofa (concept), 153–154
Santos, Juan Manuel, 87–88, 100n6
Sarah (film), 214–215, 217–218, 218n1
Sara: My Whole Life Was a Struggle (Cansiz), 105–112, 116
Sara: Prison Memoir of a Kurdish Revolutionary (Cansiz), 105–112, 116
Sarat, A., 41
Saturday Night Mothers, 167
Şaylemez, Leyla, 108
Scheme, Caribbean domestic workers, 201n1, 201n3, 201n6, 201n8
Schirmer, Jennifer, 26n14
Schwartz, J., 64
Scott, Dennis, 156
Seela (mother), 20
sentencing, 30–31, 33, 35–41
Sepur Zarco trial, 72–75, 77–78, 80–85
servitude, 187–202, 196n1
settler colonialism. *See* colonialism
sexual harm, 72–73, 75–79
sexuality, 6, 50–52
sexual violence, 82–84, 110–111
sexual violence in conflict, 6
Sharpe, C., 11, 162, 171, 216–217
Sicilia, Javier, 175–176, 178, 182
Sicilia, Juan Francisco, 175
Siegl, Audrey, 67
Sierp, A., 5–6
Sikhs, 47–48
Silva, Dilki de, 24–25
Simpson, Betasamosake, 62
Sinhala community, 24
Sinhala language, 18, 21
Sisters in Strength, 69
Sistren Theatre Collective, 150
situated knowledges, 90–91
Slater, Jessica, 69
slavery: from Africa, 101n12; ancestors of, 209–218, *211*; in Black feminism, 13–14; in Canada, 218n1; colonialism and, 32, 38–39, 41–42; Japanese Military Sexual Slavery, 79; legacy of, 11, 161–162; Middle Passage, 153, 155; in transnational feminism, 31–32; in United States, 165
Smith, V., 60–61
socialism, 117n1

social media, 74, 118n7, 177–178, 185–186, 217–218
social repair, 87–90, 95–96, 99
Social Sciences and Humanities Research Council of Canada, 86n1, 220
Son (multimedia installation), 148
Song for the Beloved (performance-installation), 13, 147–151, *152*, 153–159
Sontag, Susan, 26n10, 179
Sordo, Teresa, 179
sound memory, 87–90, 99
South Africa, 3, 5
South Asian feminists, 49
South Korea, 25n9, 137–138
Spain, 92–93, 180, 183–184
Specters of Marx (Derrida), 11
Springer, Kara, 147–148, 155
Sri Lanka: de Alwis and, 83–84, 165–166; Archive of Memory project and, xiii; Easter bombing attacks in, 137; forced disappearance in, 18, 25n2, 25n9, 26n11, 26n13; Guatemala and, xii, 6, 74–75; history of, 21–22; JVP in, 18, 20–21; LTTE in, 18, 25n7; Mothers' Front in, 20–22, 25n9; political communities in, 24; Tamil community in, 25n6; transnational feminist research project in, 75–76
Stalin, Joseph, 109
statues. *See* monuments
Stoler, A. L., 34, 64
Stoll, David, 81
suffering, 41
Suharto, 130–131, 134–136, 140–141
suicide bombers, 112
Sukarno, 131–138, 140, 143n5
survivor guilt, 19
Swarr, A. L., 8
systemic racism, 29–30, 36, 37

Taiwan, 143n7
Tamil community, 18, 21, 24, 25n6
Taylor, Breonna, 2
Taylor, Diana, 84, 132, 151
teleology, 4
Tell the Truth and Shame the Devil (McSpadden), 163, 170–171
testimonios, 12, 79–84
Till, Karen, xii
Tiruchelvan, Neelan, xiii
Tomlins, C., 35

Tracing Absent Presence (de Alwis), xii–xiii
translocality, 90–91
transnational cultural practices, 138–139
transnational feminism: approaches in, 1–7; Black, 162–163; defiance in, 105–106; leadership in, xii–xiii; methodology for, 7–16; queer diaspora and, 46–48, 50–54; slavery in, 31–32; transnational feminist research project, 75–76
transnational historical context, 165–166
transnational maternal activism, 166–167
transnational public memory, 75–79
Tribunal of Conscience, 75
Trotz, D. Alissa, 147, 148–149, 151
Truth and Reconciliation Commissions, 135–136
Tuhiwai-Smith, L., 61–62
Turkey, 6, 13, 105–106, 110–111, 167
Turner, Camille, 147–148, 153, 218n1. *See also* Afronautics
Turner, J. W., 165
Turner, Raynette, 168
2SLGBTQQIA+ people, 59–62, 65–67, 70–71
Two-Spirit people, 67–68

Ujian, 141
United Kingdom, 183–184
United Nations (UN), 64–65, 76, 79, 143n1
United Nations Declaration on the Rights of Indigenous Peoples (UNDRIP), 64–65
United Self-Defence Forces of Colombia (AUC), 92
United States: activism in, 148–149; anthropology in, 81; anti-Black violence in, 1–2; Asia and, 134–135; communism in, 109; culture of, 24; decolonialism in, 2–3; Europe and, 116; foreign policy, 174–175; gender in, 6–8; in geopolitics, 131, 134–135; in Iraq, 143n3; maternal activism in, 167–171; Mexico and, 167, 178–186; monuments in, 9; Mothers of the Movement in, 13–14, 161, 167–169; race in, 169–170; racialized capitalism in, 172; slavery in, 165
University of Toronto, 9
1/40,000 Ante el Dolor de los Demás (art project), 178–179
Unsilencing the Archive (virtual lab), 209–218, *211*

Unspoken Words (Patterson), 68
Urban Indigenous Advisory Committee, 67

Valenzuela, Ada, 73–74
Valero, Marcela, 181
Venus in Two Acts (Hartman), 212
Vera, Rayl, 175
Vergara, Aurora, 93, 96, 100n9
Vertigo Sea (Akomfra), 212–213
Vietnam, 109–110
Vietnam War, 5
Vigil for Roxy (play), 150–151
Villas de Salvacar massacre, 175
violence. *See specific topics*
Viswanathan, Padma, 46–48, 50–54
vital force, 93
Viva Ganefo, 138, 141

Walcott, Derek, 156
Walk With Us (painting), 65–66
Wall of Tears (monument), 25n9
war crimes, 79, 82
War on Drugs, 173–178, 184–186
Wayward Lives (Hartman), 212
Weerasinghe, Lichchowi Nishanthe, 21
We gat so much god we ain't gat room for nuttin else, 187–202, *193, 199*
Western culture, 10–11, 14, 24, 48–50, 61–62, 66–67, 79
Western feminism, 130–131
Western liberalism, 154
Williams, Eugene, 150–151
Williams, Raymond, 33, 161, 171
Wilson, Michael, 118n6
Wilson, Shawn, 68
Winter, J., 4
With the Omani Revolutionaries (Afraz, M., & Afraz, R.), 106, 114–115
Wok the Rock, 138
women. *See specific topics*
Women in Conflict Zones Network (WICZNET), xi–xii
Women Mobilizing Memory (Altinay, A. G.), 6
Women's International War Crimes Tribunal, 79
women survivors, 130–133, 135–138, 142
Women Transforming the World, 80
Woodly, D., 162–163

260 • Index

World Human Rights Day, 25n9
worlding, 14–15
Wright, Michelle, 204
Wüstenberg, J., 5–6
Wynter, Sylvia, 10

Yasawathi (mother), 20
Yemen, 115

Yildiran, Esat Oktay, 111
Young, J. E., 5, 9–10
Yugoslavia, 76

Zarei, Aziz, 105–106, 112–114, 116, 120
Zarei, Fataneh, 112–114, 120–122, 124, *128*
Zarei, Fatemeh, 112–114, 120–122, *128*
Zong (slave ship), 162

Available titles in the Genocide,
Political Violence, Human Rights series:

Nanci Adler, ed., *Understanding the Age of Transitional Justice: Crimes, Courts, Commissions, and Chronicling*

Bree Akesson and Andrew R. Basso, *From Bureaucracy to Bullets: Extreme Domicide and the Right to Home*

Jeffrey S. Bachman, *Genocide Studies: Pathways Ahead*

Jeffrey S. Bachman, *The Politics of Genocide: From the Genocide Convention to the Responsibility to Protect*

Andrew R. Basso, *Destroy Them Gradually: Displacement as Atrocity*

Alan W. Clarke, *Rendition to Torture*

Alison Crosby and Heather Evans, eds., *Memorializing Violence: Transnational Feminist Reflections*

Alison Crosby and M. Brinton Lykes, *Beyond Repair? Mayan Women's Protagonism in the Aftermath of Genocidal Harm*

Lawrence Davidson, *Cultural Genocide*

Myriam Denov, Claudia Mitchell, and Marjorie Rabiau, eds., *Global Child: Children and Families Affected by War, Displacement, and Migration*

Daniel Feierstein, *Genocide as Social Practice: Reorganizing Society under the Nazis and Argentina's Military Juntas*

Joseph P. Feldman, *Memories before the State: Postwar Peru and the Place of Memory, Tolerance, and Social Inclusion*

Alexander Laban Hinton, ed., *Transitional Justice: Global Mechanisms and Local Realities after Genocide and Mass Violence*

Alexander Laban Hinton, Thomas La Pointe, and Douglas Irvin-Erickson, eds., *Hidden Genocides: Power, Knowledge, Memory*

Douglas A. Kammen, *Three Centuries of Conflict in East Timor*

Eyal Mayroz, *Reluctant Interveners: America's Failed Responses to Genocide from Bosnia to Darfur*

Pyong Gap Min, *Korean "Comfort Women": Military Brothels, Brutality, and the Redress Movement*

Fazil Moradi, *Being Human: Political Modernity and Hospitality in Kurdistan-Iraq*

Walter Richmond, *The Circassian Genocide*

S. Garnett Russell, *Becoming Rwandan: Education, Reconciliation, and the Making of a Post-Genocide Citizen*

Tatiana Sanchez Parra, *Born of War in Colombia: Reproductive Violence and Memories of Absence*

Victoria Sanford, Katerina Stefatos, and Cecilia M. Salvi, eds., *Gender Violence in Peace and War: States of Complicity*

Irina Silber, *Everyday Revolutionaries: Gender, Violence, and Disillusionment in Postwar El Salvador*

Amy Sodaro, *Lifting the Shadow: Reshaping Memory, Race, and Slavery in U.S. Museums*

Samuel Totten and Rafiki Ubaldo, eds., *We Cannot Forget: Interviews with Survivors of the 1994 Genocide in Rwanda*

Eva van Roekel, *Phenomenal Justice: Violence and Morality in Argentina*

Anton Weiss-Wendt, *A Rhetorical Crime: Genocide in the Geopolitical Discourse of the Cold War*

Kerry Whigham, *Resonant Violence: Affect, Memory, and Activism in Post-Genocide Societies*

Timothy Williams, *The Complexity of Evil: Perpetration and Genocide*

Ronnie Yimsut, *Facing the Khmer Rouge: A Cambodian Journey*

Natasha Zaretsky, *Acts of Repair: Justice, Truth, and the Politics of Memory in Argentina*

Julien Zarifian, *The United States and the Armenian Genocide: History, Memory, Politics*